Comic Performativities

Comic Performativities: Identity, Internet Outrage, and the Aesthetics of Communication studies patterns of criticism and public debate in the relationship between humor, identity, and offense. In an increasingly reductive and politically charged debate, right-wing pundits argue that leftist politics has compromised a free and open discussion, while scholars take right-wing critics to task for reifying systems of oppression under the guise of reason and respect. In response, Goltz scrutinizes twenty-first century "comedic controversies," the notion of "political correctness," and the so-called "outrage machine" of social media. How should we appropriately determine whether a joke is "sexist," "racist," or "offensive"?

Informed by communication, performance, and critical identity theory, Goltz examines infamous controversies involving performers like Sarah Silverman, Amy Schumer, and Seth MacFarlane, and the social media backlash that redefined these events. He investigates the ironic interplay between spoken word, identity, physicality and, as a result, the contrasting meanings potentially construed. Consequently, the book encourages a greater appreciation of the aesthetics involved in comedic performance that help signpost interpretation and emphasizes the role of the audience as self-reflexive and self-aware.

This book highlights the significant parallels between the nature of performance art and comedic performance in order to elevate analysis of, and discussion around, contemporary comedy. In doing so, it is an important critical contribution to the field of performance studies and cultural criticism, as well as communication studies, at both the undergraduate and postgraduate level.

Dustin Bradley Goltz PhD, MFA, is an Associate Professor of Performance Studies in The College of Communication at DePaul University. He is a scholar and artist and has authored several works, including *Queer Temporalities in Gay Male Representation* (2009) and *Queer Praxis* (2015).

Comic Performativities

Identity, Internet Outrage, and the Aesthetics of Communication

Dustin Bradley Goltz

Routledge
Taylor & Francis Group
LONDON AND NEW YORK

First published 2017 by Routledge

2 Park Square, Milton Park, Abingdon, Oxfordshire OX14 4RN
52 Vanderbilt Avenue, New York, NY 10017

Routledge is an imprint of the Taylor & Francis Group, an informa business

First issued in paperback 2018

British Library Cataloguing-in-Publication Data
A catalogue record for this book is available from the British Library

Library of Congress Cataloging-in-Publication Data
Names: Goltz, Dustin Bradley, 1974- author.
Title: Comic performativities : identity, internet outrage, and the aesthetics of communication / Dustin Bradley Goltz.
Description: London and New York : Routledge, 2017.
Identifiers: LCCN 2016054851 | ISBN 9781138742604 (hardback : alk. paper) | ISBN 9781315181967 (ebook)
Subjects: LCSH: Stand-up comedy–Social aspects--United States. | Information technology--Social aspects--United States. | Internet–Social aspects--United States. | Mass media and public opinion--United States. | Comedy--Philosophy. | Group identity--United States.
Classification: LCC PN1969.C65 .G65 2017 | DDC 792.7/60973--dc23
LC record available at https://lccn.loc.gov/2016054851

ISBN: 978-1-138-74260-4 (hbk)
ISBN: 978-0-367-20213-2 (pbk)

Typeset in Times New Roman
by Taylor & Francis Books

Contents

Acknowledgments

I had no idea when I started this book several years ago how drastically the United States would have changed by February 2017. The fight to preserve complex debate and critical discussion in contemporary US culture has become an increasingly radical effort. We are in a moment when we desperately need our artists to challenge us, push at our discomforts, and expose injustice. I dedicate this book to those bold comedians who stand up to the culture—those dangerous embodied voices who call upon us to see our moral failings and shine a light to our better and more just selves.

The process of writing this book has spanned a significant period of time and there are many people who helped foster, challenge, and shape the ideas in these pages. The works of performance studies scholars, rhetorical scholars, critical identity scholars, authors of historical and theoretical volumes on humor, and lineage of bold, disruptive and hilarious artists have been deeply inspiring to me and this project. I want to acknowledge the backing of DePaul University, the College of Communication, and my DePaul colleagues for their ongoing support and encouragement (including a College summer research grant to help initiate the project, as well as the ongoing support of DePaul's University Research Council). My college filled with amazing folks who I am lucky to work with, and who have encouraged the project every step of the way. Thank you to Paul Booth for being willing to sit down and knock around ideas about audience when Chapter Three was in its early stages. Thank you to the amazing leadership in my college, which is always there to encourage faculty, faculty research, and foster an amazing climate to live and work in. I would like to express a special note of appreciation to my chair Barb Willard, Associate Dean Lexa Murphy, and Dean Salma Ghanem, whose encouragement, generous leadership, and patience is deeply appreciated.

The foundation of this book project was a journal essay published in 2015 in *Text & Performance Quarterly* under the editorship of Frederick C. Corey and the editorial assistance of Kimberlee Pérez. Through the extensive process of developing the article "Ironic Performativity: Amy Schumer's Big (White) Balls", both Fred Corey and Kimberlee Pérez offered valuable and significant questions to the project that strengthened and developed the larger frameworks on this page. In addition, I wish to express appreciation and recognize two anonymous reviewers in that early process who pushed me further into important foundational directions. Significant portions of this 2015 essay appear in Chapter One and Chapter Three, through the granted permission of Taylor and Francis.[1]

Intellectually, there is an interpersonal lineage of scholars, mentors, and friends who have worked to shape the ideas here, and that list is too long to detail here. From National Communication Association's annual conferences and The Annual Performing Artist Weekend, to discussions at various universities, the processing of these ideas has occurred in a range of discussions, relations, and contexts. I want to specifically thank my students in three previous sections of INTC 369: Performance of Humor (formally CMNS 330 Performance Topics, Performance of Humor) at DePaul University (Autumn 2016; Autumn 2014; Autumn 2012). Your performance work and our classroom discussions have informed many dimensions of this project. I want to thank my best friend Ryno for bouncing ideas around with me about comedy. As a comedian himself, I know he seems baffled (if not amused) by the ways I (as an academic) choose to approach these discussions. Ironically, as I talk about comedy, it is the academic jargon he finds the most humorous.

Abby Escatel helped to refine and clarify many of the points and arguments through the project. As my research assistant in the development of several of these chapters, we spent hours talking through early drafts of chapters, and her feedback and insight was invaluable. In addition, I want to thank everyone at Routledge, especially Erica Wetter, Felisa Keyes, Kitty Imbert, and Lucy Loveluck for their commitment, support, and work in developing this project—as well as the anonymous reviewers of the book.

I wish to thank Kimberlee for all her support, enthusiasm, and dialogue for this extended project. In addition, thank you to Roshan for always being in my corner, and for jumping in, offering feedback, and helping me whenever I need it. Finally, every stage and each movement of this project was shared with my guy, Jason Zingsheim. He knows the project as well as I. He has hacked his way through countless sloppy drafts. He has endured hours of my preoccupied ramblings. He has made an imprint on every single page. His patience is unwavering and his multiple contributions are too many to be counted. I'm a lucky man. Thanks, Jay.

Note

1 Goltz, D. B. Ironic Performativity: Amy Schumer's Big (White) Balls. *Text & Performance Quarterly*. 35.4. 266–85. Reprinted by permission of publisher (Taylor and Francis Ltd. http://www.tandfonline.com).

Introduction

What Rock *said*: Don't Tweet this

> Thinking is difficult, that's why most people judge.
>
> (Carl Jung)

> Umm, no @chrisrock. Using little Asian kids to joke about math stereotypes and child labor is not funny.
>
> (Grace Hwang Lynch)

> It's unfair and impossible to ask a comedian to push boundaries without giving them room to write material that sometimes falls short, or pushes too hard.
>
> (Sims)

The polarity, volume and clutter in contemporary political debate comes in a never-ending wave of offense, contest, argument, outrage, and repeat on the 24-hour cable news cycle. People stand on the mountaintops of their laptops and deliver sermons through impersonal dissemination, misleading headlines, comment battles, trolls, and endless exercises in futile reasoning. Journalism has been overtaken by click bait, and somewhere in the flurry of vitriolic outrage that accompanies our everyday newsfeed, nuance and complexity are reduced to falsely constructed sides, slogans, distractions, binary attacks, and reductive mini dramas. In the midst of this shifting techno-political landscape, where the lines between news and entertainment feel indecipherably enmeshed, the cultural and political stakes of comedy are often positioned at the center of the storm. It seems every week brings forth another comic controversy eating up headlines, serving as a metonym for culture wars around systems of racism, sexism, nationalism, Islamophobia, heterosexism, and a broad range of "politically correct issues" in the contemporary discursive landscape. Comedy has become (or perhaps, always was) very, very serious.

Amidst months of protests and boycotts, all eyes were on comedian Chris Rock when he took the stage to host the 2016 Academy Awards. As the #OscarsSo-White protests drew attention to two consecutive years of all white nominees in all major categories, alongside the nationwide Black Lives Matter movement putting issues of police brutality and systematic racism front and center of the national consciousness, Rock had a weighty responsibility. In this moment, Rock was not "just a comedian" and the work he presented was not "just a show," for he was poised to speak to the sociopolitical dimensions surrounding the event. He was expected to confront, interrogate, and negotiate a complex web of tensions surrounding race, representation, and structural inequality—through humor.

The broadcast opened with a montage of several of the year's most acclaimed films, to which Rock did not miss a beat citing and engaging the controversy framing his performance. He walked out after his introduction to a wave of applause, saying "Thank you, thank you. Whoa! Man, I counted at least 15 Black people on that montage." He pushes in a joke before his intro applause has even dissipated. He wears a white tux and a black tie, in front of a glimmering gold backdrop. His smile is characteristically bright, plastered, always served with a layer of overly pleased irony. "Well, I'm here, at the Academy Awards. Otherwise known as the White People's Choice Awards. You realize, if they nominated hosts, I wouldn't even get this job. That's right. Y'all would be watching Neil Patrick Harris right now!" He opened with a bite, offering a delivery with punch, but also familiarity, as Rock fell right into his trademark cadence of delivery, ironic lingering grin, and borderline-playful antagonism. He laughs at his own joke, layering his critique with an "all in good fun" delivery of a huge frozen smile that reads posed, caricature, and just one step ahead. His movements are somewhat mechanized, from clasped hands to wide gestures in a way that feels contained and intentionally stilted, like a marionette commenting upon itself. The multiple strings pulling at this performance are ever-present.

He leaps right into the mess of it all, marking how this Oscars is "the wildest, craziest Oscars to ever host because we got all this controversy – No Black nominees." He reflects on how he is being told over and over that he should boycott or quit, his voice cracking and creaking on the hard consonant sounds at the end of his sentences, liked scratched records. His gestures remain contained and abrupt, as he questions, "Why is it always unemployed people telling you that you should quit?" His arms and hands remain out, stiff, and he turns and pivots, into the wave of laughter. The joke received a loud laugh, but the cut to the audience zoomed in on actress Cate Blanchett's face, which was somewhat stilled, as if studying his joke, unsure how she yet felt about where he was headed. He continues, arguing the Oscars are going to go on with or without him, "And the last thing I need is to lose another job to Kevin Hart!" The camera cuts to Hart who, with a large smile, shares in the laugh.

Rock was doing his job, marking the controversy, while working to diffuse the tension in the room. His body is energized and engaged, where his stiff yet shifting physicality draws attention to the body in presentation, a body performing to the weighted expectation of the crowd. As a Black man, his body carries a broad range of meanings, historical and cultural legacies that are subtly referenced in his poses, his frozen beats, and the sharp grating punctuation of words that cut through the air with a winning lingering grin. Rhetorically, you have the less comfortable Blanchett, alongside the more-willing to laugh Hart and Rock, marking a careful negotiation of the tensions in the room.

Here, in this space, racial tensions are being engaged, performed, and examined. Race, in this space, is being *done*, conjured into negotiation and examined through a range of channels. It is happening in the room and Rock, along with the various audiences, are engaging it from multiple modes and positions. It is tied to his words, for sure, but also the gesture, the pause, the rhythm of his movement, the uneasy (or too easy) laugh, his response to the laugh, and the affective shifts and bends that occur moment by moment. To say it is an intricate dance would make it seem too graceful and choreographed. At points, it's more like a chaotic field of battle.

The question about this specific Rock performance, and the larger question of this book, is not about determining whether or not Chris Rock was funny. Rather, the question at the outset of this project seeks to understand what Rock (and other comedians like him) accomplish, performatively, through their comedic work. What their humor *does*, how what they *do* is far more complicated than what they *say*, and how the complex workings of political humor are often reduced to words.

Once Rock's monologue moved explicitly to the #OscarsSoWhite boycott and protest, he posed a series of rhetorical questions to the audience, asking, "why *this* Oscars? It's the 88th Academy Awards. It's the 88th Academy Awards, which means this whole 'no Black nominees' thing has happened at least 71 other times." His demeanor remains typical Rock stand up, repeating points for emphasis, asking questions he clearly has his answer to, soon to be followed up with a playful, but fully still committed, claim to meaning. To answer why people did not protest back in the 1960s, he argues, "Because we had *real* things to protest at the time." Here he makes a shift, explicitly including himself in the "We," just as he trivializes the 2016 protest, calling into question the "realness" of the critique. Applause and support follow this declaration, and it builds, unfolds and escalates to include increased applause and vocalized support. We see a quick shot of Jennifer Lawrence with her head thrown back and her mouth open in laughter. The camera cuts to Whoopi, who is smiling in appreciation and amusement. Rock's tone and physicality carries a slightly parodic claim to being "reasonable," and the audience is loving it. He is telling the Oscars audience exactly what they want to hear—that these protests are not that important—feeding and legitimizing the audiences' willingness to laugh them away. Yet, as he builds, feeding the crowd the exoneration they are wanting, he ups the brutality of his content. "You know, when you, when your grandmother's swinging from a tree, it's really hard to care about best documentary foreign short!" Here there was a rupture, as upon dropping the first part of the line (ending with "tree"), there was already a quick audience laugh—one Rock pushed through with a tensed jaw and squinted eyes in order to finish the line. The laugh felt too easy, where the audience got caught up in his rhythm and permission to such an extent that the severity of the line failed to interrupt or disrupt the momentum.

The rhetorical trajectory of the set moves to mark how suddenly this year, everyone "went mad." He repeats this refrain, marking how "Spike went mad" and "Jada went mad." He references the anger, but his intonation and punctuation of "mad" suggest the response was out of proportion. He argues, "Jada boycotting the Oscars is like me boycotting Rihanna's panties. I wasn't invited!" The camera cuts to Priyanka Chopra, laughing in clear confusion, not fully taking in the joke, and then Sofia Vergara who is fully laughing with the appreciative crowd. There is conflict in the joke's reception, even if a laugh emerges, with the triumphant meaning emerging from Vergara's enthusiastic applause. The clapping and laughter is a shut-down to Pinkett-Smith, appearing to call her out and put her in her place in a way that seemed to be received with delight.

Rock follows this up immediately by referencing that Jada was mad because her husband Will Smith was not nominated for *Concussion*. He jokes about how that may not be fair, but it's also not fair that Will Smith was paid $20 million dollars to appear in the box office flop *Wild Wild West*. The camera cuts to actress Brie Larson on this joke, and her face, while amused, performs a sympathetic pout, as if to say "poor Will." She's a reluctant audience to the joke, marking tension and dis-ease. There is something a bit too easy, and thus troubling, about Rock choosing to center this joke on Pinkett-Smith, rather than the many males who called for the boycott (Soloman). It seems Rock is working to downplay the racial criticisms launched at the Oscars, but chose to do so in a way that was potentially couched in sexisms, by individually attacking Pinkett-Smith (and using the Rihanna underwear simile). Yet, immediately after the seeming exoneration of the Academy, he drops that the *In Memoriam* package is going to take a different approach this year, featuring only African Americans "who were shot by the cops on the way *to the movies*." This line brought on a slow applause that built, almost like the slow clap that was quintessential to many 1980's teen films. The clap was not about humor, or laughter, but support and recognition. Matt Damon is featured negotiating his clap, which slowly builds along with the momentum of the crowd. Rock bursts in, "Yes, I said it, alright!" It is unclear whether he is speaking to those who fear he will mention it, fear he won't mention it, or perhaps both.

So Rock marks the presence of racism and racial violence in the world, and then returned to the boycott, once again, suggesting that if people want Black nominees every year, they should have Black categories. The audience is uneasy, as it seems he is moving to argue for segregation of categories, which, for a moment, he is. He draws attention to the ridiculousness of acting categories separated by gender, arguing "It's not Track and Field. You don't have to separate them." He draws out the "them," arms open, pleading his case in a way that marks the tacit acceptance, yet absurdity of the divide. You know, "Robert De Niro has never said, 'I better slow this acting down so Meryl Streep can catch up!'" He has his hands on his hips, posed as a caricature, his voice embellished to play the ironic fool. He is subtly calling out ignorance while also embodying ignorance from racist Black stereotypes. He breaks from it and laughs at his joke, once more. He turns meaning over once again, as he starts to name the Black categories, like "Best Black Friend." He again, adopts his fool pose for a moment, and what was first an argument of logic (why a gender divide) quickly returns to calling out racial inequity, as the only category for Black actors would have to be supporting. He jokes, this "Black Oscar" would go to Wanda Sykes for the eighteenth consecutive win, not only citing the lack of leading roles, but also the limited number of Black actresses in the supporting category. Just as his body shifts from ironic caricature adopting the fool to more reasoned indictment, and just as the laughter is constantly moving between laughing with the audience to resisting that connection, Rock's position on these issues continues to slip and slither. He refuses a fixed position of critique, for once you think you have him located right in front of you, he's poking you from behind.

Later in the monologue, after mocking the #OscarsSoWhite boycott, Rock posed the question rather directly, "Is Hollywood racist?" He performs a struggle to respond, noting that this is a more complicated question. He, through his body and tone, refuses a quick or easy answer. Instead, he troubles the question. "Is it burning-cross racist?" "No," he quickly replies without much struggle or necessary consideration, but his expression is pinched and performs an uneasiness with the question. "Is it fetch-me-some-lemonade racist? No," he squeals in adamant rejection. He launches into a story that takes some set up, where he was at a Hollywood event with President Obama. He delivers it straight, no deep irony or excessive affect. He asks the President, in a quick exchange, to look out at the room of the Hollywood elite, which is almost entirely white. Rock recounts himself saying, "Mr. President. You see all these writers, producers, and actors?" Rock smiles and very earnestly breaks the news, "They don't hire Black people." There is a completely silent moment, as he lets that sink in, before, "and they're the nicest white people on earth." He says this line with a giddiness, like this is the ultimate punchline. "They're liberals, CHEESE," as Rock leans in, turns his face out, and puts his arm out like he's posing for a picture. This moment, this pose, this realization becomes an index to make sense of Rock's entire performance, the posing, the big fake smile, the "this is the reality and I'm trying to make my way through this." He returns to his question, "Is Hollywood racist? You're *damn right* Hollywood's racist … but it's [racism] you've grown *accustomed* to. Hollywood is *sorority* racist. It's like, 'We like you, Rhonda. But you're not a Kappa.' That's how Hollywood is." The applause was far less easy and far less comfortable than earlier in the set, when Pinkett-Smith was being disciplined, and the audience took delight in the protests being reduced to "not real." It was one of the most complicated, uneasy, layered, and productive negotiations of meaning between Rock and his audience. It was the uneasy laugh that all the big laughs were driving towards.

Yes, race and racism were central and recurrent topics in Rock's monologue. Journalist Shaun King, argued, "while the monologue was still peppered with a few more good yucks, much of what Rock *said* was distasteful, uncomfortable, and just plain wrong" (my emphasis). I am not in agreement or disagreement with King in his assessment, but rather want to question where he is placing his attention—what Rock *said.* In the current cultural climate where comedy is so often at the center of controversy, too often we engage comedic work as if it were parallel to political speech. Rather, from an aesthetic communication and performance approach, the political workings of comedy involve much more complicated processes than merely "what was *said.*"

Throughout the broadcast, Rock continued examining issues of race and racism in Hollywood from a range of positions and approaches. In, perhaps, the most awkward and uneasy moment of the night, Rock introduced actress Stacey Dash as "The director of the Academy's new minority outreach program." Her appearance was an uneasy and tense moment of satire. Dash, an African American actress famous for her role in *Clueless*, has recently been a conservative voice regarding race in Hollywood and a vocal opponent to the boycott. Dash, unclear if she was in on the joke (and it was not exactly clear the direction or intention of the joke, overall), made for several moments of uncomfortable giggles as she walked "onstage to wave at the crowd in a bit many people in the audience and on social media didn't seem to understand" (Deggens). The dis-ease was elongated, palpable, and not immediately clear, frustrating the critics and audiences in search of assumingly linear, direct, and unambiguous positions.

An additional satiric segment included theatergoers outside a Compton multiplex, in a series of street interviews with Rock, responding to questions about the majority of the Oscar nominated films from the previous year. Rock asked one African American male, mid to late twenties, "Did you see *Spotlight*?" He replied, almost bothered, "No, what the hell is that?" In the next clip, Rock asks an early thirties African American woman, "Did you feel that *Trumbo* should have been a bigger hit?" The woman, simply responds, "What?" clearly marking that the discussion is simply not one she is a part of or cares about. He lists a series of movies from the year, and the interviewees continually repeat, one after another, that they have not seen them. When he asks a woman about *Bridge of Spies*, she breaks into laughter, if not disbelief, saying, "Where are you getting these movies from? You're making up some, you're messing with me, right?" Rock interjects, insistently, "No, these are real movies." The woman, still laughing, argues, "No, it's not. I watch movies, I come to the movies all the time." When Rock insists, "These are real movies" she asks, in disbelief, "like in London?" Given the absence of award recognition for *Straight Outta Compton*, which many of the interviewees had seen and liked, it marked a rift between Oscar celebrated films and the movies that were viewed and embraced by this sample of audience. Rock worked to challenge the "liberal-tinged self-congratulation of a typical Oscars ceremony with the different world people of color – even those who go to see films regularly – inhabit beyond the bubble of Hollywood's film elite" (Deggens). The bit highlighted a disconnect between mainstream film audiences and Oscar recognized films—especially along racial lines. In an award show that overly congratulates itself for the importance of cinema to the culture and the movie-going audience, the segment found a way to satirize everything the

Oscars holds sacred. The segment gave voice to persons and bodies, as well as positions that are actively ignored in the Oscar fanfare, enacting a critique of exclusion, audience indifference, and cultural elitism, arguing how many audiences do not recognize *your* movies either.

With all the racially themed humor during the broadcast, critical backlash was seemingly inevitable in the age of Twitter. Rock was accused of "perpetuating racial stereotypes" (*Oscars 2016 …*) in a moment that garnered the most social media controversy, yet was not explicitly referencing the #OscarsSoWhite boycott. Although the vast majority of Rock's racial critique was focused on Black/white racism, it was a (problematically) single moment involving Asian bodies that generated the most visible and sustained outrage. It happened in a recurrent portion of the show that has historically been the dullest moment in previous Oscar broadcasts. Rock introduced the accountants who have tabulated and secured the results for the Oscar voting process. Rather than the usual three accountants from Price Waterhouse, out walked three kids "who turned out to be three Asian children in suits" (*Oscars 2016*) providing "an embarrassing nod to stereotypes about Asians being good at math" (Deggens). In addition, one of the kids was given a last name that was Jewish. The audience responded with a conflicted discomfort. Rock, anticipating and ready for this engagement, replied, "If anybody is upset about that joke, just tweet about it on your phone, which was also made by these kids."

The whole bit infuriated many, especially given the absence of Asian-American actors represented in the awards show and the reduction of much of the racial commentary to Black/white binary frames (Deggens). The critical response was absolute and definitive that this joke was racist. "Rock has been criticized for a joke he made while hosting the Oscars ceremony, at the expense of Asian-Americans" (BBC). Constance Wu, actress from the ABC sitcom *Fresh Off The Boat* tweeted "To parade little kids on stage w/no speaking lines merely to be the butt of a racist joke is reductive & gross. Antithesis of progress." The bit was quickly concretized as "anti-Asian" (Soloman) and could only possibly be understood as "perpetuating racial stereotypes" (*Oscars 2016 …*) Rock was taken literally and simplistically, without any possible consideration for additional irony or complexity. The presence or mere invocation of a stereotype was swiftly and linearly determined to mean and enact the outright support and perpetuation of oppression. Rock's follow up comment, that anticipated the offense, called for the audience to be self-reflexive of how they, in fact, are regularly benefiting from child labor, yet this was either ignored or used to further bolster the "racist" charge. What are the limitations and shortcomings of taking humor at face value, where the introduction of a racist meaning is instantly disciplined as racist? What does it say when Rock anticipates the expected offense, calls for the audience to be self-reflexive of their own complicity in oppressive systems, and that call is actively ignored?

Chris Rock's Oscar performance provides a point of entry into a broad range of issues explored in this text. It marks the weight and expectation that lingered and framed Rock's performance before the event started, suggesting that his performance was always more than just about jokes and humor, but actually was central to a larger social and political context. Many framed and then critiqued Rock's role as political voice as much, if not more so, than as a comedian. For example, King criticized that, "Sadly, though, Rock is missing out on the fact that more unarmed African Americans were killed by police in 2015 than were lynched in any single year in the history of the Oscars. While it may be hard for some to think of our present day problems on that scale, these are the cold, hard facts." King's critique suggests a couple of key assumptions, most notably that Rock carries the burden beyond entertainment. Rather, he has a political platform where he is responsible for far more than just making the audience laugh. Additionally, Soloman created a lengthy bullet pointed list of issues, points, and facts surrounding the current state of racial oppression that Rock failed to engage, mention, or address, ranging from Trump, to the housing market, to gun reform and the murder of trans women of color. As a comedian and a cultural critic, there is a pronounced political expectation, role, and weight lingering over Rock's performance. However, in the face of this weighted expectation, critical attention remains primarily fixated on his words—what Rock said—fully privileging the spoken text of the joke, while downplaying or completely erasing the role of Rock's body, his voice, his expression, the context, the audience engagement, and a wealth of additional factors that operate in the construction of meaning in the comic context.

The remainder of this introduction will set a context for the larger book, beginning with a discussion about the serious role comedy plays in contemporary political discourse. Next, the introduction sets up a performance-centered framework of analysis, which will drive and shape the analysis over the next five chapters. Within the performative framework, the project looks to the aesthetic performances of comedians, but also enlists a performance frame to analyze how critics and critical patterns engage and respond to comedic work. Thus, there is the comedian's performance, but also the performativity of critique, which is equally central to the larger project. The introduction will then provide key points of entry for the larger project, identifying social, technological, and discursive factors that have come to shape the recurrent ritual of "the comic controversy" that plays out regularly across social media. Next, there will be a brief overview of the five chapters of the text. Finally, the introduction offers some additional framing about the stakes, investments, and risks of the project, and works to situate my role, as author, in this discussion.

The seriousness of comedy in the new millennium

> If you don't want to get insulted don't go to comedy clubs.
>
> (Masada qtd. in Odell)

> Liberals must learn to distinguish between 'things that truly count as profound injustices and … things that just kinda piss you off but you gotta get over it.' … My side, the left side has gotten a little unreasonable when it comes to separating the trivial from the profound.
>
> (Seth MacFarlane qtd. in Keller)

When proposing strategy to the Senate Subcommittee on how to handle ISIS militant extremists, Bono argued, "Don't laugh, but I think comedy should be deployed … It's like if you speak violence, you speak their language, but you laugh at them when they're goose-stepping down the street and it takes away their power … I'm suggesting that the Senate send in Amy Schumer and Chris Rock and Sacha Baron Cohen" (Kickham). There is a long history where the arbitrary lines between politics and comedy have been blurred beyond recognition. Satiric comedy such as *The Daily Show* with Jon Stewart or Trevor Noah, Samantha Bee's *Full Frontal,* John Oliver's *Last Week Tonight*, or Bill Maher's *Real Time* take on the role of political commentary in our contemporary culture. Steven Colbert, as his ironic persona of Steven Colbert, testified before Congress on immigration policy. *The Daily Show*'s Hasan Minhaj's powerful plea before Congress about gun control was one of the most important political speeches of 2016. The comic interventions of Ali G have shaped and impacted the political careers of a broad range of political figures. It is a now trite truism that many people get their primary news from these comedy programs, which are active in political discourse, yet have a habit of claiming they are "just doing comedy." This volume bypasses this false binary of political commentary/comedy, engaging the work of many comedians as inescapably both, and does so without apology or hesitation. In 2004, Jon Stewart famously appeared on *Crossfire* with Tucker Carlson and Paul Begala and took the hosts to task for being "partisan hacks" who contribute to a culture of screaming, false dichotomies, and the erosion of journalism. He begged for their help to stop "hurting America." The hosts were flustered, calling upon Stewart to be funnier, saying no one wants to see this angry and serious side of Jon Stewart. Stewart refused, begging for them to step up and do better. It was a singular moment in contemporary culture that emboldened a shift in the role of comedy in contemporary political culture, and the comedian became the truth teller and cable "news" was unmasked as toxic entertainment. While this was not a new tension, the line between news and comedy has since remained blurred, and the critical capacity to engage with the work has struggled in this negotiation. Comics do more than "tell jokes" and the jokes they do tell do more than merely solicit laughter. Comics have emerged as voices for a range of social positions and issues, from body shaming and police brutality to Islamophobia and gun control. As Soloman identified in the list of all the topics Rock did not address in his Oscars monologue, comedians are now part of the political process, a voice for the voiceless, and spokesperson of specific platforms. Comedy is serious business. Comedy is also dangerous as hell.

The "just a joke" defense no longer flies in contemporary culture, as the political significance of comedy resists this easy excuse. To say one simply doesn't get the joke or does not understand the joke and is being too sensitive seeks to absolve the comedian by diminishing the weight, value, or significance of humor. This book project takes a sharp 180-degree turn from this retreat, arguing jokes deserve more time, more consideration and more seriousness than we, as a culture, tend to allow them. Comedians, the ones I am most interested in here, have positions they wish to promote, ideas they wish to examine, and meanings they seek to interrogate. That is to suggest they have more going on than merely "things they want to say," but in a more complex mode of communication, they have work they wish to do. Yet there is a rift in our cultural dialogue around comedians, too often reducing what they are *doing* to what might have been *said*. It should go without saying that if you wish to satirically engage racism, you need to deal with racism. The same logic goes for misogyny, or homophobia, or ableism, or xenophobia, or any broad range of social fear and ignorance and oppression. As Borns argues, "In order to satirize trash, the satirist must, in a sense, wallow in it himself [*sic*] … does this make the final product trash?" (cited in Peterson 37). Too often, in contemporary discourse, these are lazily conflated. In our current climate, how we talk about these ever-present systems is carefully monitored, like a delicate dance to make sure we never set off a trigger. The way we, as a culture, discuss volatile topics such as race is like a careful, systematic tiptoe around a field of landmines. These topics present dangerous terrain that, in our current climate of comic controversy, is more and more explosive. This project works to speak to that terrain, to call attention to our reductive and simplistic focus on speech, to investigate the limiting patterns that shape our own criticism, and to claim a greater range of questions and possibilities for what comedic performance can do.

When we engage a comedian, what level of sophistication do we grant the meanings being examined? In our current soundbite culture, where tweets and op-eds are forcefully driving—if not fully replacing—much of "the news," complex communication processes are too often reduced to catchy *BuzzFeed* headlines and 140 character tweets. A citizen journalist from *Huffington Post* declares a joke offensive and homophobic, a Facebook friend shares the "article" with the comment "homophobic jokes are bad," a parade of "likes" follow, and we should all be expecting the comedian's apology in the morning. Ronson in his bestselling book *So Now That You've Been Publically Shamed* marks that social media has led to a public shaming renaissance (10), where Twitter and Facebook present a stage for "constant artificial high drama" (78)—a pattern of rigidly drawn courtrooms of heroes and villains where everyone goes for the hanging (51). The form tends to privilege emotional reactions (60) over intellectual complexities, and obscure the distinction between an attempt at humor and outright hate speech (Wallenstein qtd. in Ronson 75). This reflects a broader trend where individual thought requires too much labor in contemporary soundbite culture—where there exists a "breakdown of a consensus that the pursuit of knowledge is good" (Williams). As Williams argues in *Anti-Intellectualism and the Dumbing Down of America*, "Thinking takes too much time: it gets in the way of the immediacy of the online experience." Our speech and judgments become trained into a pattern of reacting and reactions, and the repetition of this pattern over and over begins to shape and define who we are as a culture. The stakes of this discussion are nothing short of preserving the role of intellectualism and artistry within our public discourse and insisting slogans and soundbites do not come to fully replace rigorous debate.

The artistry of comedy

> The goals inspiring the richest comedy are the same steering all art: to say what is usually suppressed and also speak truthfully.
>
> (Stone xiv)

> One of the tasks facing those who would alter identity-linked structures of privilege and oppression is to study performances that maintain, mimic, or modify such social relations.
>
> (Peterson vii)

The patterns playing out on a daily basis are likely not new to any reader, as the perpetual spiral of clickbait, outrage, polemical comments, escalation, and on-to-the-next moment is the mediated scream-fest we currently live within. Looking at recent controversies of comedians who "went too far," such as Daniel Tosh, Tracy Jordan, Katt Williams, Sarah Silverman, or Don Rickles, their humorous offense is usually reported (and evaluated) through a short textualization of the spoken words. Aesthetic craft, bodies, temporality, context, and audience are erased through a disembodied and decontextualized record. For this book project, which seeks to intervene into this ongoing pattern of comic controversies, the core proposition is quite simple—comedy is a complex art form. While hardly a revolutionary claim, there are several implications of this premise that call for some reflection.

First, too often comedy, if ever considered in the realm of artistry, is approached as popular and lowbrow, where critical stand up comedy "straddles the border between high art and popular culture" (Peterson viii). The presence of words, or spoken language, trips us into the deceptive faith with which we engage our daily interactions and all other modes of speech. In other words, if I can assign meaning to what you have said, I "understand" it. You laugh or you don't. In communicative terms, we engage comedy as a mode of fast messaging, rather than slow messaging (Hall and Hall). A fast message would be considered a cartoon, television, or something that has "easy familiarity" (165). Slow messages, on the other hand, would be more along the lines of art, poetry, and would be understood to take and demand a different speed and form of engagement. Approaching comedy as a fast message leaves little room for challenging an audience, pushing at discomforts, troubling sedimented meanings, or cultural interrogation. Consider the sense of humility, of openness, of patience, and commitment one must offer to enter and engage an art museum? A ballet? An opera? Consider the cultural authority these forms carry, as well as the attention and investment they demand. Humor, particularly the more critical political humor I am examining in this volume, requires more of us in order for us to get more out of it. In an interview about comedy, comedian Ricky Gervais addressed this point:

> I've seen people say, "Ricky Gervais made this terrible joke." And they say the joke, and it is terrible, but they've got it slightly wrong. Or they've misunderstood it because they've missed a word or changed one side of the pun or play on words and I think no, you didn't get the joke. You're allowed not to like my jokes. When I go up and I do stand up, I cherish the gasps as much as the laughs because they're like, "(Gasp) You shouldn't be saying that," and then they laugh because they get it. So I don't mind people not liking my stuff, but to criticize it, I think they should understand it.

In this text, the approach towards comedy that I am advocating for places far greater responsibility on—and opportunity for—the audience. It is about self-reflexivity and challenging how our ideological commitments and privileges shape how we come to humor. There is a small scene in the film *Ted 2*, where Ted (the "live" talking teddy bear) amuses himself by attending an improv show and calling out very serious topics. So, when the overly perky and enthusiastic improv comedian asks the audience to call out a historical event, Ted yells, "9/11!" Flustered, the performer suggests a different route, asking for a person. Ted calls out, "Robin Williams," who recently killed himself. The performer tries to redirect, but Ted yells "Robin Williams on 9/11!" When asked for a location, Ted yells, "The offices of Charlie Hebdo," "GermanWings cockpit," and "Ferguson, Missouri!" The performer pretends that someone called out "Starbucks," and tries to move forward with their show. The scene works because engaging these deeply heated and serious topics in improv is extremely dangerous. Off the cuff, in the moment, and at the will of fellow improv members is not how a comedian wants to take these ideas to an audience. I use this example, because it helps to set up an important comparison between the flippant and improvised engagement with these topics, and the comedians who mindfully, skillfully, and intentionally choose to wade into these issues in their comedic work.

This project generously engages the comedian as a form of anthropologist (Kozinski cited in Peterson 33), who enlists various genres of comedy to make "covert culture visible" (33). It is about an ongoing process of questioning the work we are comfortable with and what are the implications and investments of those comforts. This larger project insists on a more complicated and complicating discourse around comedy, that pushes past whether something is funny and investigates what the humor is seeking to do beyond the laugh. Even when satiric irony is "working" or doing critical performative work, the result is not always "funny." The "boo," the groan, and/or affective audience discomfort mark a different valuable aesthetic for interventionist humor. The gasps, groans, and awkward grumblings in "racy" comedy are part of the communicative process and the negotiation of meanings. One comment pushes a delicate or offensive topic, and these vocalizations or pained silences mark a dialogic response. There is great risk/value in these ironic moments—the "Oh damn" and the "they did not just say that,"—for they open up a space, a discomfort, and a performative doing. Discursive meanings are breached. The transformative laugh is not usually the easy one. The "Can I laugh?" "Should I laugh?" and "Why am I laughing?" moments open up and potentialize the very self-reflexive interventions that doing comedy can elicit.

Thus, this project follows the work of cultural critics such as Stone who advocate for "treat[ing] stand up comedy as solo theater" (xii). Stone suggests we "put aside the categories performance art, one-person theater piece, and stand up" asserting that "sass and craft are my criteria" (xiii). Wherein performance art, like stand up, is permitted to challenge social taboos (34), the degree that stand up is considered popular and more mainstream seems to impair its more complex operation. Borns argues, "In stand up, as opposed to other art forms, people are far less willing to stand back and let the 'experts' tell them what is and isn't high art. Unlike a Jackson Pollock painting or a John Cage quartet, with comedy, everyone 'gets it' to some degree, so everyone becomes an expert critic" (cited in Peterson 36). Perhaps, as Peterson suggests, the distinction between performance art and comedy should be dropped altogether (36), opening an ever-present awareness of the role of interpretation, and appreciation of the centrality of aesthetics to the production of meaning, and the navigation of complex codes. In that space, perhaps audiences will attend less so to the crass and grating obnoxiousness of Gilbert Gottfriend's voice and intolerant rantings, and more fully be able to engage how his work "reveals the poison of ethnocentrism" (Stone: xxvii).

Now, to be clear, just as I am not dealing with improv groups, the work I am interested in is not the work of all stand up comedians. There are those comedians who are doing this anthropological work, calling upon us to interrogate our own social commitments, privileges, and moral failures, and then there is work that merely panders to our lesser selves. Comedian Albert Brooks helps to articulate this distinction, recounting, "My friend Harry Nilsson used to say the definition of an artist was someone who rode way ahead of the herd and was sort of on the lookout. Now you don't have to be that, to be an artist. You can be right smack-dab in the middle of the herd. If you are, you'll be the richest" (Apatow 70). This project seeks out and tries to provide greater critical language for those satiric artists who follow in the traditions of Richard Pryor, George Carlin, Lenny Bruce, and Dick Gregory, but also Whoopi Goldberg, John Leguizamo, and Spalding Gray. Stone argues that "Satire is opposite to cynicism, because it thinks about its targets" (xxix). Satiric work not only invites the audience to laugh, to take pleasure in the workings of a joke, but presents the "implicit invitation to the audience to consider the 'meaning' of the work" (viii).

It is a common argument that the ultimate determination of the comedian's work is whether or not they get the laugh. As a slow medium of communication (Hall and Hall), one that requires time, reflection and contemplation, the critical evaluation of this form of humor must look beyond the simple criterion of the laugh. Just as humor is a slippery process that is impossible to nail down with a singular theory or interpretation, laughter is a complicated process that occurs for a broad number of reasons. Beyond the range of emotions, reasons, and stimuli that she lists in her taxonomy of different laughs, Rayner marks the "invaded laugh" (2012: 34), where she finds herself laughing at a joke she does not find particularly funny because she was caught off guard. While not "funny," or even offensive in its content, the timing, rhythm, pace and delivery of the joke cues or prompts laugher. Thus, the performance of the joke and its structural eloquence can elicit laughter yet this may not provide insight or understanding into the workings of the joke, the performative effect, or the rhetorical dimensions of the communicative exchange.

On the flipside, the absence of laughter should not always mark a joke as a failure. As many comedy historians have marked, Lenny Bruce, one of the most celebrated satirists in stand up was often not very funny. Furthermore, engaging culturally sensitive and volatile topics can produce knee jerk reactions, where the mere mention of a topic elicits discomfort, frustration, and even offense. Gervais elaborates that, "People use things like 'targets of your jokes' and I don't consider them targets, I consider them subjects. And that's where offense comes most awful – when people confuse the target of a joke with the subject of a joke" ("Ricky Gervais on"). Considering our opening example of Rock, was Pinkett-Smith the *target* of the joke? At one point, it appeared she was, yet only to build up the exonerating audience laughter and then turn this back on them. So, the larger subject was the boycott, and Pinkett-Smith became a way to isolate and diffuse the critique (a momentary target) until he led into critiquing the types of racism he does see happening. The language of targets, offenses, "the" audience, and the embodied and temporal negotiation requires a more sophisticated engagement. If anything, by the metric I am carving out, the much laughed at Pinkett-Smith joke marks Rock's weaker moment, and his uneasy and not so laughed at conclusion of sorority racism defines his uncomforting success.

At this moment in time, as it has in many moments in our history, comedy marks a dangerous terrain, rife with risk and pitfalls, particularly "edgy" or political comedy. The political right is screaming everything is "political correctness," the left is destroying reasoned debate and free speech, attacking character over substance, intuiting motives rather than engaging ideas, and weaponizing "outrage for ideological and partisan ends" (Ham and Benson 21). This form of "lazy debate" is criticized for "impugn[ing] your motives rather than debating the merits of the idea" (Ham and Benson 82). The political left is calling out microaggressions, encrypted racism and sexism, and "political dog whistles" (105) in the never-ending debate around the (perhaps, over exaggerated?) "outrage machine."

Speech, in its most textualized and literal modes, is under great scrutiny. The risk of comedy, particularly when enlisting irony, body, and audience negotiation for satiric intervention, has reached a boiling point. This project traces and examines the multiple fears and anxieties that underscore the risk, danger, and anxiety that sits at the foundation of comic controversies. The comic controversy can be defined as a broader cultural outrage and debate—often via social media—regarding a word, phrase, or specific joke from a comic set or event. One key feature to the comic controversy is the process of decontextualization and recontextualization, where the joke (often isolated from a larger set) in question is extracted from the initial space, audience, and larger comedic frame of the intended event, and reframed in a different forum (ex: a critical tweet or online article). Often this decontextualization strips away a wealth of communicative information, such as body, affect, audience response, ironic cues, and resituates the mere words of the joke within a polarizing frame (Is this joke homophobic when X said Y?). The comic controversy works to reduce the artistry of comedy to text, and tends to focus upon some absolute notion of rightness or wrongness of wording. It sets the terms for a cultural debate that works to reproduce a binary, simplified and circular pattern of outrage that feeds the clickbait machine.

One significant assumption that sits at the heart of many comic controversies is that when a comedian speaks or references an existing cultural stereotype or prejudicial meaning, the audience's bias will be always and only reinforced and the prejudicial attitude will be blindly adopted. Such a fear operates with some, if not all of the following assumptions:

1 The speaking or reference to a stereotype is equal to the endorsement of a stereotype.
2 The speaking or reference to a stereotype is always linear and fixed in its meaning.
3 The comedian has the power to influence the minds of the audience.
4 The audience is primarily passive in the reception of meaning.
5 The interpretation or projection of hegemonic meanings by the audience is the comedian's fault/responsibility.
6 The meaning of a joke resides in the words spoken.
7 Context of the joke is peripheral to meaning.
8 For a younger minority viewer, the potentially stereotypical meaning can diminish self-worth and identity.

The anxiety that feeds the comic controversy is partially fed by a highly simplified understanding of communicative processes, both in terms of artistry, but also in terms of polysemy. Communication is polysemic, offering a broad range of ways a text or message can be read, navigated, and endowed with meaning. Entering into the realm of the aesthetic, where artistry is highlighted, and strategies of irony, parody, and camp are centralized, meaning is a complex, negotiated and heterogeneous process. Just because the language of a dominant or hegemonic system is enlisted, it does not mean that the work is not coaching highly resistant and subversive meanings. Even extending beyond the assumed intention of a comic, the polysemy of comedic texts can be taken in, taken up, negotiated, appropriated and surely employed passively, strategically and/or resistively by audiences (Shugart and Waggoner 2008: 8). Audiences both take the experience of the communicative exchange, and then they also *make* the experience.

A performance-centered analysis to the comic controversy

> Explicit body performance artists have deployed the material body to collide literal renderings against Symbolic Orders of meaning.
>
> (Schneider 3)

> Apatow: I saw you and you seem like a different person onstage.
>
> Sandra Bernhard: Well, you have to be. You have to have some sort of persona onstage to get your point across.
>
> (Apatow 747–8)

Central to this book is a performance studies approach to humor and communication, which draws its attention to several dimensions of the communicative process and how meaning is produced and reproduced. Performance, and specifically theories of performativity, turn their eye to the patterned conditions of culture, tracing what Schechner calls "twice-behaved behavior." Performance and performativity look to the ritualized, the repeated, and the sedimented in cultural behavior to understand the process of naturalization and normalization through *doing*. Thus, to approach culture, or identity, or gender, or even criticism from a performative frame is to take a step away from essential understandings of what something or someone *is*, and look to how something or someone is *done*. Diamond famously framed performativity as a dual analytical framework of the "*doing* and the thing *done*." From this theoretical perspective, working from Butler's groundbreaking work on gender performativity, many performance scholars have examined how all areas of identity and culture mark performative accomplishments. By zeroing in on the moment-by-moment doings of race, or nation, or our daily performances at work or in public life, we can trace the spatial, bodily, temporal creation and ongoing recreation of norms that produce the seemingly essential and concretized systems we exist within. Furthermore, by tracing the moment-by-moment reiteration of discursive norms, we can open up a critical space of intervention to do otherwise. Not merely to repeat and reflect the pattern, but to challenge the moment-by-moment concretization of cultural forms.

With specific regard to comedy and the comic controversy, a performative framework assists in asking key questions that are too often absent from the cultural discourse. First and foremost, a performative frame places temporality at the center of discussion, with a core focus on process and the processual. This is the emphasis on how we do, rather than what we are. Second, performance centralizes the body in the heart of the analysis and study of communication. Although our scriptocentric (Conquergood 1998, 2002) culture tends to privilege the written and textualized word, the physical body and the broad range of meanings and relations it carries is always central to how meaning is produced. "The explicit body in representation is foremost a site of social markings, physical parts and gestural signatures of gender, race, class, age, sexuality – all of which bear ghosts of historical meanings, markings delineating social hierarchies of privilege and disprivilege" (Schneider 2). Bodies carry a wealth of meanings, stories, and histories. As Derkson argues, physical bodies are always met with assumptions and cultural codes (236). In comedic work, where the comedian takes on and presents a persona, "The body of the persona and performer are put in critical dialogue with one another" (236). In enacting cultural scripts and logics through the eyes and voice of the persona, these scripts are not merely a flat and mindless reiteration, but open a space for interruption, for play, for reflection, for critique, for resisting the gaze, and for rearticulation. Existing and not yet existing cultural meanings are "performed; deformed; enjoyed; and imagined" (Derkson 245). This is not merely wordplay, but an understanding that bodies carry meanings, discourses, histories and assumptions that, in the performative encounter, are central to how a performer and audience work through and navigate one another. Just as Lenny Bruce can now be understood through the terms of "performance art" (Peterson 38), comedians like Sarah Silverman also engage this work, as we are always engaging Silverman's humor and cultural criticism *through* her body (Lowery 62). Her body is not just a medium of communication, but a site of analysis and intervention. Her comedy does not merely speak from a white female body, but is about interrogating the process of speaking *as* a white female. As Rebecca Schneider writes, "Unfolding the body, as if pulling back velvet curtains to expose a stage the performance artists … peel back layers of signification that surround their bodies like ghosts at a grave" (2).

Too often in cultural criticism we leave the body to the unstated, resisting the active and central role it plays in navigating meanings. The body does speak, but not always in a manner that we are trained to hear. The body carries a politic and a wealth of discursive content that is always, ever-present. Rock, as an African American male, speaks in and through a body that carries meanings and codes that he draws attention to and engages in a variety of strategies. His work as the ironic fool in his set cites racist legacies and that citation *is a central part* of the joke. Judd Apatow once asked Sandra Bernhard, "Do you think comedians should make a statement, like a political or social kind of?" Bernhard replied, "I think if you're really good, you do that without trying to. You invoke emotions from an audience without being obvious about it." The politic of comedy is not only what is said or stated obviously, but happens in the affect, in the pause, through the body, in relation. A performative frame, with its eyes to processual meanings, body, and context seeks out these operations with and through that which is explicitly spoken.

Alongside the focus of the processual and the embodied dimensions of communication, performance attends to the spatialized dimensions of communication. Communication happens in specific contexts and the design and inhabitance of those spaces shapes how meaning is produced. This includes the physical comedy space, as well as the implication of recording the event, placing it in a mediated environment, trimming a ninety-minute set down to a three-minute joke, and embedding the clipped joke with a specific camera angle into a web article with a leading headline. Clicking on that link, the physical bodies of the audience are removed, the groans, the giggles, the screams of support, and the negotiated affect of the room.

In the negotiation of text, audience, body, affect, space, and context, performance more immediately attends to the aesthetic dimensions of communication (Pelias and Van Oosting). It privileges not merely what was said but how it was said, knowing the how works to shape and reconstruct the what. It approaches stand-up comedy as an embodied act, an affective and interpretive negotiation that occurs between heterogeneous audience positions and the comedian. It places focus on the physical and the subjective in how meanings are interpreted and narrated to self.

PC and the performativity of critique

A performative frame, however, introduces additional points of value and intervention to the comic controversy, through the attention to extended patterns of behavior—that of critical reception. The comic controversy, these virtual debates about the potential offensiveness of a comedian's joke (and the often demanded apology for the offense), marks a secondary performative site of analysis. Herein, critical patterns for marking offense and dialoguing offense depict an additional pattern of behavior, a repeated social process, that works to solidify and normalize limiting and circular critical patterns. Burke looked at symbolic rituals of punishment through his framework of "The Iron Law of History" which sets forth a circular and ongoing pattern of repeated violence and punishment. Burke grounds this work in the symbolic capacity to produce perfection—a state or ideality that does not exist in nature but lives through discursive production. Only through symbolic systems can something be the negative, can an utterance or a tree or person *not be* (a bush or thinner, etc.). The negative produces an always present falling short, a failure, a imperfection that needs to be dealt with and purged. It requires some form of disciplining and punishment. This can take the form of mortification (i.e., self-punishment) or victimage—wherein a scapegoat is identified and sacrificed to temporarily restore order. There is release, cleansing, and a form of self-righteous reward in the process of punishment—a rebirth. We also find a place, a home, a root, a cause in which to place our angers, failures, and social shortcomings, particularly when it comes to the most durable and hideous of our failures—racism, sexism, homophobia, ableism, xenophobia. The critical calling out and disciplining of one for the good of the whole works to isolate and (falsely) contain the threat, while distancing the critique from the broader social ill. It is a performance of innocence through designating a guilty. Resisting the false right wing rallying cry of "political correctness" or "PC," this project seeks to recast this troubling and limited assignment of meanings with a performative approach, wherein "PC" works to call out and unpack the Performativity of Critique (PC). A performative frame works to both highlight this ongoing ritual, but also works to disrupt its normalization and reification. Our use of theory and how we make sense, where we are offended, how we voice that offense (and where and when we are not) are also performances in need of interrogation.

The multiple variables at work here, and the manner by which we try to simplify and explain humor goes back to a simple truth from Lewis Black: science is not equipped to deal with comedy. The only way to understand humor is to "go tell jokes" (as cited in Rayner 29) or in other words, to *do* it and investigate and reflect on the embodied, contextual, affective process. Performance approaches the aesthetic event as a laboratory, one filled with sedimented hegemonic weight, but also fueled with critical promise. The bodies of the comedians, the critics, and the audience are all called into the discussion, and asked to put themselves on the line. While certain bodies invoke and can engage discourses with greater authority and experience, all bodies are positioned by these discourses and all bodies have work to do. Approaching these performance artist comedians with complexity, nuance, and performative modes of engagement provides a greater space for these cultural workers to continue their irreverent inquiries—attend to the performativities that map their (and our) bodies as a means to bend and push and disrupt our comforts. We need spaces where we can reflect on these doings, find hope, joy, release, shame, and maybe, a good complicated laugh.

Comic performativities: Points of entry and tracing trajectories

At the outset, it is important to mark that the organization of this project is not linear. There are those book projects that set up a theoretical framework in the introduction, which is then deepened and applied in a selection of case studies and contexts. There are also those projects that begin with a problem, and the volume traces an interlocking system of theoretical tools to engage the issue. This book falls more into the latter category. *Comic Performativities* is not a systematic "how to" guide but a tool of complication, offering a constellation of theoretical frameworks to trouble the existing already linear modes by which we engage controversy in comedy. I am not suggesting we do not take comedy seriously. As a culture, we take it incredibly seriously, which leads to the ongoing debates of offense, and the political stakes of comedy.

What does seem to be lacking is a willingness to wholly engage the comedian as an artist, as a cultural worker, and as a distinct contributor to our political discussion—to take comedians seriously. Comedians are celebrated when they make us laugh, and they are respected when they tell jokes that help us feel good about our beliefs, values, and commitments, yet our cultural discourse seems to have grown less and less willing to let comedians challenge us. This is not surprising. We live in a cultural moment where intellectualism is vilified, speech is carefully monitored, and partisanship is explosive. I sit writing this introduction in summer 2016, amidst the rancor and demonization of the presidential election. Our country is standing in a moment where videos of police killing innocent Black bodies testify to a truth many have argued for decades. I type in the wake of the Orlando massacre at the Pulse night club, in the immediate aftermath of targeted murders of police officers, and the reinvigorated Republican attack on women's rights, LGBTQ rights, and the seemingly clear and necessary demand for Black lives to matter.

We have stopped trusting comedians in much the same way we have lost faith in our journalists. Rather than challenging us to think, the emergence of social media and cable news has made it convenient to create bubbles of our own rightness, righteousness, and homogeneity. Yet the failure to come to the comedian as an artist, to let the joke be a cultural mirror, only scratches the surface of a much more complicated set of issues. The comic controversy is not merely about our lack of faith in comedians or our trust in comedy. Rather, there is a complex web of intersecting factors that have worked to shape this current phenomena, determining who and if someone can tell which joke, and what is the correct response. In other words:

WHO can tell that joke?
Who CAN tell that joke?
Who can tell THAT joke?

1 *Scriptocentrism*: When it comes to comedy, we tend to privilege what was said over the entire aesthetic experience of the event, erasing body, affect, and audience relation. Thus, our talk about the workings of a joke will tend to focus on a simplified transaction of what was said, versus a more complex integration of factors shaping what the joke does.
2 *Decontextualization*: Social and digital media have allowed us to audience a joke in contexts never intended by the comedian. Any mediated version of a joke can be cut to any length, trimmed down, uploaded to YouTube, and embedded in any number of spaces. The original audience of the joke, as well as any necessary context preceding the edit is lost.
3 *Recontextualization*: Social media has allowed us to recontextualize and thus rewrite the meaning of jokes. When a joke is textualized or embedded as a video link onto a post or blog entry, there is a new frame established to read and interpret the joke. If the text above the Facebook

post of the video clip says "Bill Maher's transphobia is NOT okay," the very meaning of what will be watched is already driven.

4 *Online Anonymity*: Social media has allowed us to critique and demonize a comedian without having to face them.
5 *Essentialism*: It's hardly earth shattering, and actually tacit cultural knowledge that certain people and certain bodies can say certain things and tell certain jokes. We have all heard the disclaimer, as well as the meta commentaries on the disclaimer of "It's okay, I'm gay," "It's okay, I'm Jewish," "I can say that, my mom is Mexican," etc. Identity politics have come to define, in very regimented ways, which persons are permitted to engage which topics. YOU can't tell this joke speaks to how certain jokes, culturally, cannot or should not be performed by certain identities. The question is "why?" It's about both body and identity. It's not merely the saying of the joke (You can't TELL that joke), but a complex negotiation of the speaking body in relation to existing discourses, aesthetic delivery and text. What meanings and possibilities reside in the performance of certain bodies and what stories and histories do they cite and carry?
6 *Anti-Intellectualism*: Cultural shifts have worked to devalue the role of intellectualism, while privileging how one may feel as the primary political compass. Our cultural discourse, in a culture of Facebook likes and Twitter retweets, works to privilege limited engagements from a menu of six variations of like, all that situate a response in the realm of feelings (like, laugh, angry, surprise, sadness). We are encouraged to trust our feelings about candidates, about issues, and about social problems rather than vigorous and nuanced intellectual debate. In the realm of art, where sometimes the goal is not to make you feel good, this works to severely limit the types of artwork that is appreciated or supported.
7 *Dog Whistles*: Cultural shifts have worked to mask explicit statements of racism, sexism, and homophobia, preserving their existence, while disguising their presence in directed speech. This encrypted form of speech can be characterized as "coded messages that are intended for a narrow, discrete audience, while passing unnoticed by everyone else" (Ham and Benson 105).
8 *State of Paranoia*: Jackson talks about how coded language, as a result of "political correctness" has led to a cultural state of paranoia, wherein bias is relocated to implicit subtext. Racism is ever-present, but silenced in polite speech. Thus, when racism is made explicit (even if in the context of critically engaging its operations) it sets off alarms. Coupled with the anti-intellectualism mentioned prior, this leads to a lazy conflation between enlisting references to existing cultural bias and plainly endorsing that bias. For the comedian, particularly the satiric and ironic comedian, there is a perpetual reduction of calling up oppressive systems (such as engaging racism) and supporting those systems (being a racist).
9 *Critical Innocence*: In this moment of anxiety, the calling out and disciplining of comedians seems to provide a sense of superiority, pleasure,

and self-righteousness, where the critic can demonize the violator and rhetorically position their own pristine distance from oppressive systems (I can't be racist because I critiqued them for being racist).

10 *Triggers and Challenging Art*: Generationally, there are trends occurring where audiences resist being challenged or offended as a productive, valuable, and expected dimension of comedy and art.

The variables and factors contributing to the comic controversy are many, and the above list of ten merely trace out some of the significant trends in contemporary culture giving rise and shape to these events. This can be summed up, imperfectly, by what Gournelos and Greene refer to as a characteristic of post 9/11 humor and politics, marking "the increased importance of negotiated media, image, and discourse through a rapid and complex interaction between politicians, media sources, texts and audiences" that is far more complex than production and consumption (xvii).

Comic controversies and the goals of this project

> And I didn't go out there to ruin everyone's day or undermine the moral fabric of America. I was making jokes. And I'm the butt of my jokes as well ... But it wasn't a room full of wounded soldiers – this was a room full of some of the most privileged, rich people in the world with some idiot from England teasing them a bit. And I really think offense is the collateral damage of freedom of speech and freedom of speech is one of our greatest privileges.
>
> Ricky Gervais ("Ricky Gervais on ...")

We live in a cultural moment where "comic controversies," "Political Correctness" and the "outrage machine" of social media produce an endless and circulating stream of social dramas of offense, indictment, and apology. Right wing pundits argue leftist politics have brought an end to cultural discussion and debate, while critical scholars take right wing critics to task for reifying systems of oppression under the guise of reason. This book project traces and disrupts these cultural patterns of who gets to say what, who can tell a certain type of joke, who gets to laugh, and how meaning is assigned to the message. Resisting simplified understandings of who can and cannot make a particular joke or author a particular position, the project works to investigate the dynamic ironic interplay between spoken word, asserted identity, bodily performance, and the differing meanings produced through diverse audience positions. It asks how we, as a culture, determine whether a particular message is "sexist" or "racist" or "offensive," and what are the stakes and implications of these designations. *What does that designation accomplish, both for the accused and the accuser? How does this pattern of response work to strengthen and reaffirm exiting social hierarchies?* Interrogating these questions, the project sets forth a conceptual framework to examine how a particular utterance might do racism, do sexism, or do offense in differing ways that may or may not work to subvert these systems. Working in the fields of communication theory, performance studies, rhetoric, critical identity studies, and humor, the book is structured around a series of contemporary comic controversies and the social media backlash that worked to write these communicative events.

From a mainstream pop cultural position, the book is an examination of critical patterns that exhaustingly rehearse themselves around humor, identity, and offense. Focusing on a broad range of "comic controversies" from the last ten years, the project works to trace, interrogate, and disrupt the workings of this ongoing social media ritual. Recasting the now deflated charge of "PC" from "political correctness" to identify the "Performativity of Critique," the book project seeks to examine the rhetorical implications and limitations of these ongoing patterns, while offering alternative models and modes of intervention. It aims to help coach us to engage these dialogues more critically and reflexively.

Theoretically, the project is a critical investigation of how bodies and bodily discourses—the meanings that precede bodies and are mapped onto bodies—present complex and layered disruptions that fall outside "what was said." Digging deep into the long, contested and heavily theorized concepts of irony and camp, the performative approach of the book is less concerned with defining what these terms are, but tracing the performative dimensions of what they can *do*. This is accomplished through the primary theoretical export of the text, ironic performativity, which mines a tradition of speech act theory, performativity, and irony to theorize the complex negotiation between bodily action and bodily discourses working to frame and define bodily meanings.

At its core, the book works to more solidly position performative dimensions (relation, body, context, aesthetics, affect) into the study and engagement of communication, for aesthetic dimensions of communication (which include a range of strategies and channels beyond the spoken word, most immediately including camp, various forms of irony, parody, sarcasm, and audience) are central to the process of assigning and constructing meanings. The book disrupts and challenges flat and linear theories and models of human communication through the entry point of humor. Critical and public engagements with controversial ironic work, which have been quickly and wholly labeled as oppressive (ex. racist, sexist, or homophobic) are troubled through performative engagement. The text develops a vocabulary and method for tracing how a particular text engages with oppressive discourses (i.e. how it DOES racisms in ways that can be potentially resistant).

The next five chapters will engage these interlocking issues through the analysis of a broad range of comedic texts, as well as larger comedic controversies. The texts selected, and the broader cultural events, were chosen based on a series of criteria. First, the larger controversies selected were the ones that garnered the most attention. Comedians like Jerry Seinfeld, Sarah Silverman, Chris Rock, Louis C.K., Daniel Tosh, Margaret Cho, Bill Maher, Ricky Gervais, Eddie Murphy, Dave Chapelle, and Amy Schumer are celebrity comedians who have been frequent figures at the center of comic controversies. In turn, close attention will be paid to their most controversial works, in order to trace and unpack how aesthetic dimensions to communication and performative processes are actively removed from the cultural discussion. In addition, smaller moments of outrage and productive counter-examples will be used to assist in tracing key patterns. This will include lesser-known comedians like Jim Jefferies and Rebel Wilson, or non-comedian celebrities such as Darren Criss, Brad Paisley, RuPaul, Eva Longoria, and Kanye West.

The multiple channels and embodied complexities of current "comic controversies" require an analytical approach that can trace and unpack aesthetic dimensions within and beyond the words spoken (ex. "She said X"). Chapter 1 opens with specific attention to how the aesthetic dimensions of a communicative act—particularly in densely layered and highly subjective communicative exchanges such as comedy—complicate and disrupt the "doing" (the telling of the joke) and the "thing done" (the effect) of any performative action or communicative exchange. By centralizing the critical lens of performativity in the analysis of communication, this optic draws attention to the ways all communication marks an unstable space of contestation and political effects, wherein subjects are constituted, social hierarchies are structured/struggled over, and the us, them, and we of audiences are reproduced (Langellier 1999). Thus, exploring the performativity of comic controversies turns our attention to the political/social/discursive/constitutive reverberations of the aesthetics of communication. Where a performative approach to communication draws our attention to the ever-present negotiations of power and control, attention to irony marks the twiceness inherent in the communicative event, wherein bodily citation and spoken text each work in, through, and against existing discourses. Through this framework, the chapter grounds and mobilizes the guiding concept of *ironic performativity* through the study of Trevor Noah, Brad Paisley's CMA "Blackish" joke, and Amy Schumer's breakout performance in the *Comedy Central Roast of Charlie Sheen*. A frame of ironic performativity works to closely trace this struggle and negotiation to map the layering of meanings between words and aesthetics. Ironic performativity traces the struggle, the moment-by-moment power negotiation in the communicative event, detailing the instability and the potential reworking of political meanings that occur through words, bodies, and patterned systems of meaning. The chapter offers a close read of Schumer's break out performance, wherein her four-and-half-minute set enlisted and eviscerated a broad range of gendered expectations that framed her arrival.

Transitioning from Schumer and the foundation of ironic performativity, Chapter 2 begins with a broader overview of the patterns that make up and repeat themselves in the ongoing parade of "comic controversies." The analysis is framed by a close analysis of Sarah Silverman's controversial appearance on the *Conan O'Brien Show*—perhaps the first "comic controversy" in the age of social media. While this is a regular occurrence, and has been a site of struggle and frustration for most political comics (e.g. Bill Maher, Amy

Schumer, Louis C.K., Joan Rivers, Don Rickles, Lenny Bruce, George Carlin, Kathy Griffin, Daniel Tosh, etc.), this comic controversy takes on a unique ritualized pattern in contemporary culture.

This chapter, extending the processual shift from the examination of ironic performativity, interrogates this performative pattern of textualization, offense, and indictment. Calling for a shift in the language of tragic judgment (wherein a joke, a comedian, or an event is framed as racist, sexist, ablest, etc.), a performative approach coaches a dialogic engagement (questioning how racism, sexism, misogyny, ableism is being *done*). Such an approach—as theorized through Butler's conception of judgment and Burkean comedy—offers a more complex and processual approach to understand how subversive comedy not only rehearses oppressive discourses, but also, potentially, unpacks, disrupts, and reimagines them in a range of complex and situated ways. Communication, especially complex sites such as humor, need to be engaged as *more* complex, *more* intricate, and offering layered information that demands close attention to performative effects. To open a performance frame where meanings are multiple, negotiated, and contextual, the overall determination of meaning, however, resides in the audience—an interpretive space that requires its own critical self-reflexive investigation.

The chapter contextualizes this work in an historical tracing of the term "political correctness," and specific sites of analysis, including William Shatner's *Roast* appearances, Kanye West's response to President Bush following Hurricane Katrina, Jerry Seinfeld's recent indictment of "PC College Kids," Sarah Silverman's controversial *Conan* appearance, Chris Rock's "N***ers and Black People," white parody on *Orange is the New Black*, Bill Maher's Caitlyn Jenner joke, and Jon Hamm and Jane Krakowski's use of blackface on *30 Rock*. Questioning the linguistic tendency to assign fixed descriptions of solidified judgment to our interpretations (i.e. Schumer is "racist" or Maher is "transphobic"), this chapter offers a performative model of analysis as a corrective.

The third chapter moves from aesthetic complexities and naming practices to the role of shifting audience practices and processes within the comic controversy. The chapter examines how audience social positions and investments inevitably co-author the interpretive processing and "understanding" of ironic performativities—centralizing the importance of critical self-reflexivity in the audiencing of this work. Phrased in a more colloquial manner, how we read ironic performativity is as much, if not more, about the audience as it is the speaker/performer/comedian. Whether an audience reads offense, subversion, or hope into a joke has as much to do with the specific audience member and the context, as the content of the joke, itself.

Extending discussions of comic controversies involving Rebel Wilson, RuPaul, Eddie Murphy, Chris Rock, and Amy Schumer, the chapter turns to the experience of offense into a self-reflexive resource. Where we find and assign offense, humor, or pleasure requires critical self-reflexivity. Context, timing, audience, and our own investments in hegemonic systems of power and privilege enable and goad our laughs, and—as shown by how we make sense of specific moments—our offense. Our own values, beliefs, and expectations dictate reception. Thus, jokes that have crossed the cultural lines of "too much" or "too soon"—often marked as failures or missteps—also provide important insights as tools of cultural investigation. They mark our cultural avoidances, fears, and anxieties as well as our comforts and commitments. As ironic performativity is never stable enough to eliminate any potential ambiguity, there is reason to believe we can always see what we want to see, what we choose to see, or what our positionality allows us to see (or not see). Ironic performativity requires that we, as audience, accept and examine our role, our commitments, and our complicities.

The chapter begins by tracing the contextual shifts that have occurred in comedy, moving from the live audience engagement (primary audience) where audiences actively worked to shape meanings with comedians in the moment (what can be called *audienceship*). The contexts of comic work have since shifted to mediated forms of comedy, where the initial context of the event is stripped and potentially reframed. In addition, in the contemporary comic controversy, there is the networked audience, wherein the joke is reframed, retold, or perhaps fully reconstructed in the act of textualization. Herein, the critical audience is not merely repeating a joke but is, in fact, re-authoring the joke, crafting a narrative about the joke, and thus taking the joke and making it into something new. Whether it's an improvised comment found to be transphobic by Darren Criss on stage in *Hedwig and The Angry Inch*, or a joke by Sean Penn about his friend Alejandro González Iñárritu at the Academy Awards, the reduction of the communicative event to the textualized message to the cultural indictment is a pattern now commonplace in the daily news cycle. This pattern is theorized as a paranoid mode of audiencing (Sedgwick) that works to reproduce *critical-norms* of cultural debate. A critical norm, to provide a brief definition of this concept, enlists critical theory to reproduce a cycle of tragic indictment—a halting of dialogue and punishment—rather than a vigorous inquiry to further dismantle systems of power. This chapter explores how to locate, interrogate, and process our own personal investments and blind spots through the various ways we understand ironic performativity, find humor, take offense, and position ourselves within and across comic controversies. When considering the "understanding" of ironic performativity, the effect and intelligence of a comedian can only be as smart, subversive, or critical as their specific audience allows or enables.

Extending projects of Fiske and Shugart, amongst many other cultural studies theorists, Chapter Four seeks to afford audiences a range of positions and agencies beyond merely "that of cultural dupe" (Shugart and Waggoner 2008: 8). This chapter digs deeper into the range of audiencing possibilities and potentials that exist when making sense of ironic performativity through an exploration of camp as a critical resistant practice. Taking a cue from RuPaul, who argues drag is the opposite of trans discourses, the playful irreverence and rebellion of authorship inherent to camp is positioned in tension with the very seriousness of identity based discourses. The chapter begins with an analysis of

Daniel Tosh, specifically his parody reenactment of Selene Gomez's "Good for You" music video. The analysis frames Tosh through a lens of a mainstreamed and distinctly "bro" form of camp. The chapter situates the notion of "bro camp" within a long lineage of camp literature, as a concept and an audiencing practice with key foundations such as Sontag and more current theorists such as Doty, Cleto, Halperin, and Meyer. Following this theoretical foundation, this chapter will discuss a contemporary and mainstreamed manifestation of "bro camp" codes, as exemplified through the infamous Seth MacFarlane musical number "We Saw Your Boobs"—the opening number he performed as Academy Award host that was lambasted as crudely "sexist" and "over the line."

In order to assert an alternative range of subversive performative engagements beyond the critical norm, the chapter seeks to reclaim resistant audiencing practices as powerful and generative spaces of defiance/production. Such practices, even if overtly cued by the aesthetic dimensions of the MacFarlane number, are resisted through the text-flattening practice of the critical norm of Internet outrage. Thus, what offered the potential to read MacFarlane's number as a bold camping of hegemonic masculinity—a read that was continually coached by MacFarlane and the number's producers—was resisted in support of re-patterning critical narratives of offense and violence. The chapter centralizes how a performative engagement with a text not only attends to the role of audience, and offers self-reflexive possibilities based on meanings generated, but reclaims the agency of audience through construction of meaning and sharing of that meanings (whether in a laugh, boo, sigh, silence, clap, or analysis). MacFarlane and Tosh's enactment of "bro camp" is placed into dialogue with uncomplicated performances of misogyny, enlisting the example of Australian comic Jim Jefferies.

The fifth and final chapter looks to explore the limits and resistances of comedic interventions by focusing on recent comic engagements with race, racism, and whiteness. The chapter examines the question of what unique forms of engagement can the white body execute in anti-racist comedy. The performative concept of "whiteface-saving" (Jackson)—a strategy for performing one's identity as removed or innocent of cultural racisms and complicity—marks the central focus, wherein seemingly critical and resistant stances against the racism of a text or a person work to further bolster and support white innocence, white supremacy, and structural racism. Thus, satire works to both indict racist capitalist systems of oppression through the use of humor, yet allows the audience rhetorical distance and "whiteface-saving" innocence from these structures. Sarah Silverman's controversial use of blackface in the episode "Face Wars" from *The Sarah Silverman Program* is closely examined to mark the limitations of critical white irony. In addition, the chapter turns to comedian Louis C.K., whose controversial 2016 SNL monologue sought to invite audience self-reflexivity and identifications with racialized systems. Louis C.K. explicitly enlists his body, as a site of white male authority and carrier of racist discourses of violence, to performatively disrupt whiteface-saving patterns of engagement. Enlisting an ethical framework derived from the works of

Kenneth Burke, Shannon Jackson and Judith Butler, the chapter extends the criticism of whiteface-saving strategies and Margaret Cho's criticisms of "white fragility" to the anti-racist work of comedian Sarah Silverman. The chapter seeks out alternative modes of intervention that resist the work of face saving to implicate and interrogate the messy ways both performer and audience are enmeshed in ugly, unpleasant, and complicated complicity of structural oppressions. Revisiting the role of body and identity as sites of mobility and restriction to examine certain systems of meanings, the chapter revisits the Chris Rock 2016 Oscars performance, which opened the text, to complicate the complex web of negotiations operating in concert between body, context, audience, and aesthetics.

What I am and what I am not

> Comedy isn't polite and it isn't correct and it isn't accurate, even. It's just a mess. So that's the way I approach it.
>
> (Louis C.K.)

As the author, I come here with a range of investments, experiences, and concerns that shape every corner of this project. I am a white, able-bodied, Jewish, gay, cis-gendered male. My Ph.D. is in Communication Studies with a focus on performance studies and rhetoric. My M.F.A. was in studio performance art. I have been drawn to radical interventionist performance work most of my life, and firmly belief in the transformative power of art, of artmaking, of radical trust in audiencing, and the power of discomfort. I'm drawn to the repellant and haunting wail of Karen Finley's performative deconstruction of the male gaze, or Diamanda Gala's affective terror in the loss of her brother to AIDS and government silence.

I sat on a panel of humor scholars earlier this year, and when I was discussing this project, there was an audible gasp by a claim I made. I said, "I really don't care if the work is funny, or if you think it's funny, or if someone else finds it funny. It's not what I am studying." The study of humor has a long detailed set of theories that seek to understand why humans experience a joke and break into laughter. While a worthwhile and interesting area of research, it is not this project's focus. My interest is in the performative possibilities of critical interventionist humor, and how our critical patterns, as a culture, are failing to take this work up with the complexity and nuance I believe it deserves. This is a question not usually centralized in humor studies, but one that is well suited for the work of performance and communication studies.

A danger of this project, and one I want to address directly and immediately, is that this work is not designed to support, endorse or embolden the current cultural trend of "PC pushback." In addition, the move to complicate the labeling of work as wholly sexist or racist or homophobic is not to eliminate our need as a culture to call out violence and oppression. There is really awful humor out there that I believe does far more damage than productive work. I aim to call that out. However, the project is about elevating our discourse and seeking to preserve and protect spaces of artistic intervention that, I believe, are in the end sacrificing important modes of inquiry and examination. The shift to the performative language is about more critical engagement, not less, offering a more complex understanding of what different forms of comedy (and knowledges generated through comedy) can *DO*.

I come to this with a history as a performing artist with the firm belief that silencing art should never be a standpoint of the left. I've had my work protested, referred to erroneously as hate speech, and received hate mail (back in the quaint old days of trolling when someone had to actually put a stamp on it and drop it in the mailbox). I've watched protesting discourses quickly expand and explode, learning that so often the protest and offense is not really about the work, the art, at all. I have, through most of my work, enlisted humor as a means for understanding culture, to broach the seemingly forbidden, to use it as an exposing art form. Humor has a way of breaking in and through, finding pleasure in resistance and pleasure in the reflexivity. Humor is "one of the most powerful tools available to humans in their communicative endeavors" (Apte 67). Humor is a communicative mode of political expression and articulation, one with the power to constitute an activated and reflexive audience in unique and valuable ways. I believe our willingness, as a culture, to curb or limit its scope, reach, or strategies should be challenged, and much more carefully considered.

In possibilities

> In so doing, we hope to contribute to broader cultural studies conversations regarding the media as a dynamic and shifting site of contestation and, more broadly, opportunities for resistance in a context of constraint.
>
> (Shugart and Waggoner 2008: 7)

> One of the most useful things about employing the entirely subjective 'offense' of the listener to draw the limits of acceptable speech is that literally anything can be offensive to someone.
>
> (Ham and Benson 20)

The choice to invoke and bring in some of the conservative critiques around political correctness is not to bolster or endorse these positions, fully, but to also mark a strong sense of limited speech, to consider the implications of experience, and question why comedy is the space where speech is facing such a strong cultural pushback. These are messy questions, and the objective of this text is nothing short of seeking to shift the discourse. When Sarah Silverman or Steven Colbert engages controversial topics through the perspective of their ironic personae (Gournelos and Greene; Lowery, Renegar, and Goehring), this communicative process is qualitatively and aesthetically different from Fox News or Rush Limbaugh "reporting" the news. Yes, these interventions have an inherent aggression to them and they carry danger and anxiety, but that anxiety is the price we pay for the potential opportunities and pleasures afforded by humor (Rappoport).

During the 2013 Academy Awards, when *The Onion* tweeted a "joke" of calling Quvenzhané Wallis a "cunt," (Glenn) any satiric openings afforded by this tweet were overshadowed by the weight, weakness, and desperation of the effort. This is not aesthetically complex, but a text attempting to enlist verbal irony (juxtaposing a happy and proud, nine-year-old African American female who was so excited to be at the awards show with the foulest insult imaginable for a female). Yes, it created a stir, which is what much satire claims is its goal, but a stir for what reason and at what expense? What was opened up or exposed in the stir? How was pain being examined or transcended? Rather than determine it sexist and racist, can we allow a space to say it is doing sexism and racism. We should have that discussion. While arguably satiric, the expected ironic sensibility of *The Onion*, as a contextual cue, was insufficient to invert the joke. Who was this comedian? Where is their body in this exchange and what meanings extend from, mobilize, and construct where and how they speak? The invited laugh solicited an audience to participate in something that was far more externally violent than personally self-reflexive. Let's talk about its failure with specificity and break down how the joke rides on a legacy of racism and sexism in ways that merely wound and transcend nothing. We should turn the joke back on us all and question if it made us laugh, who gets to laugh, why they are laughing, and what meanings are at play.

Allowing the performative space for anxiety and risk is not to argue that comedy is simply a free zone, however, wherein dismissals of "just a joke" and "lighten up" seek to excuse all communicative acts that claim satiric or ironic elements. Rather, humor and comedy need to be engaged as *more* complex, *more* intricate, and offering a greater complexity of communicative information that demands closer attention to their rhetorical doings. Daniel Tosh's words offend. Lisa Lampenelli's words are nothing short of foul. They enlist words that conjure offenses and hurts and violences, yet to understand the functions of their work requires a contextualization of their bodies, their strategic uses of irony, and the distinct personas they construct that are central to their "comic stylings" (i.e. aesthetics of humor). We learn through the processing of the work, the self-reflexive investigation of the work, and a more complex communicative engagement to what they are *doing*, trying to *do*, failing to *do*, and what they *do* to and through us. Personally, Lampenelli's work has always been deeply uncomfortable and offensive. We should struggle with her "free for all" assault of "ist" humor where no one is safe and all bets are off. It's risky and dangerous, yet to process and invest more in her work allows us to consider the affective value of her work. At her best, all of her disrespect actually opens up a space for honest and respectful exchange. She digs into the silences, the politeness, and the unspoken hostilities that so often inhibit discussions across difference. We should approach her work with caution, but also with complexity.

Comedy is an art form, and the work of opening up new ways of thinking, new approaches to speaking, and new modes of being must permit some allowance for offense, pain, and discomfort. There ought to be limits, for sure, as the reckless infliction of pain should not be excused. Humor and comedy, if not held to scrutiny, can too easily become a place to disguise and defend the uncritical regurgitation of oppressive meanings.

The form and ethic of engagement I am attempting to trace in this project are not easy ones. The cynic might scoff at the effort, arguing there is a shift in the culture through our current technology that inevitably sacrifices nuance. In a sea of "likes" and retweets, the performativity of critique and the uncomplicated perpetuation of outrage and tragedy are the world we now live in. Perhaps the lines for interpreting irony are just too permeable in this historical moment of Trump's presidency, in a moment when Sarah Palin satire and Sarah Palin are indecipherable, where meaning has no footing except for the self-sustaining drive of our individual investments.

From a communication perspective, we know the dangers of words and the violence they can and might bring forth. Surely, the term "offense" is not always enough to hold the weight of the violence that they carry. Still, our work for opening, complicating, and democratizing public discourse needs to consciously factor in the role of performance, processual meaning-making and communicative aesthetics. We must continue to develop complex alternatives to "just a joke" dismissals, textualized (and decontextualized) condemnations of "ists," and "you are being too sensitive" refusals to engage the complex doings of humor. When engaging humor, we need to attend to a broad range of channels that shape meaning and how our labeling of communication phenomena works to potentially open up (or foreclose) audience responsibility and reflexivity. Although it's common logic in any critical theory course that we are all somewhat racist, homophobic and sexist, as we are all part of these social systems, we often resist this truth in our language. In marking "them" as sexist, the implication is we are not. Rather, as "they" do sexism, how it's done and how we are part of their work opens up a broader systemic focus. This critical project is even further extended in reflecting on who can, who will, and who refuses to read humor in different ways. For example, how does my affinity with whiteness permit me to read productive doings of racism in Schumer's work? How does my gayness resist ironic interpretations of Eddie Murphy? Who gets to laugh? How is the meaning/knowledge we generate, through humor, tied to our bodies, relations, and subjectivities? We can provide the tools and sophistication to stop looking at comics and comedy as the symptom of our problems, and understand stand up as one of the few places—and irony as one of the few strategies—left to discuss, process, interrogate, and—perhaps—transcend our collective pain.

1 Ironic performativity

Amy Schumer and the conventions of embodiment

> Embodiment is both the "act of embodying" and the "condition of being embodied," just as performance is the immediate act of doing and the thing done.
> (Diamond 155)

Too often in daily life, it is taken for granted how slippery the process of communicating meanings can be. Although the field of human communication has long-troubled linear and uncomplicated transmission models of symbolic exchange, we continue to act and respond with the determined faith that communication works, that meanings can be transferred, and that understanding is not an arbitrary process riddled with limitations. We toss out messages and receive them with a deceptive sense of comfort and confidence. Still, we read intention, relational bias, our personal selections and perceptions, and our own interpretations as "the" meaning, "the" truth, "the" facts. When it comes to ironic, contradictory, or layered messages—wherein aesthetic dimensions of the exchange present a range of variables to be navigated—a quick and confident "I know what you mean" becomes increasingly fraught: especially in the case of jokes or styles of humor that are "transgressive," "edgy," "not PC," or "irreverent."

White country singer Brad Paisley, during the *2015 Country Music Awards*, delivered a seemingly simple joke that received a lot of attention in the days following. He said, "If any of you tuned into ABC tonight expecting to see the new show *Black-ish*, (pause) yeah, this ain't it. In the meantime, I hope you all are enjoying (longer pause, searching for word, gesturing to room, with uncertain upspeak) … White-ish?" The moment elicited some laughter but also audience criticism and speculation of his intentions via social media. The negative response was, in part, because country singer Darius Rucker—one of the very few successful African American country singers in the industry—made an appearance right after Paisley's joke. Was Paisley mocking Rucker? Was he calling out the normative whiteness of country music? Was his hesitation and then declaration of "White-ish" marking an unstated norm, critiquing a norm, or reifying a norm? More importantly for this project is the question of how this moment and this joke would have operated differently from a different body. Had Rucker stood in front of the audience and delivered the same joke with the same inflections, the response would surely differ. Imagine Rucker joking, "If any of you tuned into ABC tonight expecting to see the new show *Black-ish*, (pause) yeah, this ain't it. In the meantime, I hope you all are enjoying (longer pause, searching for word, gesturing to room, with uncertain upspeak) … White-ish?" Would the indictment have been more pointed? Would it be more acceptable? Would it have read as angrier, even if the affect were identical? Paisley's delivery had a performed nervousness to it, a staged discomfort that if adopted by Rucker would have exposed and indicted a different physical threat and vulnerability in that space. Rather than the removed and ambiguous/whitened commentary from Paisley, the role of Rucker's body in the performance of that joke would cite a different set of discourses and histories that would radically alter the interpretation, meaning, implication, and assumed intention.

Yes, it's hardly earth shattering, and actually tacit cultural knowledge that certain persons, identities, and bodies are differently constituted to speak to certain systems and tell certain jokes. We have all heard the disclaimers, as well as the meta-commentaries on the disclaimers, of "It's okay, I'm gay," "It's okay, I'm Jewish," "I can say that, I'm half Mexican," etc. Although Chris Rock has publicly stated he will not perform his infamous set "N**gas and Black People" (Hartsell, 7/5/2012), his performance of this routine, while surely not without controversy, would carry a radically different set of meanings if performed by Billy Crystal or Robin Williams—or even African American comedians like Dick Gregory or Kevin Hart. At the same time, Chris Rock would be more quickly criticized for performing the rape jokes in Sarah Silverman's stand up routine. "He can't tell that joke!" The question under consideration, beyond tacit knowledge, is "why?" It is tied to identity, for sure, yet the boundaries and lack of fixity of identity require a deeper examination. From headline personalities such as Rachel Dolezal and Caitlyn Jenner, to South African comedian Trevor Noah, identity is not, and never has been, a stable or clear-cut endeavor. Thus, these tensions are about identity (in all the ways that identity is shifting, contextualized, historicized, performative and subject to failure) *and* the body. Furthermore, when we look to the body, this includes the co-presence of the physical/material and the rhetorical/discursive body—the act of embodying and the condition of being embodied (Diamond 155). For Rock (or Paisley or anyone else), it's not merely the speaking of the joke (*She/He can't TELL that joke*), but a complex negotiation of the speaking body in relation to existing discourses, aesthetic delivery, text, and audience:

SHE/HE can't tell that joke (identity and rhetorical production of body).
She/he CAN'T tell that joke (There is an inability for differing bodies to tell the same joke as the body partially writes the joke).
She/he can't tell THAT joke (The text is restricted by cultural norms).

In addition, there is a glaring absence in this statement, wherein the audience/speaker is assumed, but not explicitly marked:

She/he can't tell that joke, AS I UNDERSTAND IT (the interpretive audience).

The quick short-cut answer is to rely on a rubric of identity politics, where a marginalized identity is allowed greater space and leeway to name/discuss, unpack and interrogate a marginalized experience and critique systems and identities with greater access to social power (Rappoport). Louis C.K., as a straight white male, *can* make jokes about racism, but to evade the risk of swift criticism, the jokes need to be unambiguously not racist. In addition, the jokes also must be clearly anti-racist in ways that are fairly constraining. However, Wanda Sykes, as an African American lesbian, can explore the complexities of racism with far greater abandon, messiness, and leeway.

The belaboring of this tacit cultural standard works to anticipate the focus of this chapter, which seeks to explore the relationship between the spoken text of the joke, the aesthetic delivery and the performing body, as text. This negotiation of body, aesthetics, and text has the potential to open up a broad interplay and proliferation of meanings—particularly when these elements work in ironic tension/production. The multiple channels, reiterations, and embodied complexities in this communicative event require an analytical approach that can trace and unpack aesthetic dimensions within and beyond the word. Attention to the performative elements of communication challenges legacies of scriptocentrism (Conquergood 2002), highlighting the significance of context, body, relation, audience, and aesthetics to the processes of meaning making (Pelias and VanOosting). Aesthetics do not merely enhance or beautify a message, as if somehow beside or extraneous to meaning. Aesthetics are active in both the construction of a message and the relationship between that message and the larger discursive context in which the message operates. Aesthetic dimensions of a communicative act complicate, lace, and disrupt the "doing" and the "thing done" (Diamond 66) of any performative action or communicative exchange. Performativity, as a core conceptual tool in this study, examines how social identity and systems are produced through repeated, often taken for granted, discursive practices. When we introduce performativity to our analysis of communication, we draw attention to the ways all communication marks a space of contestation and political doings (Langellier 1999: 128–9), wherein subjects are constituted (134), the social is structured/struggled over (128), and the us, them, and we of audiences are reproduced (130). Thus, exploring performativity turns our attention to the political/social/discursive/constitutive reverberations of the aesthetics of communication.

While any embodied communication event, through a performative lens, is fraught with risk and opportunity, enlisting irony as a central method animates a subjective and multidimensional field of meanings that must resist fixed or reductive assessments. Irony, at its best, is "a very messy subject" (Booth 2), and "Nobody escapes troubles with it" (76). The chapter begins with a conceptual grounding of irony, emerging from a literary, rhetorical, and performance tradition. Next, the chapter looks to performance literature, rhetoric, and literary criticism to conceptualize the framework of ironic performativity. Finally, the chapter turns to the *2012 Comedy Central Roast of Charlie Sheen* to demonstrate the application of *ironic performativity* by analyzing the breakout performance of comedian Amy Schumer. Beyond verbal or written ironies, ironic performativity simultaneously draws attention to a range of aesthetic and discursive factors to be negotiated in constructions of meaning (e.g. context, gesture, body, affect, pause, identity). Examining the slippery and contested space of "understanding" irony, the concept also works to more directly implicate the audience and/or critic in their productions of meaning in later chapters.

Irony (undefined): A review of approaches

> Irony is usually seen as something that undermines clarities, opens up vistas of chaos, and liberates by destroying all dogma or destroys by reveling the inescapable canker of negation at the heart of every affirmation.
>
> (Booth ix)

To unpack, process, and theorize the multi-channeled complexities of embodied communication and ironic performativity, humor offers a productively unstable point of entry. Humor exploits and examines the messiness that is always present in communication exchanges, seizing the dangerous, ambiguous, and elusive relations between words/bodies/relations for intervention, disruption, and shock. While dominant theoretical frames of superiority, incongruity, surprise, and psychic release remain foundational to studying humor, it is commonly argued that humor resists theorizing (Nelson). Theory, by definition, operates in abstraction, working to map and trace concrete experiences and events through recurrent patterns of behavior. We can analyze transcripts of humorous moments to mark how certain patterns emerge, but the workings, doings, and experiences of humor exist within the bodily repertoire of a situated, localized, felt, temporal experience—a tension between the archived record of "what happened" and the embodied experience (Taylor).

Perhaps most elusive, and yet most diligently tracked down (only to slither away, once again), is the paradoxically indefinable (de Man) concept of irony. Much of the scholarship on irony has approached it from a literary perspective, wherein irony is engaged on the page, and driven by modernist commitments for the correct or preferred interpretation—those of the author. For example, Booth works to locate and detail what he labels stable irony, "those passages that are unquestionably ironic" (3)—freed from the infinite process of continually undermining understanding. He details four steps in stable ironic reconstruction, wherein literal meanings are rejected, alternatives are tested, authorial intent is weighed, and new meaning is selected (8–10). Booth works to distinguish the (perhaps seemingly more) clear rhetorical intentions of stable ironies from the more slippery infinite ironies, yet the location, designation, or properness of irony's presence or meaning will always resist, by its very character, solid ground (de Man). Thus, when Sean Penn jokes at the 2015 Oscars, "Who gave this son of a bitch his green card?" as he presents an award to his friend and past collaborator Alejandro Iñárritu, the assigned meaning and the reading of irony is never fixed. Even though Penn has "Absolutely no apologies" about this joke and Iñárritu "found it hilarious" (Bahr), the comment continued to draw criticism as "racist." Penn argued: "'I'm always surprised by flagrant stupidity. I keep having more hope,' said Penn of the widespread outrage that followed the moment" (Bahr) "In fact, I have a big (expletive) you for every … anybody who is so stupid not to have gotten the irony when you've got a country that is so xenophobic," said Penn. Yet, for many the irony was lost, misread, or resisted.

In *A Grammar of Motives*, Burke locates irony as one of the four master tropes through his application of the dialectic. Irony, according to Burke, pushes through relativism to see or generate meaning beyond one single set of terms (512). Irony develops dialectic through opposing points of view that interanimate and coach new understandings through expanded perspective. Thus, irony generates liminal, prevaricated, and potentially subversive spaces for new meaning (Shugart 1999: 435). This marks the collision and proliferation in irony that de Man (165) and Booth (15) suggest is inherently performative, a mobilized twiceness that rubs, disrupts, and creates/negates (what is said/meant, what is doing/done). Likened to Brechtian *verfremdungseffekt* and the ironic wedge it draws between actor and character, as well as "the historical subject and the actor's function" (Diamond 160), performativity marks a perversion and estrangement in its reference (Parker and Sedgwick 3). Northrop Frye defines (written) irony as "a pattern of words that turns away" (cited in de Man 164). This enlisting of bodily metaphor, the turning away, works to capture the action and performativity inherent to ironic processes.[1]

Articulated through a Burkean lens, Lowery, Renegar, and Goehring examine the performativity of Sarah Silverman's ironic persona in her comedy film *Jesus is Magic*. Through the conceptual optic of *perspective by incongruity*, they explore the productive use of irony in her comedy film to expose and undermine hegemonic systems, rules, and behaviors. According to Burke, perspective by incongruity can offer a comic corrective, wherein rigid and restrictive modes of thought can be expanded. Through comedy—a frame of mistakenness where rigid designations of good/bad and right/wrong are rejected for error, mistake, and education (Attitudes 41)—"people can be observers of themselves, while acting" and cultivate "maximum consciousness" (171). Arguing Silverman's ironic persona presents a form of embodied perspective by incongruity (Lowery, Renegar, and Goehring 60)—a performative "double vision" where restrictive orientations are clouded, interrogated, and extended (Goltz "Perspective" 8), Silverman enlists the performative twiceness of irony through her use of body, gesture, and a range of performative cues. We, as audience are coached to engage her humor through her body (Lowery, Renegar, and Goehring 62), wherein physical and affective cues of raced and gendered innocence and ignorance are sharply juxtaposed with racist, sexist, and intentionally offensive statements. This ironic work, this situated enactment of perspective by incongruity in speech and body (63; Olson and Olson 27) pairs opposing meanings into a generative tension, a crashing and colluding with seemingly incommensurable ideas, that works to potentially open up new modes and perspectives. For example, when locating the workings of her ironic white privilege, Silverman states, "I don't want to be labeled as straight or labeled as gay. I want people to look at me and see me, you know, as white" (cited in Lowery, Renegar, and Goehring 66). The performed ignorance in her delivery cues audience distance, wherein she both presents racial privilege and also works to display its operations in ironic tension.

Extending these foundations that examine the performative dimensions of irony, this chapter sets its attention on the embodied act, embodied performativity, examining the complex interanimating processes of spoken words, bodily action, citation of previous performances, and the discourses that shape and constrain the meanings attached to and negotiated among the relations of bodies. For example, when South African comic Trevor Noah narrates his "Dream to come to America," because he's "always wanted to be Black," there is a flurry of co-present meanings at work. His own story and body contextualize his statement, for as a South African man born (illegally under Apartheid) to an African mother and a Swiss father Noah was not, in South Africa, seen as either Black or White. He was labeled "mixed." Thus, his chance to "get to be Black" is also grounded in cultural truth, for he is told, "You come out to America, they will label you 'Black.'" "Really?," he excitedly asks. "Hell ya," he responds (performing the second person with a dryness and clear absence of enthusiasm). Additionally, in this joke, there is the ironic twist of "*getting* to be Black," which pairs Noah's excitement and sense of opportunity with the reality of racism and oppression faced by African Americans in the U.S. Thus, Noah's wink and smile coaches the audience to laugh at this "dream" and "opportunity," even as he expresses his excitement about it. The ironic working of the joke is further complicated as the story is by Noah, told by and through Noah's body and voice, who continually jokes that he is lighter skinned than most Americans' expectations of Africans. He parodies this assumption by bouncing around on stage, performing a Disney-fied stereotype of the African primitive, leaping and dancing. Throughout the sketch, he continually draws attention to his lighter than "navy" but darker than white skin, while shifting from his native South African English accent to a range of ethnic dialects. The entire joke leads up to his dream of "getting to be Black," and his arrival in the U.S., playing on how the U.S. automatically frames mixed persons as not white, as other. Thus the co-presence of Swiss and African heritage is his body is played against U.S.-based discourses that rhetorically produce race. He plays on this malleability of race through a joke about his Swiss father, saying, "My father *was* white." He quickly corrects himself, in faux panic, saying "He *is* white," and overly reassures a white person in the audience that being white is stable and they need not worry about that changing.

The audience is asked to factor his body, and the meanings we have been trained to map onto his body, into the processing of his ironic humor. He actively plays with the limiting discourses of African-ness, Blackness, and whiteness that are mapped onto his body based upon physical and vocal choices he adopts, and as quickly as he embodies and cites these discourses, he tosses them aside. He practices a performance of U.S. Blackness on the entire flight over, polishing up performance cues that signify authentic Blackness in the U.S. He adopts moments of slang and Black English, examining the extreme economy of the expression "now mean?" (Translated to "Do you know what it is I mean?"). He plays and explores assumptions and recognitions tied to both speech and body, and then elevates this ironic play about finally getting to "be Black" to the next level. Upon arrival to the U.S. (specifically New York), he sees another man, who sees him, and he narrates a profound moment of recognition and familiarity. The man immediately approaches Noah and as Noah readies his performance of Blackness (finally), the man begins speaking Spanish to him. He is mistaken for Puerto Rican. The punch line is, once again, ironic failure of misrecognition, yet Noah ups the stakes in this joke by embodying and performing the Puerto Rican male with full commitment. In this performance, through his body and adoption of a Puerto Rican dialect, he also presents this misrecognition as *understandable*. His failure is our failure. We, as audience, see how his body *can* be read as Puerto Rican, and how race, as a seemingly fixed but flawed system in the U.S., is more tied to context, performance, recognition than essence or materiality. Yet, because of the flexibility of his body in relation to racial discourses, he can maneuver through a range of contested and complicated discourses. Thus, Noah's work exposes how both with, but also outside of identity, discourses are cited and ever-present through the body and these profoundly shape and impact ironic messages.

Further examining the performative engagements of irony, de Man takes up Schlegel's use of the rhetorical term *parabasis*, which generally marks a disruption in a pattern or narrative. Enlisting theatrical metaphor, the parabasis is the break to the audience, the interruption, the aside of the ongoing fictional narrative. The parabasis is "The interruption of a discourse by a shift in the rhetorical register" (178). Yet, de Man argues, "you have to imagine the parabasis as being able to take place at all times. At all moments the interruption can happen" (178). Performatively, it marks the existence of the pattern, and the always-present potential for ironic disruption of the pattern, just as performativity highlights the ever-present attention to the moment-by-moment possibility for a transgression in the "discursive compulsion to repeat norms of gender, sexuality, and race" (McKenzie cited in Langellier and Peterson 156)—that critical space "Between someone's body and the conventions of embodiment" (Diamond 5). Using the example of Trevor Noah, the presence of patterns of racial categorization and the parabasis of ironically "getting to be Black," are ever-present within his set, and his embodied ironic play continually works to expose, undermine, and shift away from the flow and ease of these patterns.

These conventions of embodiment reference "the reiterative and citational practice by which discourse produces the effects that it names" (Butler 1993: 2). In other words, the performing body is always negotiating this tension, this critical space, between the physical doing and the discursive effects of its thing done. In Derkson's examination of gender parody in the performance of Karen Hines's "Pochsy's Lips," she explores this tension in the staged comedic act, suggesting the performing body, in this case the female body, is always met with assumptions. Thus, "The body of the persona and performer are put in critical dialogue with one another" (236). In Pochsy's Lips, Derkson argues that Hines performs specific highly gendered movements to draw attention to and undermine their expected effects (237). Through this parodic gender mimicry, the audience is invited into an awareness of the cultural patterns and gestures that produce and reproduce gender. The parody, and ironic tension, is enacted in the twiceness of the effect, for Hines is not offering a mere repetition (237), but coaches and invites critique of the mechanisms of workings of gender performativity. In a complex interplay, Hines both invites and resists the gaze (241) wherein gender is "performed; deformed; enjoyed; and imagined" (245).

Irony exploits and mobilizes a mischievous and messy tension between what is explicit and the intended message. Irony presents a minefield of potential meaning making, a critical space between a "doings" relation to "a thing done." The objective of this theoretical set up is not to wade into the fraught project of defining irony with any degree of firmness. Rather, I will be approaching this historically slippery concept/term/trope through an exploration of what irony does. Irony is approached as a method (Colletta 860) and a rhetorical device (Booth; Kreuz and Roberts) for opening ambiguous spaces between real and appearance, between what is meant and what is said (Colletta). Irony is approached as a strategy for generating/disrupting meanings, splicing and activating the doing/thing done tension. It provides an incongruous perspective (Burke) that simultaneously offers up multiple frames of meanings (Scarpetta and Spagnolli). It opens spaces for dialogue, tension, and critical analysis, through resistance to fixedness, completion, or understanding. Irony is a destructive force—it is the tearing or interruption of form (de Man). Enlisting bodily metaphor, irony is the pulling and prying apart of the muscles and tendons of meaning—an ache, stress, and strain of the musculature and naturalized reiteration of compulsive discursive patterns. Ironic performativity traces the struggle, the moment-by-moment power negotiation in the communicative event, detailing the instability and the potential reworkings of political meanings that occur through words, bodies, and patterned systems of meaning. As with Trevor Noah's constant push and pull, he calls attention to his body, cites the expectations mapped upon him, experiments with the malleability and possibility of these meanings, and highlights the spaces for play and negotiation that are pried open between bodies and bodily discourses. Thus, "The body of the persona and performer are put in critical dialogue with one another" (Derkson 236).

"Understanding" postmodern irony: Cultivating paradox and incongruity

At its best, ironic humor, such as Silverman's, Noah's, or Hines's, can do satiric work,[2] wherein it challenges and disrupts oppressive discourses and meanings. Audiencing irony and constructing understanding of and through ironic messages, however, is more "processing intensive" than non-ironic messages (Kreuz and Roberts 106). While an ironic comic might provide some form of a wink or nod to cue an ironic read—such as Silverman's use of extended stares, overly performed ignorance, and side comments of meta-awareness (Lowrey, Renegar, and Goehring)—ironic comedy is always drenched in some level of ambiguity. There is no absolute nor sure-fire manner to mark correctly an ironic moment, trace its impact, or solidify its meaning (Gournelos and Greene). Hutcheon argues the strength "of postmodern irony inheres in its ability to cultivate rather than transcend paradox" (cited in Shugart 1999: 436). Irony will complicate, rather than simplify, with the potential to forge new ways to speak, think, and experience an issue (xxiv). Ironic comedy will speak the language of the dominant culture, while simultaneously suggesting an alternative meaning, and thus always plays in the risky waters of whether or not the audience "gets it" (Shugart 1999: 435). This is "irony's edge," the constant play of meanings, affects, and potential subversions that code ironic comedy with risk and political charge (Gournelos and Greene xxiii–xxiv). So, even though the impulse to control irony is to find understanding, what "if irony is always the irony of understanding, if what is at stake in irony is the question of whether it is possible to understand or not to understand?" (de Man 166).

Assisting this tension, "understanding"—from a communication perspective—does not assume or suggest a shared comprehension or transfer of fixed meaning, but can be defined more generally as a process in which one assigns a meaning to a message. Intentionally highlighting the arbitrary and fraught workings of this process, to "understand" irony is only to have assigned *some* meaning or interpretation. Thus, this volume rejects notions of stable irony (Booth) or a "two available meanings" approach to irony that assumes a more predictable interplay between the literal and the intended (Shugart 1999: 434). A postmodern approach to irony embraces its capacity for subversion, yet tempers this capacity with greater attention to its multiplicity and fragmentation of meaning (434). Thus, "although postmodern irony functions subversively for select audiences, it may well function hegemonically for others" (434). As Booth argued, "Every reader will have the greatest difficulty detecting irony that mocks his [*sic*] own beliefs or characteristics" (81). In an illustrative study, wherein liberal- and conservative-identified audiences assigned "understanding" to *The Colbert Report*, the political investments of the audiences were significant in how they interpreted his work (Lamarre, Landreville, and Beam). In short, individual political belief shaped how they understood Colbert's ironic humor, what they assumed about his political leanings, and what made them laugh. Even more complicating, regardless of the audiences' political leaning and interpretation of Colbert, audiences found him funny (Lamarre, Landreville, and Beam).

When considering the "understanding" of ironic performativity, the effect and intelligence of a comedian can only be as smart, subversive, or critical as their specific audience allows or enables. It is no surprise that this shift, movement, and fragmentation of meaning in ironic comedy has garnered greater attention from rhetorical critics in communication (Shugart 1999, 2001; Lowery, Renegar, Goehring) who can define a singular text and audiencing location in order to trace ironic subversions. Performance scholars have been less attendant than rhetorical scholars to irony in their analysis, as the messy interplay of words, bodies, contexts, and postmodern frameworks of reception are muddied and frustrated in the critical study of ironic communication. Asserting ironic performativity as a conceptual framework to help argue, if not loosely trace, the performative operations of ironic comedy, this chapter turns to the case study of comedian Amy Schumer to more fully and necessarily centralize the role of body and aesthetics in the study of communication.

The ironic performativity of Amy Schumer

The 2011 *Charlie Sheen Roast* embraced and celebrated a hyper-masculinity in honor of the self-proclaimed "Rock Star From Mars." Renowned for excessive drug use, soliciting female prostitutes, domestic violence, and a notorious "fuck the system, I'm winning" rebelliousness during his very public exit from *Two and a Half Men*, Charlie Sheen was 2011's Hollywood renegade "bad boy." Roastmaster Seth McFarlane and roasters Jeffrey Ross, Patrice O'Neil, then-newcomer Anthony Jeselnik, and Jon Lovitz, alongside William Shatner, Mike Tyson, and Steve-O, populate his dais. There are only two women on the dais (not uncommon for these roasts), actress Kate Walsh of *Grey's Anatomy*, and then-up-and-coming comedian, Amy Schumer. In her 2015 cover story interview with *Entertainment Weekly*, the now highly successful Schumer reflects on this "infamous" and "breakout," appearance. "I watch the Charlie Sheen roast and I'm like, who the fuck is this kid? I can't believe the balls on me" (30).

At the opening of the roast, a film montage of Sheen is cut to Survivor's "Eye of the Tiger"—a nod to Sheen's much-reported claims to drink "tiger blood." Sheen is rolled onto stage, amidst smoke machines, while seated at the front of his own "crazy train," as Guns N' Roses' Slash pounds out a guitar solo. The event was an unapologetic championing of misogyny, where Sheen's violence towards women and excessive use of cocaine was celebrated—a badge of honor and admiration. Roaster Jeff Ross, commenting on Sheen's ex-wife Brooke Mueller, states, "She's not too bright, unless Charlie's throwing a lamp at her." The camera cuts to Mueller, in the audience, laughing along at her violent past with Sheen. Political/identity-based "ism" (Kramarae) humor (i.e. racism, sexism, classism) and efforts to shock are commonplace at roasts and were well established forty-nine minutes into the show, as Amy Schumer claimed the stage in her career-launching four-and-a-half-minute set.

The jokes flung at Amy Schumer by the earlier roasters included generically base "slut" jokes (suggesting she had to "suck a dick" to be on the roast) and jokes that mocked her lack of status. Prior to her set, Schumer sat politely on the dais, an unassuming "girl next door" with a chipper smile that conveyed deference, humility, and accommodation. When faced with a joke, she would nod in recognition, playing the good sport without visible resistance. MacFarlane asks, "What can I say about Amy Schumer? I actually say that sincerely, I've *never* heard of this woman." Schumer slightly nods her head up and down, accepting this introduction. "Please welcome the fourth runner up of the fifth season of *Last Comic Standing*, Amy Schumer!" Rock music and applause accompany her walk to the podium. Schumer moves with playful confidence, bouncing slightly to the guitar playing. As she steps down the stairs, she gently accepts the assistance of Jeff Ross, extending her hand to Sheen as she passes. Schumer gracefully steps to the podium in a silver poufy dress, cut above the knee that she deliberately presses down and straightens as she approaches. She plants hands on both sides of the podium, pops her head to the dais, and looks directly at Tyson. She flashes a bright smile, her eyes and expressions playful, and her energy upbeat. She energetically shifts back and forth from the dais to the audience, and, at the end of each joke, she squints her eyes in a half-committed gesture of confusion, as if to say, "explain this to me, I'm not sure I get it." Her smiley accommodation, however, is layered with a slightly forceful assertiveness—a quickness in her shifts of the head and her facial meta-commentary that cites a docile femininity, yet simultaneously undercuts it. At times she looks to Tyson as she speaks and cocks her head with a self-conscious toothy silliness that feels like a 1980s sitcom tag line, "Oh, *that* Mike!"

From the outset, it is important to mark an inherent contradiction throughout this project, wherein the investigation of embodied communication is executed through a written analysis. In order to push against, though never resolve, this limitation, the second part of this chapter hovers within a specific communicative context and works to actively write the body explicitly into the analysis. So, Schumer gracefully steps down, plants her hands on both sides of the podium, pops her head directly at Tyson (not Sheen) and says, "Mike Ty-thh-hon. Am I saying that right?" She squints and looks to him with performed confusion that is never fully committed to, before turning fully to the audience. Thus, in this uncommitted confusion, she references a gendered "ditz" performance, a parodic performance of femininity (Shugart 2001) layered with ironic complication. She uses passive female confusion ironically as her opening assault to both Tyson and the masculinist belittlement that has preceded and attempted to frame her. Tyson laughs out loud, clapping, over-demonstrating 'good sportsmanship' and amusement to an extreme that reads nervous and condescending. Energy in the room abruptly shifts, as there is a clear break in tone, relation, and intensity from what has preceded Schumer—the set from

Steve-O that was defined by choppy, stilted one-liners, and Steve-O willingly running his face into Tyson's fist. Schumer continues with Tyson, cheerful and sarcastically glazed over, "Wasn't he great up here?" She focuses directly on the audience, "No, I'm asking, I couldn't understand a fucking word he said." The authority and ease in her dismissal of Tyson visibly takes Tyson by surprise. She is speeding up the pace from previous roasters, cutting into laughs. Tyson tries to counter her, vocalizing and attempting to command authority, but she railroads him. She holds her quickened rate of delivery, her face still pleasant, her smile bright, without a glimpse of apology. "Mike, your voice sounds like a girl crying. Every time you speak, do you give *yourself* an erection?" She poses the question with a partial commitment that straddles "ditz," a tone of sarcastic 'I'm confused' and assertive indictment. Tyson is flustered, starts to answer, "Sometimes …" but Schumer continues in rhythm, cutting him off, "Hey, hey, Mike, *here's* something you'll never hear: 'Great tattoo!'" She quickly throws the sarcastic line to him and then returns to the audience with her now familiar "confused squint." "You have a slutty lower back tattoo *on your face*," she addresses to him directly. The audience roars and Tyson claps wildly, in an exaggerated manner, eyes squinting, pointing at her as if they are all having a great time. She drops any trace of the parodied femininity and runs with it. "Men don't know whether to be scared of it or *finish on it*!" While this particular line was one highlight of the roast, and commonly referenced in the post-show recaps, the performative struggle for control that was happening on stage during Schumer's brief set—a moment-by-moment renegotiation of power taking place between bodies, relations, and affect disruptions—was absent from the transcript.

A performative approach to communication draws our attention to these ever-present negotiations of power and control. A quick camera cut to the dais early in Schumer's set shows Kate Walsh clearly applauding, Shatner (slightly labored) and Jezelnik smiling, Ross with his smile obscured, and an uneasy stoicism from Steve-O, Seth MacFarlane, Jon Lovitz, and Patrice O'Neil. The rhythm and pace of Schumer's Tyson attack was quick, impatient, and dizzying—a performative violation of femininity that was an affective challenge to masculinity. While the audience was rolling with her, the dais appeared thrown in ways that are distinct from previous sets.

The very vulnerability of the body, specifically a female body in a highly masculine and aggressive context of staged comedy (Pelle 28) creates a space for intervention and change (Lee cited in Pelle 33). This is particularly relevant for performers such as Schumer, who pose direct threats to gendered expectations. Female comedians, historically, have had to adopt a limited range of personae to intervene in this world, either embodying aggressive models of the "bitch" or "bawd" or more passive "reporter" or "whiner" roles (Gilbert). Schumer, thirty at the time, is a normatively attractive and feminine white blond woman who strategically uses her bright smile and rosy cheeks to pander to and then upset gendered norms. Her delivery most immediately follows in a tradition of Gilbert's bitch posture (108–14) and the whiner (114–24), yet pulls and borrows from the broad range of postures to contextually and strategically deploy whatever works (131). Her body, in comparison to the hyper-masculine dais, signifies and deploys traditional femininity (exemplified by Ross helping her step off the platform in her heels, while Schumer, with demure and deliberate repetition, flattens her pleated flared-out dress). Her ironic performativity—the interplay of her words, her gestures, and the discursive field that precedes them—continually plays with and against sexist expectations of politeness, cuteness, and white feminine modes of accommodation. For Schumer, whose body cites (at times parodic) femininity with each gesture, to criticize Tyson and Sheen's history of violence toward women, accomplishes an intervention that is profoundly distinct from what Ross or MacFarlane's jokes can produce. There is resistance and revolt, rather than just masculinist play and "busting each other's balls." Thus, when she launches into her set, her rapid-fire pacing, driving affect, and quick wit upsets the normative commitments of the room. She executes this with unfazed calm, devoid of hesitation, while claiming command, power and authority over the space. As comedy can be understood as, always, an 'exercise in power negotiation' (Gilbert 176), there is clearly an affective triumph in Schumer's set, both launching a shaming sexist critique at Tyson, while resisting feminine apology, accommodation, retreat, or search for approval.

Although Tyson was a popular topic for many of the early roasters, the "just kidding, please don't hit me" fear of teasing boxing legend Mike Tyson was an ongoing disclaimer for the men in the roast. Mostly, their Tyson jokes were tinged with boyhood admiration, resisting any penetrating interrogation of his sexism or history of violence against women. Much like Sheen, whose drug addiction, sexual exploits, and domestic violence were often referenced, the ease by which these references were made by the men failed to directly indict the behaviors. Thus, when Schumer took the stage and immediately tied Tyson to sexist violence, while refusing to honor his masculine authority, the shift in content/affect/energy/politics was highly pronounced.

Schumer did not miss a beat in shutting down Tyson's failed efforts to reassert himself. Tyson, whose 'good sportsmanship' grew labored, asks Shatner if "we" need to take this. Shatner, with a frozen, uncomfortable 'playing along' smile, comments that "we" have to. Tyson, somewhat playfully, but clearly processing a visceral response to being mocked, says, "We got to get her back!" Tyson, in a disciplinary move, attempts to reassert power, yelling, "If Amy had as many dicks coming out as she did going in, she'd look like a fucking porcupine …" Schumer interrupts, "… Is his interpreter here?" unfazed, refusing to surrender. The audience laughs louder. Tyson, apparently still amused with his porcupine comment, unsuccessfully seeks validation from the dais and audience. Not surprisingly, as he is not a comedian, his "joke" lacks aesthetic complexity, merely offering up a predictable form of misogyny. His body cites multiple discourses, including athleticism and Blackness, yet his response, posture, and positioning forefronts masculine power.

Still, the historical tensions of the White female and the Black male cannot be ignored, also conjuring legacies of White innocence, the production of the Black male body as dehumanized threat, and the emasculation of the Black male body for white pleasure. Tyson's struggle for control, and his failure to claim it, is exposing itself. Following Schumer's "Ryan Dunn" joke, discussed in a later section, Tyson yells out, "Fuck You, Amy!" She half-heartedly states, "Oh Mike, stay away from me," as if Tyson is not even worth the energy to shut down. The demeaning and condescending "Oh Mike," is coupled with her directive, "Stay away from me," where Tyson's violent past is performatively cited. He is positioned as both pathetic and threatening. Schumer does not retreat or flinch, but continues calmly, working in a mode of plastic smiling irony that channels denigration towards Tyson. He is marked as threat, yet she claims power in her dismissal. The audience is with her. To appropriate Sheen's own line, in that space, she is winning. Tyson is no longer heroic, but shamed and squelched. Her witty retort, but also the speed, calm, command, and belittlement in her energy knocks Tyson down. It is one of the main reasons Schumer's set stood out in the event, for "making the master laugh is one thing; unseating him from a position of power is quite another" (Gilbert 21). It is notable that Schumer's set had the most consistent heckling and vocalized resistance/aggression from members of the dais, as the power struggle produced visible and audible tensions, resistance, and efforts for reassertion.

When Schumer moved past Tyson to other members of the dais, the ironic performativity of her set continued to disrupt and upset sedimented gendered norms of the event. In a playful and resistant twist, spotlighting the male bodies on stage, she mocks Ross's and Shatner's physical attractiveness, O'Neil's weight, and Jezelnik's "Hitler Youth" looks. She indicts Sheen about the constant fear his wife must have experienced in their marriage—what she calls her *Platoon* (the Vietnam film Sheen was in) because "she [his wife] was constantly in fear of being killed by Charlie." Across the dais, with the exception of her contemporary (and boyfriend at the time) Anthony Jezelnik, there is an uneasy resistance of "who is she" that straddles the interpretive line of "who does she think she is?" This was underscored by the constant mocking her as a "nobody" by the men prior to her set. She refused the traditionally accommodating female posture of merely laughing at and appreciating men's jokes (Gilbert 27), and resisted the tacit norms of the roast that comedy is primarily a male genre (41) and a boys' club (68). Holding her own with a subversive winning smile, Schumer seized this aggressively masculine event. Notably, the one person she avoided criticizing in a subtle act of feminist solidarity was the other female on the dais, actress Kate Walsh. Instead, when she got to Walsh, she threw out a weak *Grey's Anatomy* joke about Shatner's testicles and moved on.

During her set, she transitions awkwardly from Tyson to O'Neil with a cheap one-liner. She narrates how Mike's face is all "dark and wrinkly and constantly getting pounded, it's like, Patrice's grandmother's asshole after a gospel brunch." She then turns to O'Neil and offers the aside, "I'm just assuming she raised you." The first line—drawing connections between the two persons of color on the dais and the reference to dark skin—explicitly invokes race, but draws its humor from violating norms of proper femininity and insulting Tyson's face. The follow-up, however, is clearly entrenched in racist/class-based stereotypes. O'Neil looks shocked, as the joke was cheap and a bit labored, but rather than offer nonverbal comfort or "check in," Schumer looks down, refusing him approval or reaction. Her attack-then-break from him resists the possibility of connection or reconfigured relation. She performs a white femininity and invokes his Black masculinity, but refuses them to be in any form of complicated or inventive dynamic with one another. Her turn away resists their meeting or negotiation. This moment hit an affective register that fell short of fully mobilizing an ironic performativity to disrupt racial hierarchy. Unlike Tyson, wherein the invocation of domestic abuse highlighted embodied discourses of gender power negotiation, Schumer's joke to O'Neil cited racial discourse in a way that felt base and uncomplicated. Her delivery had a tinge of aggression in the tone that, if it were pulled back or allowed time for an extended cue of ironic ignorance, might have offered, propelled or instructed a stronger ironic reading. The performativity of racism was not turned away from with irony, and thus seemed to reiterate rather than disrupt. Tyson claps excitedly, if not awkwardly.

Schumer continues deriding O'Neil, mocking his weight and diabetes, suggesting tonight is not only a roast for Sheen, but also "a farewell party for Patrice's foot." Schumer delivers this line with peppy zeal, playing the clueless and shameless[3] enthusiast—an extreme version of ignorant white femininity smiling to the camera in unaware/aware repulsiveness. Physically, this was one of her largest gestural moments, wherein her line delivery is punctuated with a pleased smile and a strong head nod that lands on the word "foot." There is wickedness in her delivery of this punch line that is excessive, cold, and seemingly delighted. Following the "grandmother" joke, the performativity of this exchange accentuates the ever-present racialized discourses between this white feminine woman and this larger Black male—legacies of white innocence, brutalization and castration of Black male bodies, and the overall dehumanization of Blackness. The performativity was citing these discourses, but her ironic cues did not offer enough to interrupt, turn away from, or redirect them. Unlike a comedian like Sarah Silverman, who has crafted a persona of ironic white ignorance to unmask and interrogate privilege, Schumer's "pep" with the foot line conjures something more sinister, inhumane, and difficult to negotiate—the dehumanizing festivity of lynchings. Her delighted smile, her heightened perkiness enacted through her white feminine body, alongside the verbal reference to the severing of an appendage, cites historical discourses of racist torture without a clear disruption of their meanings. There was not the "simply incredible" demonstration of ignorance that coaches the audience into knowing and taking faith that she knows what she is doing here, and that she is doing something productive (Booth 57). In that moment, she is grotesque. Schumer's rapid delivery seems less layered in its hurry, and ambiguously cruel. It does not tear at meanings, but paves over them. Visibly a bit thrown, O'Neil says to the rest of the dais, "Holy shit. Evil. I've been sitting next to this bitch the whole time, I didn't know this was coming." On the dais, the only two persons of color were O'Neil and Tyson, yet O'Neil was constantly the recipient of race-themed humor. Tyson's masculinity was often referenced, but O'Neil was continually and explicitly marked and engaged as a Black male. O'Neil called attention to this absence, saying it was disappointing how comfortable white people had come to be around Tyson.

Schumer invokes discourses of race in a manner that is open for ironic/satiric reads, but the mere presence of satiric irony should not be enough to define or explain her ironic performativity. Rather, it is important to discuss what her ironic performativity does (or attempts to do). Although Schumer is satirically holding up a mirror to cultural stereotypes of African American children being raised by grandparents (absent fathers, teen pregnancy) and the dietary crisis in poor communities, are these stereotypical invocations providing any critical intervention into the underlying ideological systems? At points, this race-themed section of her work is similar to Madison's narration of her student's performance, as "fenced off from rhetoric, or more precisely, from conscious rhetorical performance" (2014, 112). Madison elaborates,

> The [student] performance was arguably an uninterrupted reflection upholding the violence of a foundational, racist rhetoric that lacked, in turn, a rhetorical performance hammer to crack that reflection. This hammer would manifest in added performance devices: gesture, symbol, language, tempo, movement, sound, etcetera. This rhetorical performance hammer is constituted by a critical aesthetic, by moments of intentional and deliberate creative intervention.

Certainly, performers can never assume critical awareness in their audience; does Schumer provoke, aesthetically propel, or coach critical awareness in an effort to shape and drive the ironic performativities of her race-themed work? While irony carries the potential to be "a highly complex rhetorical, social, and political tool" (Gournelos and Greene xviii) to shift oppressive meanings, it can also work to merely reify and reproduce inequity. A frame of ironic performativity works to trace this struggle and negotiation. Reducing the aesthetic complexities to dismissals of "just a joke" or a totalizing "it was ironic" undermines the critical possibilities of humor while also providing shelter for jokes that work to primarily reaffirm oppressive logics. As seen in the not fully resistant, yet potentially subversive race-themed work of Schumer's set, the performative workings of ironic satire demand deeper and more layered considerations.

Processing ironic performativities: Schumer and Shatner

Central to a processual shift of ironic performativity is to push against the knee-jerk judgment in our interpretations (i.e. Schumer is racist or even

Schumer's "foot" joke is racist). This functions to challenge the myth of a fixed and correct read (Gournelos and Greene xxv), placing symbolic focus on the processes of becoming (Madison, 1998). Schumer, in her interaction with O'Neil, is neither simply racist, nor so easily not racist, but is embodying racisms in potentially complex ways that are tied to her body, her multiple subjectivities, and how she is audienced. Arguing the powerful cultural critique of the stereotypical performances of Carmelita Tropicana, José Esteban Muñoz ties Tropicana's ability to camp, critique, and subvert dominant images of the Cuban Latina to her lesbian and Cuban identity (120). Her strategic critical resistance to and reworking of dominant norms—her doing and redoing of Latina representational critique—relies upon a set of distinct meanings mapped onto her body, which are informed by, but not determined by, her identity. Similarly, Schumer's performative doing of femininity and disruption of sexism is particularly enabled in her body, in a manner that her doing of racism through her white feminine body (in reference to O'Neil) is limited and discursively directed. The obvious result of this argument is that Schumer's identity, and how she is read, enables her to execute certain comedic performativities (and not others). She is a white feminine woman, and the body she inhabits provides differing and specific access/capability to intervene into gendered and sexist discourses. While she may be culturally sanctioned to speak about different things, this is always in relation to the cultural meanings mapped onto her unique body that permit her to performatively engage specific discourses from specific ways.

Yet, one of the things Schumer can tackle, and does take on with varying degrees of success, is embodying an excessive ironic performance of whiteness that potentially pushes against, or at least investigates, dominant logics. While she could be read as "racist," depending on how and by whom she is audienced, this labeling solidifies and simplifies a communicative process of far greater complexity. Attention to ironic performativity ought to resist the final and reductive either/or logics of "ist/not ist." Through the lens of ironic performativity, the invocation of racist stereotypes—"I just assumed she raised you"—is more than an untroubled recitation of racism. Thus the performative effect is complicated if her delivery aesthetically cues an audience otherwise, and operates to disrupt the steady reiteration of racist performativity. Rather than silenced, avoided, or disguised in inferential racisms, we are actively (and potentially, critically) watching racisms being stretched, pulled, and engaged (i.e. "I just assumed …"). The ugliness is unleashed in this forum in a manner that allows it to be identified, reflected upon, interrupted, and possibly negated/turned away from.

Ironic performativity and attention to the engagement with racist discourses both reflects concretized meanings (Madison's mirror) and critically exposes the ugliness and instability of these meanings (Madison's hammer). The mere presence of an "ism" (e.g. sexism) or the summoning of an "ism" through verbal language (e.g. "faggot") should not set off an alarm (e.g. you are "sexist" or "homophobic"). Indeed, such a charge may be likened to spotting a rat in the basement and screaming, "I see a rat! Over there! In the corner!" The problem is, metaphorically, the rats are always there. The basement is filled with them—racism, sexism, homophobia, and a multitude of oppressive logics are always scurrying around our every move. Screaming, "There's a rat over there!" functions to obscure the omnipresence of racism and sexism in our culture, and their power to control the discursive field. In marking "them" or "that" as racist, the implication is that we are not complicit with these systems, obscuring a broader systemic focus. Just because the rat does not squeak does not mean the rat is not there—though killing the squeaking ones seems to make everyone else feel a bit better.

Is Schumer's "grandmother" joke targeting the comedian, the audience, or O'Neil? If we audience Schumer as the Socratic ironic fool, who faithfully "believes" racist stereotypes and follows their "logics," then the ironic performativity of the joke identifies and scrutinizes racist scripts. When Schumer "just assumes" his grandmother raised him, she is exposing her (our) ignorance, as a culture, performing an obliviousness that has the potential to foster critical consciousness. As a normative white feminine female, smiling with a slightly vicious obliviousness, Schumer does some aesthetic work in her delivery to coach an ironic reading. The strongest indication of this, however, is in her extended pause after the words, when initial shock and discomfort is followed by a groan of laughter and dis-ease. She maintains her perky affect in an awkwardness that starts to unravel and expose and disrupt, if not turn away from, the citational chain of racism invoked. The camera cuts from a stunned O'Neil to an African American woman in the audience, likely in her late twenties, shaking her head in disapproval as she laughs. For several seconds, the room processes Schumer's "just assumed" ironic white innocence—her "no offense" performance is designed to shock, yet in its aftermath, it potentially opens up a space for an extension of meanings. The level of ambiguity in this joke straddles a line that leaves much up to the audience, and thus the ironic performativity interrogates racism for some and merely reflects it for others. The joke implicates all of us as part of a racist culture, yet the labeling of Schumer as "racist" dismisses ironic cues, individualizes racism, and lets the larger social system—and the noble and offended audience—off the hook. Her forward-facing and blank, perky smile momentarily suspends us in the regurgitation of racist discourses, lingering, opening the possibility for us, as audience, to turn away. However, irony should not be a free for all, nor is the doing of racism a way to shield or legitimize overt reifications of oppressive logics.

To detail a different comedic engagement with racism, the analysis turns to Shatner, the roaster who followed Schumer. Less a comedian than an ironic celebrity persona, Shatner's roasting exemplifies how irony does not always propel critical, disruptive, or complex interventions with "isms." Shatner, with smug pride, says to Sheen, "I've had sex in space with green women [as Captain Kirk on *Star Trek*]. Sure you've had sex with blue women, because unlike you, they couldn't handle their drugs." In a monologue about providing career advice, he says, "Prostitutes cost a lot of money, Charlie, hasn't anyone ever told you that actresses will sleep with you for free?" The camera cuts to a white blond woman, in her early thirties, who begins to laugh and then turns it down with a disapproving expression.

While ironic in his self-aware presentation—exemplified in his Priceline commercials—but lacking in critical interrogation of its sexist doings, Shatner seems more satisfied with the surface humor and drawing a linear parallel. His comedy relied upon sexism in its construction (women are faceless props for male pleasure; dead females due to overdose are now blue), but failed to open a critical space for the performative norms of his doings to be questioned, disrupted, played upon, or parodied. His use of body cites a performativity of hegemonic white masculinity without contest or ironic reflection. For example, discussing his career, he offers advice to Sheen to slow down and take time "to get into the right projects – just like Patrice O'Neil's family." Where Schumer's performance of the Socratic ironic fool potentially opened a space to call attention to her racist assumptions through her perky delivery, pause, and embellished postures of white femininity, Shatner's "joke" simply regurgitates a stereotype. The performativity of the joke, alongside the aesthetic elements of the delivery, merely cited and reified a racist discourse. The message did not complicate or turn away from existing meanings. Furthermore, it is worth noting that Shatner actually mispronounced O'Neil's name, calling him "Pattriss." This distancing only emphasized the generic nature of his "joke," which failed to mark or include a cue to trouble or disrupt the doing of racism in the statement. Unlike Schumer, who uses her body to call upon and disrupt cultural codes, such as the oblivious white "ditz," Shatner's white male body remains normalized and unscrutinized. Had Shatner provided a more conscious reflection in performing the "old white racist man" shtick, which O'Neil openly called out, perhaps Shatner's humor could have done more to pry open a critical space for who gets to laugh at the racist discourses he seems to enjoy. In other words, rather than work against oppressive logics, Shatner seems to be standing comfortably on their shoulders.

When O'Neil finally takes the stage, his responses to Schumer and Shatner are qualitatively different. He never addresses Schumer explicitly in his set, although he did generally note the coldness of joking about his diabetes (from which he passed away two months later). However, as O'Neil fumbles with his notes, he explains that he had prepared jokes, but is now thrown. He says he is speechless, bothered to find out Captain Kirk was going to be all "quasi-racist." He then turns to Shatner, and says directly, "You're an asshole." His performance manages a hint of labored playfulness in accordance with the context, but is also an unequivocal indictment of Shatner's humor. He shakes his head in shock and disgust, calling out how "everyone (in the audience) is all giggling."

Clearly, Schumer and Shatner are both working with racism, but the ironic performativity of their jokes are coaching and soliciting vastly different types of engagements with and through racisms. These dissimilarities are reflected in O'Neil's response. This critical project demands even further reflection through questioning who can, who will, and who refuses to read racisms in resistant ways. How does my own affinity with whiteness, as a white gay Jewish academic, permit me to read productive doings of racism in Schumer's work? Who gets to laugh? How is the meaning/knowledge we generate tied to our bodies, relations, and subjectivities? This line of self-reflexive investigation will be explored more directly in Chapter 3. Chapter 2, however, extends our examination of ironic performativity into performative frames of critique. I have argued that there is a greater value in tracing how racisms are done in unique spaces, through differing bodies, in differing ways, through a focus on the processual. However, judging a joke or a joke-teller as "racist" fails to address the ironic performativity of the comedian's work and how these doings are unique, resistant, and/or hegemonic. Communication, especially in complex sites such as humor, needs to be engaged as *more* complex, *more* intricate, and offering layered information that demands close attention to performative effects. To open a performance frame where meanings are multiple, negotiated, and contextual, however, calls for a performative approach to how racisms, sexisms, and cultural discourses of oppression are being done, moment by moment.

Notes

1 In a brief footnote, in fact, Booth argues there are both descriptive and performative dimensions to ironic statements. He states "I don't quite know what to do with this tidbit, except to hope that some professional philosopher will digest it, and then do something with my further observation that 'ironic performatives' can apparently be employed in each of J. L. Austin's speech acts: locutionary, illocutionary, and perlocutionary" (15).

2 When coupled with satire, understood as a genre that seeks to perform a moral critique and corrective to point out faults or failings (Colletta; Kreuz and Roberts; Nelson), irony is used for critical/rhetorical ends. While ironic works without satiric content are hollow (Colletta 859), irony offers a range of performative methods for enacting satiric critique. Whether building empathy (Nelson), bridging identification with audiences (Nachman), disarming an audience (Gilbert), placing offensive language out there to be dealt with (Nachman), or opening up taboo or dangerous connections and opportunities through laughter, ironic satire creates a space that does multiple levels of work that the audience might not even be fully aware of—or at least be able to articulate easily (Nachman). Satire, at its best, works to hold up a mirror to our faults and confronts them with scorn and ridicule (Colletta). Such an approach troubles the simplified equation that laughing at a joke merely and only strengthens an oppressive meaning. Within the laugh is a broad range of potential knowledges and understandings, which is traced in this chapter and larger book project through the workings of ironic performativity.

3 Much of Amy Schumer's comedy, especially her very successful television show on Comedy Central, deals with shame and gendered norms. This work of hers is strongly informed by Pelle's analysis of the stand up comedy of Margaret Cho (26), and the relationship Cho builds with her audience. The roast, however, presented a different context and her work with shame was notably and necessarily absent, for

the looming presence of the highly masculine dais and the central positioning of Sheen limited some of the work she could do (while enabling other types of work). Although overt negotiations of power struggle and affective resistance were highly pronounced, there lacked a space of trust and vulnerability for her to delve into issues of shame in the manner than she could in a one-woman performance (where the audience is there for her and she is in control of the setting the context.)

2 The end of the discussion

The crisis of judgment

Introduction: "Sarah Silverman: Funny Woman or Foul-Mouthed Racist"?[1]

> We've become so good at anticipating the other's next move that there is little need even to listen out for the trains rumbling across the racial tracks dividing us from an assortment of thems.
>
> (Jackson 14)

> When you are playing with racial slurs you are playing with fire, and if you are playing with fire, expect to get burned.
>
> (Guy Aoki on Politically Correct)

> Increasingly I've spent my time thinking about how do I try to break out of these old patterns that our politics has fallen into. Which is part of the reason why I'm here.
>
> (Barack Obama on "President Barack Obama," WTF Podcast)

It was perhaps one of the first "comic controversies" in the new era of social media and the Internet, after Sarah Silverman famously sat down for an interview on the *Conan O'Brien Show* on July 11, 2001. Silverman is seated next to Conan, with his earlier guest comedians, Penn and Teller, to her right. The then 30-year-old comedian narrates her experience with a drawn out, dazed, dismissively giggly, and slightly "stoner-ish" delivery. She wears a casual black tank top, throwing her hands down in annoyance, "I got. Cause I got a jury duty (she deliberately pauses with extended stare) notice. You know, you have to like fill it out (mimes writing action, rapidly and routinely) and send it in (mimes again) and they select you randomly." She stares forward after "randomly" for a moment like it's almost traumatic. She stammers, from the exhausted annoyance of the process, performing an over the top whiney, lazy, and privileged persona. She breaks into conversational frustration. "There's just, I don't, there's *nothing* funny about jury duty, except for the obvious, (she smiles) you know the *duty* part." She pauses for a moment to laugh at the word "duty" in self-amusement. The audiences takes the cue, and as she laughs at a juvenile "doody" joke, they connect with the sensibility and laugh—seemingly *at* her laughing, rather than at the preschool-appropriate joke. She returns to the whine, "But I, jury duty, I don't want to do it, and I'm filling out this form and everything, and my friend is like, 'why don't you write something, like, really inappropriate on the form, like 'I hate chinks.'" She delivers this matter of factly and directly, in a straight narration, punctuated by a stern, direct and unflinching delivery of, "I hate chinks." Each of the three words are equally emphasized and set forth in a steady offering in front of the audience, somewhat removed. The audience responds with a wave of uneasy laughter and surprise/shock. Her straight expression moves to a smile, as she raises her arms up in a gesture to imply, "I know, good ideas, right?" She does get out a muffled, "good idea," but Conan jumps in, somewhat nervously. He states, over explaining, to clarify "But it sounds crazy, but people sometimes do that just so they can't be on the jury." He's cut into her rhythm a bit, overstating her subtext, so she adapts and works off him. She nods, sarcastically, and in a slightly condescending but a playful way, says, "Exac … *Nice* point," identifying he's stating the shared pretense of the joke a bit too explicitly for her taste. Conan drops in a "Thank you," which is followed, without a beat, with Sarah saying, "That was sharp," extending her condescension by offering no emphasis or weight to "sharp"—rendering it hollow.

Silverman pushes on, working to get her joke moving, "So, I'm thinking to myself …," but Conan interjects, "I'm trying to help you out here, Pal …" Silverman again, determined, pushed forward without pause, over the nervous laughter, "… I know, really, you are." The joke is now getting drawn out a bit too long. In a rapid, perhaps nervous gesture, she awkwardly licks her finger, wipes it, and then launches directly back into the joke. "I wanted to do it, but then I'm like, I don't want people to think I'm racist or something, I just want to get out of jury duty," she says, very calmly, with a relatable sense of reasonable honestly. "So I just filled out the form and I wrote, "I *love* Chinks."

As she delivers the punchline, she turns to the side, mimes writing casually, and places just enough emphasis on "Love" to mark the shift in wording, as if to highlight a brilliant, but subtle shift or maneuver. The audience laughs, Conan laughs, and Penn and Teller (on the sofa next to her) nod their heads in awkward agreement. The laugh is not uproarious, but uneased and negotiated. "And who doesn't!" Silverman exclaims, in a sarcastic burst of ironic punctuation, as she leans outwards, with a goofy smile, and her arms hanging forward. Conan jumps in, "So, you are not going to be on that jury anytime soon. That's very nice"

Silverman's use of the racial slur "chink" received a strong, and very public condemnation from Guy Aoki of the Media Action League for Asian Americans (MANAA) and was a topic of controversy on the morning show, *The View*, the following week. Aoki launched a public campaign insisting the offense be addressed. NBC quickly apologized and agreed to never air the uncensored episode again. Aoki argued that the network apology was only a start. He argued Conan should make an apology on the show, and Sarah Silverman should also issue an apology for hurting anyone. Silverman wrote a long email[2] to Aoki apologizing if he was offended, stating this was not her intention. She also explained her use of irony and her ironic persona of the ignoramus to examine racism in the social unconscious. She asks, "Some people react to buzz-words before listening to the context of those words. Isn't that ignorance?" (146). While arguing she and Aoki should be on the same side, even if they have different approaches to combating racism, she questions his framing of her as the bigot to his victimhood (146). In her email, Silverman called for a face to face dialogue, rather than arguing in soundbites in the press, but Aoki resisted the invitation. Rather, Aoki wrote a curt response, distributed her email to all the members of MANAA (so she could get months of hate mail) and continued leading the public outcry against Silverman. Silverman appeared on Bill Maher's talk show *Politically Incorrect* to respond to the controversy, arguing Aoki was personally going out of his way to attack her and was using her to gain attention. It is important to mark that the persona Silverman embodies and performs publicly, in response to this controversy is distinct from the more analytical voice she adopts when writing about it, as her public persona is tied to her ironic comedic persona. In a whiney, and slightly too over-performed to be read entirely sincere plea, Silverman pouted, "It hurts" and "I want an apology from him."

The controversy continued to build, and on a later episode of *Politically Incorrect* airing August 23, 2001, Silverman and Aoki were brought together (along with guest stars David Spade and Anne-Marie Johnson) to address the dispute face to face. To "set the stage" for the dialogue, Silverman had to tell the joke (rather awkwardly) again, "as quickly as you can." She rapidly recounts the joke, nervously, and even though the context of the joke is now very different, it receives some laughter. Understanding that the joke cannot work the same way in this space, Silverman follows up, and says, "It's a joke that …," but Actress Anne-Marie Johnson leans over, interrupts her, and asks, rather directly and accusatorily, "Where *is* the joke?" A loud burst of supportive applause emerges from a portion of the audience, and it becomes clear that there are strong divisions already staked out in the issue. According to Silverman's book *Bedwetter*, the auditorium for the show had 120 audience seats, for which sixty seats were reserved by Aoki for his supporters and fellow protestors (149). Before the issue was even introduced for discussion, the room was, literally, split.

What ensued throughout this show was an intense debate about the role of language and the license of comedy. Silverman argued, "I believe comedy reflects society and I feel that joke is a joke that points a finger at racism, just like it's your job to point your finger at racism, and I think it's inappropriate and it's counterproductive to demand an apology for someone, who, like you, is illuminating racism just for doing it in a different way than you do it." Aoki responded, "I think you give yourself too much credit. I think that, first of all, I understand satire, she says this was satire and was taken out of context. I said there was no context. I enjoy good satire. Satire is a great device … but if you don't know how to do satire correctly, you make situations worse." He elaborated, "If you don't know how to do satire correctly, you run the risk of making people think that you really believe what you are saying, and until you know how to do satire correctly, I'd stay away from it."

The panelists spoke at one another, but there was not any indication of listening taking place. In the end, the dialogue was not really a dialogue at all, but an entrenched and polarized debate, and the guest panel never reached any sense of shared understanding. Aoki worked to claim his position by suggesting there is a cultural linkage between Silverman's use of the slur and a recent stabbing of an Asian student on a California college campus. Anne-Marie Johnson agrees with Aoki. She argues that the problem she has with Silverman's "joke" is the countless times Johnson is "at a dinner table, or I'm playing golf, or whatever, and I have to hear people say 'He really Jewed me down on that,' or 'He was slow as a [n-word],' or 'Look at the beaner run' and then I have to say …" Silverman interrupts her, appalled, amused, and in disbelief, "*Who* are you hanging out with? God!" Half the audience, along with Maher, laughed at/with Silverman, marking a range of different understandings at work in this debate. In the end, Johnson and Aoki saw it as a slur, no different than when used in a hate crime. They believed she chose the word because she thought she could get away with it, as an exercise of power and bigotry. They wanted an apology. Silverman made no claim that the word was innocent or a free for all, but argued her use of it, in the joke, was strategic to expose and examine racism and racial ignorance. She argued her use of the word was a method to bring forth and then interrogate the ignorance signified by the slur.

Silverman has since provided a range of critical responses to these events, most thoroughly detailed in her book *Bedwetter*. In the text, she mocks the simplicity of Aoki's engagement, questions the opportunism of his public outcry, and (begrudgingly) provides a thoughtful and complicated theorization of how ironic comedy works. Silverman argued her satiric work was reflecting, and also interrogating, the simple mindedness of racist postures. It anticipated and worked to coach an ironic read, and there is more to satiric comedy—and to the interrogation of racism in contemporary culture—than mere word policing.

The argument I am setting forth in this chapter is not a position on whether Silverman's joke was "good" or "bad," offensive, or an effective performance of satire about white racisms. Rather, I want to draw attention to several key issues that define both the form and governing logics of this 2001 event in order to explore the patterns and entrenched logics at work within the contemporary comic controversy. Most immediately, the mere presence of the word is the offense felt by Aoki, and for using that slur, there was a strong belief that Silverman needed to apologize to the Asian American community. Within this framing of events lie several assumptions/tensions that will be examined and unpacked throughout this volume.

1 To say the word "chink" is racist and its mention or use, regardless of context, is a racist act (as opposed to the logic that, within comedy, there are different systems at work).

2 There is nothing else in the delivery or crafting of the joke, from vocal cues, to established persona, to nonverbal delivery that could change the first point (as opposed to the argument that comedy is an art and form of cultural critique where aesthetics are central to the meaning).
3 Aoki was offended, and the experience of offense was solely about Silverman's actions (as opposed to the offense being about Aoki's interpretation).
4 Aoki's offense is shared and standard across a broader and heterogeneous Asian American community.
5 An apology is necessary and would help remedy the racist offense.

While Sarah Silverman's infamous "chink" joke on *Conan* can surely be read as "racist," depending on how and by whom she is audienced, this labeling works to solidify and simplify a communicative process of far greater complexity. The objective of this chapter is not to indict or defend Silverman's joke, but to unpack and examine the interpretive and discursive frameworks that produce this very discussion—the *is* and *is not* racist debate, the performance of "Internet outrage," and the cultural firestorm that is the "PC" debate (i.e. "the "PC" police, and "political correctness run amuck"). Through a close analysis of the Silverman debate, alongside current arguments about "political correctness" and comedy, this chapter sets forth a position that we ought resist the final and reductive either/or logics of "-ist/not -ist." Wholly judging a joke or a joke teller as "racist," just as essentially categorizing work as "ironic" or "satire," fails to address the performativity of the comedian's work, and how these doings *can have* a range of effects that might be unique and resistant, but/and also might function hegemonically to reify oppressive systems. Performatively marking and tracing the ironic *doings of* racism or sexism (examining its discursive effects), rather than applying the judgment of work *as* racist or sexist, disrupts the limited equation between engaging social oppression (the doing, undoing, redoing of multiple isms) and merely reifying those oppressions (the being an "ist."). Herein, the analysis shifts from the "language turn" in culture to the "performance turn." A performative frame would not settle into a firm judgment of what the joke *is*, but would rather invest in a deep, close and ongoing contemplation of what her joke is doing (or trying to do). Furthermore, this line of inquiry works to explore the limits of this "is/is not" framework, identifying the hegemonic systems this limited debate works to obscure and protect.

The chapter will begin by setting up contemporary "PC" debates and tracing the contours of the comic controversy, an ongoing contemporary ritual of rapid offense, outrage, and hollowed PR-approved apology. Next, the chapter looks to discuss the rhetorical workings of this ritual, with specific attention to the language of "political correctness" which often operates to reproduce tragic systems of judgment and punishment. The final two sections of the chapter enlist examples from Jerry Seinfeld, Bill Maher, and the Sarah Silverman/Aoki drama to explore the limitations and dangers of engaging in comic controversies through a tragic frame. Such a simplified and binary mode of engagement—where a joke is either good or bad, racist or not, offensive or progressive—limits the critical possibilities of comedic work and denigrates cultural discourse.

The minefield of political correctness: Historical emergence and contemporary tragedy

> "PC" needs to be addressed seriously by the left, because the critique of "PC" remains an effective and damaging strategy.
>
> (Fairclough 27)

> It [PC] has become a misnomer, being concerned with neither *politics* nor *correctness* as those terms are generally understood.
>
> (Hughes 3)

> There is a tendency to confuse verbal purification with real social change.
>
> (Barbara Ehrenreich qtd. in Littlewood and Pickering 304–5)

Before wading into the complex tragedy of the comic controversy, it is necessary to briefly define and contextualize the emergence of the contentious, slippery, and contested concept that is often—though not always correctly—invoked in these debates: "political correctness." In 1991 at the University of Michigan commencement, George H. W. Bush warned, "political extremists roam the land, abusing the privilege of free speech, setting citizens against one another on the basis of their class or race … The notion of political correctness has ignited controversy across the land" (Selfa). Early appearances of political correctness have been traced to irony and self-deprecation in the 1964 Maoist text "Mao's Little Red Book" (Hughes 63). Toni Cade's "The Black Woman" enlisted the expression, when stating "a man cannot be politically correct and chauvinist too" (Hughes 63). However, the modern usage of "political correctness" and its common shorthanded marker, "PC," has been traced to college campus in the 1980s. Hughes states, "linguistically it [PC] started as a basically idealistic, decent-minded, but slightly Puritanical intervention to sanitize the language by suppressing some of the uglier prejudicial features, thereby undoing some pasts injustices or 'leveling the playing fields' with the hope of improving social relations" (3). Fairclough traces the emergence of political correctness to the "language turn" in social political theory, where cultural studies and discourse theory challenged the value-laden and ideological effects of language (23). Signifying practices, for those outside or resistant to the language turn of cultural studies, were commonly seen as neutral, wherein there is a transparent relationship between words and what they represent (23). Approaching "culture as a 'signifying system'" (18), political correctness is a label assigned to a cultural intervention, that, at least in part, sought to change inequity in language and discourse (20). The intervention sought to diminish the use of demeaning language that reproduced historical inequity, such as the generic masculine forms of "fireman" and "policeman," the use of slurs, and the erasure/whitewashing of violent histories (ex. "Native American" rather than "Indian"). In addition, "it also manifested itself in speech codes which suppress prejudicial language, disguising or avoiding certain old and new taboo topics" (Hughes 3).

According to the predominant conservative narrative, any well-meaning efforts of "PC" have inadvertently been the root cause of "America's dysfunctional national conversation" (Ham and Benson 8). As George H. W. Bush explained in 1991, "Although the movement arises from a laudable desire to sweep away the debris of racism and sexism and hatred, it replaces old prejudices with new ones. It declares certain topics off limits, certain expressions off limits, even certain gestures off limits" (Selfa). The conservative narrative constructs a tale where this well-meaning (and laudable, even from the right) effort has resulted in empowering "The relentless, pedantic, hall monitors of our discourse" (Ham and Benson 12). These "more radical members of the left attempt to regulate political discourse by defining opposing views as bigoted and illegitimate" (Chait) through clutching one's "emotional hamstring and writhing on the floor" (Ham and Benson 33).

Yet, how any given person works to define or explain "political correctness" will quickly shed more insight into that individual's political commitments, than providing any grounding to the contested concept, itself. In 2004, Doris Lessing claimed, "The most powerful mental tyranny in what we call the free world is Political Correctness, which is both immediately evident, and to be seen everywhere, and as invisible as a kind of poison gas, for its influences are often far from the source, manifesting in general intolerance" (qtd. in Hughes 63). Conservative rhetoric has cast their conceptualization and production of "PC" as the greatest of evils. The 2016 Republican primary candidate Ben Carson has linked PC's silencing effects to Nazi Germany. He argues:

> Most of them did not agree with what Hitler was doing, but they kept their mouth shut and you see what happened. And exactly the same thing will happen to the freedoms that we enjoy in America and the kind of nation that we've had if people don't speak up. They need to rise up. They need to say to political correctness: "Take a hike! This is who we are."
> (Patrick Henry College).

Right wing conservatives have routinely cast political correctness as conformity and silencing, at best, and tyrannical censorship and the death of democracy at its worst. "PC" has been used to mark what is perceived to be a self-righteous, nit-picky, "liberal fascism," which makes a "Deplorable bid to stifle debate" (Fairclough 26). Progressive left wing liberals, on the other hand, often reject the term as a political straw man. "Few of those identified as 'PCers' accept themselves to be such. 'Political correctness' and being 'politically correct' are, in the main, identifications imposed upon people by their political opponents" (21). Clare Short, in 1995, argues "Political correctness is a concept invented by hardright-wing forces to defend their right to be racist, to treat women in a degrading way and to be truly vile to gay people. They invent these people who are Politically Correct, with a rigid, monstrous attitude to life so they can attack them" (qtd. in Hughes 16).

An interesting paradox emerges in these debates. The right wing characterizes the "nit picky" word policing of the phantom PC mobs, rejecting the notion that words have such a profound effect (it's just a word), yet the very use and deployment of the term "politically correct" from the right has been an "effective and damaging strategy" (27). In other terms, the right has enlisted their own cultural intervention to shape and alter signifying systems and representations as a means of social change (Cameron cited in Fairclough 21), even as they work to mock and debunk the very strategy. Even if the right creates a phantom characterization of an illusionary collective of "PCers run amuck," the use and framings of the PC debate have significant political and social effects. What emerges is what Jackson calls "The minefield of political correctness," where anything labeled "PC" is dismissed as "silly and pointless, a form of social censorship that makes Americans, especially white Americans, overly precious with their language … yet suppresses honest and open debate" (77). Thus, according to Jackson, political correctness has worked to complicate and obscure the "good-faith dialogues" that the initial policies sought to foster (77).

During the 2015 Republican presidential primary, FOX news commentator Megyn Kelly questioned Republican candidate Donald Trump about his multiple attacks on women, stating, "You've called women you don't like 'fat pigs, dogs, slobs and disgusting animals.'" Trump quips, "Only Rosie O'Donnell" and then continues "I have been challenged by so many people and I don't frankly have time for total political correctness. And to be honest with you, this country doesn't have time either." The response, which never fully provided an answer, received a huge wave of applause. His usage of "political correctness" and the response he received, shows the term in this context functions less as an intervention "to change ingrained prejudicial attitudes and their semantic correlatives by the introduction of new, neutral, and unfamiliar lexical forms" (Hughes 15–6). Rather, the audience seems aligned with the belief that "The formulas 'political correctness,' 'politically correct,' and 'PC' are now basically pejorative and ironic in their use" (296). After all, as Blitt argues, the term is unique in that it is almost only used ironically, for "if you label a statement or remark – or the avoidance of a statement or a remark – politically correct, you are criticizing it" (74). Furthermore, it has a unique rhetorical function of self-congratulation, for launching the charge of "political correctness" (never a compliment, but an indictment) is presented as an act of defiance, or courage, and conservative integrity (74).

Trump's usage, that was so welcomed by the audience, was an act of self-praise and pseudo-courageous bravado. The way he uses the term, when read in context of Megyn Kelly's question, has moved far away from earlier manifestations—once a project with a focus on social justice consciousness raising, even if criticized for "camouflaging social problems by polysyllabic obfuscation" (Hughes 296). PC, in Trump's usage, is watered down to mean any censorship of speech that is offensive (or obnoxious). "PC" becomes a threat to free speech, a threat to free society, and a shackling of choice—couched in a claim that honest and rational debate is being stifled. Tacitly, in this new configuration modeled by conservatives like Trump or Carson, "PC" comes to mean not being honest when expressing what one feels. It works to twist and bend its original aims for more democratized language into a democratic threat. By challenging Kelly's question with the response of "PC," Trump's response bypasses the effect or meaning of his statements in order to re-center his right to say them. Trump infers his reference to certain women as "fat pigs, dogs, slobs and disgusting animals" is a democratic act of resistance—an act of patriotic defiance against the band of liberal watchdogs grouped under the rhetorical umbrella of "PC." By embracing a stubborn, resolute, determined commitment to unapologetic misogyny, Trump works to reframe this posture as *more* American and *more* patriotic. Trump's dismissal of "PC" not only reifies the logic of an illusionary liberal community of PCers infringing upon his right to free speech, but seeks to broaden the scope of political correctness away from "undoing some past injustices or 'leveling the playing fields' with the hope of improving social relations" to a broader frame of simply being a "honest." His language choices were not so much a refusal to alter selected words of identity labels that reference legacies of inequality, so much as a misogynist finding pleasure in dehumanizing women through metaphor. Thus, while political correctness carries a history that emerged in the 1980s, where it is used, how it is understood, the meanings it carries, and how it is mapped onto others is not so easily tracked down or solidified. "Discussions of these topics will show that political correctness and its obverse, political incorrectness, are more easily recognized than defined, and that both appear in manifold forms" (Hughes 9). Thus, the charge or invocation of "PC," in itself, lacks a firm sense of grounding or shared meaning, presenting an instability that needs to be carefully attended to throughout this chapter. For this reason, the term "political correctness" and all its variations must remain in quotations moving forward.

Comic controversy as a performative ritual

> Consistently amazed at how little it takes to create 'an outrage.'
>
> (Ham and Benson 17)

> It was a little, stupid joke. There is nothing to apologize for. I made a joke. That's what I do. Calm down. Calm f**king down.
>
> (Joan Rivers qtd. in Garcia)

> All the out of context misquotes aside, I'd like to sincerely apologize.
>
> (Daniel Tosh on @danieltosh)

> I meant no disrespect, and my thoughts are with the victims and their families
>
> (Gottfried qtd, in Zakarin)

> My new goal is not to explain jokes … There's a real culture of demanding apologies, and I'm opting out.
>
> (Tina Fey qtd. in Framke)

> Every joke now has to come with an apology.
>
> (Gottfried)

In a tweet by Seth MacFarlane in April 2014, he attributes the quote "I demand an immediate apology" to the author "everyone about everything." Almost 15 years after Silverman and Aoki's public argument, the presence of the comic controversy is now a weekly newsfeed occurrence. Ironic comedy, in the age of Twitter, is a daily battleground ripe for vicious and polarizing comment threads. There was a time when the checkout newsstand, with splashy weekly *National Enquirer* and *Star* headlines fought to pull you in, draw your eye, and get you to throw an issue onto the conveyor belt. The new frontier of attracting blog hits, fighting for link shares, and retweets takes this to a whole new level—the minute by minute demand for mediated audiences and clicks has become torrential. Controversy, even if fabricated, drummed up, or simply manufactured, is big business. In 2015, if a few random tweeters make a racist comment about *Star Wars* casting choices, or the casting of a supporting role in *The Hunger Games*, it can become a huge (fleeting) news story. When a celebrity makes a comment, has a photo shoot, wears a Halloween costume, or posts a tweet that is construed by someone, somewhere, as homophobic or sexist or racist, it is quickly a front page event (and Facebook event with the expected comment thread explosion). Thus, when a comedian, especially a celebrity comedian, makes a joke that can be construed as offensive, the story is a hit (and thus worth thousands of hits). It is easy to be flippant about this process, and the rapid rate by which these momentary outrages explode and fade begs the question, why bother offering serious attention to them at all? Tomorrow there will be another story to click through. However, this rapid and repeated pattern has worked to frame, train, and constrain the ways we, as a culture, engage complicated issues of voice, humor, offense, language and oppression.

It is productive to set forth how conservative voices have conceptualized "PC" within this ritualized comic controversy. The best-selling right wing text by Ham and Benson, *The End of Discussion*, sets forth the premise that political debate and rational argumentation in contemporary US culture is being threatened by the liberal left's outrage machine. The book examines a broad range of political discussions in recent years to trace how leftist discourse enlists "political correctness," charges of racism, and discussion-silencing traps to resist true and honest debate. Central to this book's argument is the strategic use of "political correctness" and dog whistle offenses of racism to shut down and silence oppositional views, and attack unwelcome positions by "playing the race card." The book encapsulates the contemporary conservative attack on "PC" and makes a series of compelling arguments, consistently partial, limited in their depiction, or downright flippant, yet it sets forth a claim that is worthy of some suspended attention. The text reflects the authors' resistance to examining their own positions of privilege, and a deep sense of feeling wronged—as if an extended explanation of the audience's enthusiastic response to Trump's "PC" comment. "Political Correctness," in their configuration is the "end of discussion," where "outrage mongers turn this process on its head, disqualifying ideas *without* debate instead of after debate" (Ham and Benson 12). The authors cast the liberal left in the role of the anti-democratic, arguing the liberal left is constantly censuring what words can be spoken, while the right wing has never worked to repress speech in this manner.

Ham and Benson argue that once the liberal left made the social and political gains it wished to achieve, it sought to turn the whole machine down and refuse further discussion. Surely any critical and left-leaning reader, at this juncture is already scratching their head at the limitations of this position as conservative policies and voices and values are constantly weighting down and silencing a broad range of expressions—most notably words deemed "offensive" or artistic work seen as indecent, obscene, or pornographic. Where "political correctness" becomes the rallying cry against free speech for the right, there is a blinded and commonsense adoption of silencing speech or ideas or images that can be deemed offensive—whether pornographic, unchristian or somehow threatening to the innocence of children. Yes, the right has its outrage mechanisms to silence discussion as well, but the impetus and argument on this side is important to factor in the tracing and contextualizing of the comic controversy.

Tackling the obstacles and limitations of "political correctness" and impeded dialogue from a far more critical and leftist position, Jackson's *Racial Paranoia* argues the masking and cloaking of racism from explicit speech, the workings of a more "politically correct" culture, has manifested in a current state he calls *racial paranoia* (4)—"This ambiguous and nonfalsifiable sense of racial distrust is at the heart of the real reality of race in America" (xiv). Jackson's conception of racial paranoia works to mark the ways political correctness has ushered us into a new era of racism, and has produced a range of unintended consequences. Jackson argues that the racial realities and frameworks for thinking about racism from a pre-civil rights mindset are no longer effective (10). Marking what he calls *de cardio racism* or "racism of the heart" (78)—which mandates that we read the heart of a person's intention and trust one's intuition in the absence of explicit racial speech—Jackson makes a compelling argument for both the intentions and importance of "political correctness," but also its unintended consequences. He argues "Political correctness has cleaned up our conversations, but there's a catch. This cleansing means that lip service to racial equality isn't taken at face value. And racial paranoia has become one of the primary ways of divining hidden race-based animosity in someone who would never willingly show it" (21).

It is no surprise that both *End of Discussion* and Jackson routinely look to examples of comedy and political humor to ground their projects, as comedy has become a central location for these tensions to play out. Jackson's theorization in the shift to a state of racial paranoia provides a strong conceptual frame to unpack Silverman's use of ironic humor, and why it's an important strategy. In *Bedwetter*, Silverman argues (154):

> Had Guy Aoki been operating in the 70s, he might have attacked Norman Lear as a racist. The bad news for guys like Aoki is that, not only are the progressive messages out there today more refined and sense-of-irony dependent, but racist messages are more oblique too. Right wing Americans who appear in mainstream media are not out there calling black people [n-word] or saying "The Klan has good ideas." Instead, they're questioning the legitimacy of Obama's presidency by accusing him of being born in Africa, or being a Muslim. Or they are having "tea parties" and calling Obama a "communist" and a "Nazi." The entire Fox News Channel is a twenty-four-hour-a-day racism machine, but it's all coded, all implied. Lou Dobbs used to scream on CNN about "immigration" not "filthy Mexicans."

Silverman argues that humor, via irony, can enact satiric work to challenge the meanings, assumptions, and ideological investments that have been pushed beneath explicit speech.

Where *End of Discussion*, Jackson, and the entire guest panel of *Politically Incorrect* in August 2001 meet, and with differing commitments overlap, is in the understanding that dialogues around race—as well as dialogues of broader systems of identity and power—are failing. While *End of Discussion* is quick to mark the left as the primary culprit for this failure, and Jackson resists the meritocritous optimism of Ham and Benson's continual justification and dismissal of systemic racisms operating in our everyday culture, both see an ongoing pattern that has impeded our ability to engage critical issues. Both mark a limitation, a halting, and an end to discussion that manifests in an ever present cycle. For Jackson, he marks the current climate as one of perpetual distrust around race, a state of racial paranoia, where the absence of overt racist speech allows for suspicion on one end and the room for plausible deniability on the other. The racism and racial paranoia that sits underneath the surface of polite speech festers and builds, whispering contradictions in a small never-ending voice (10). Thus, in those moments when a visible act of racism is experienced in a way that is "seemingly unambiguous" (70), there is a quick and recurrent ritual where "individuals apologize, deny racist motivations, and try to move on" (70). A public moment of seemingly unambiguous racism can also work to provide "almost cathartic moments for us as a nation" (89). In these moments where racism is made visible, brought into the light, something we can point to directly, we can turn to our "antiquated methods for dealing with overt racists, everything from public shaming to legal prosecution, and shake our collective index finger at their impudence" (89).

Where the entirely diverse texts of *End of Discussion* and *Racial Paranoia* agree, and where I suggest they meet with Silverman, is in the *limits of this ritual*. The outrage, indictment, shaming, apology, and the individualized demonization that occurs in these recurrent social dramas of overt moments of prejudice are reductive, suspect, and in need of careful reconsideration. The ritual continues to divide and reaffirm two sides, two opposing forces. The ritual falsely and simply constructs two seemingly dichotomous groups where, depending on whose side one identifies, this will determine and concretize who is "good" and who is "bad." As Silverman wrote to Aoki, "You have cast me as the bigot to your victim" (146). In the land of comedy, specifically, this framing and its recurrent ritual of the often dubbed "Internet outrage machine" has led to what comedian Gilbert Gottfried has called "The Apology Epidemic" (Gottfried).

Tragic frames: Judgment, punishment, apology, and repeat

> Part of what we do when we make moral judgments is express allegiance to a team. But that can interfere with our ability to think critically. Acknowledging that the other side's viewpoint has any merit is risky—your teammates might see you as a traitor.
>
> (Lukianoff and Haidt 45)

> A person may lead a life of complete probity and intellectual rigor, but be destroyed socially and professionally by being denounced for simply using "politically incorrect" language and thus labeled as a *racist, sexist, homophobe*, or *fascist*, despite the fact that these terms are problematic both in definition and specific application. Furthermore, no distinction is commonly made between fiction, dialog, and private utterance.
>
> (Hughes 295).

> You can't even be offensive on your way to being inoffensive.
>
> (Chris Rock qtd. in Page)

Central to how Aoki engaged the entire Silverman controversy was Aoki's firm belief that Silverman needed to apologize for her joke. Silverman's first response was to write Aoki a letter, where she attempted to complicate, dialogue, and contextualize her work as an ironic satirist. This form of dialogue, however, was dismissed. Aoki's position and framing of events insisted on apology, where Silverman admits wrongdoing. Escalating the drama, Silverman enlisted her ignoramus persona once more, appearing on *Politically Incorrect* and demanding her own apology—insisting that she was the one offended and hurt. In an ironic response, Silverman mirrored (mocked) Aoki's reductive rigidity in her own public performance. In a childish and pouty delivery, she replied with, “no, *you* need to apologize” in a mode that enlisted irony to draw attention to the simplified manner that this discussion was playing out. Tensions increased. Aoki felt wronged, argued Silverman was racist, and felt he was hurt. Silverman must apologize. Perhaps what is most remarkable about these events, looking back on them fifteen years later, is that these events were remarkable at all, as indictments like Aoki’s are now a daily routine.

In order to conceptualize the rhetorical operations and effects of this ritual of indictment—alongside the demanded apology—there are two conceptual tools that are instructive in this work; tragedy and judgment. Kenneth Burke is a rhetorical and communication scholar whose work seeks to examine how language establishes and enacts motive. Burkean tragedy (1984), or what he refers to as the *tragic frame*, works to make sense of experience through a rigid and flawed dichotomous categorization. In tragedy and tragic storytelling, according to Burke, there is good and there is evil, there is right and there is wrong, and these two are clearly delineated in ways that resist complication. The tragic narrative is ever present in our political landscape. It is possible no other satirist has been more directed in their criticism of tragic framing than Jon Stewart. On the *Daily Show*, he regularly mocked CNN’s engagements with a range of complex issues for literally reducing the news to a rigid and dumbed down framework of “is this a good thing or a bad thing?” (Feldman). Through simplified and problematic designations of hero and victim, tragedy produces an interpretive frame, much like our legal system, where one is either guilty or innocent, rightly or wrongly accused. Furthermore, if found guilty, the tragic motive sets forth a rhetorical framework that requires punishment. Evil must be penalized, in what Burke calls the “Iron Law of History.” There must be a sacrifice and a ritual of penance, where either one punishes themselves (mortification) or another is sacrificed (the scapegoat of victimage). The tragic motive, then, is a motive of dichotomies, simplicities, and mandated punishment for the restoration of order. It is a rhetorical frame of absolutes and can work to not only indict the guilty, but, depending on how it plays out, fully exonerate one as innocent. Central to the tragic frame is the refusal to allow lines of allegiance and righteousness to blur or bend. When one enlists the tragic frame, the hero is purely good and the villain is purely evil—a model predicated on the act of judgment.

Judith Butler’s conception of *judgment* provides an instructive framework to examine and interrogate the tragic ritual of shaming and apology, particularly when situated in a comic controversy such as Silverman and Aoki’s. According to Butler (2005), judgment marks a severing of connection and know-ability. It denies complication or the possibility of our own complicities. Judgment rejects self-reflexive investigation, a space for potential fallibility, or a willingness to suspend a tragic frame. Judgment is the end of a discussion. When we enact judgment for another, we cut off the ties and connections and possibilities of where we are connected, where we share some of the same humanness. We rhetorically separate ourselves from the person and the crime the person has committed. In other terms, our judgment of one's guilt works to shore up and define our innocence. Beyond more general judgments of evil or bad, Butler's conceptualization of judgment becomes very useful in interrogating the workings of the now commonplace "call outs" of a joke or a comedian being tragically framed as "racist," "sexist," "homophobic" or any firm and absolute judgment.

In his words, Aoki recounts his preparation for appearing on *Politically Incorrect*. "Before leaving the green room, I'd reviewed the sound bites from my clipboard, but now, backstage, I'm having trouble remembering them. C'mon, dammit!, I think, what were those lines?! All right- 'playing with fire.' 'stay away from satire.' 'the hate crime in Laguna Hills.' 'wounded bird. multiply your pain by.' OK. Got it.' His narration is instructive in helping to locate where and how tragedy was framing and dictating the outcomes of this "discussion." Part of his approach must surely be attributed to enlisting strategy for the greater good—a commitment to his politics and the beliefs he genuinely is passionate and dedicated to. He narrates, "I already had two pages of sound bites I'd had in my head for days. But I need to be flexible and in the moment to respond to whatever they throw at me. Can't be stiff. Have to smile whenever I can. Show I'm a reasonable guy so they can hear the message" (Aoki). Attention to presentation makes sense, and the type of press he was getting on a discussion about Asian stereotyping for MANAA was huge. Yet, tragedy seems to overtake his approach, as he moves into his description of the taping. He narrates, "Here comes the sound bite to put Silverman away. It was the one everyone I'd 'previewed' it for nodded their head and agreed it would just nail her." He appraises the show by his ability to fire off a soundbite, gain audience applause, and tear down Silverman—almost as if a video game. His description of the discussion, in his own terms is, "The Sarah vs. Guy issue" marking both the degree that this is personal but also tragic in his framing. He was willfully adopting the frame Silverman criticized, wherein he was victim to her bigot. He engaged the show as a fight to determine guilt and innocence, a tragic judgment, yet the show was framed under the false pretense of "having a discussion." This false pretense of "having a discussion," when really there is not one desired, enters into some murky waters. The tragic frame, the motive of judgment, and the construction of the apology epidemic might appear to dangerously legitimize the positions of Ham and Benson's *End of Discussion*. They argue "By disqualifying someone as prima facie bad, wrong, and backward, you've shut down their ideas without much intellectual exertion, guaranteeing they don't receive a fair hearing" (20).

In Jon Ronson's *So Now You've Been Publically Shamed*, he carries out an extensive interview with several persons who have been the object of Internet shaming and controversy. Mike Daisey, publicly shamed monologist and fabricator of information concerning Apple products overseas, argues, "It's a lie because they don't want an apology … An apology is supposed to be a communion – a coming together. For someone to make an apology, someone has to be listening" (191). Daisey goes on to reflect on how apology involves a power exchange, and he does not believe his public shamers are interested in apology. Rather, "What they want is my destruction. What they want is for me to die … They never want to hear from me again for the rest of my life, and while they're never hearing from me, they have the right to use me as a cultural reference point whenever it services *their* ends" (191–2 his emphasis). The narrative speaks importantly, not to the rightness or wrongness of Daisey's actions, but the motive and function of his accusers. His actions not only took something away, but rhetorically give his accusers something for "their ends." They get to be righteous and heroic in their damning of him, and use him as the "cultural referent" to their cause, their outrage, their position. Herein, Daisey (as well as Silverman, and many more), in their efforts to apologize, engage the controversy as an interpersonal relationship, wherein they are fallible and complicated people. However, in these public Internet controversies, through tragic framing, Daisey is less a person than a visible moment of wrongness to be seized upon—a cultural referent to an ill, a problem, or an injustice demanding punishment. Silverman's ironic workings, her political commitments, or the aesthetic complexities of her joke—just as her apology—are not the point. She is now a (and for a moment "the") cultural referent to Asian prejudice.

Once again, it is important to mark that this analysis is not arguing whether or not a particular joke or comedian is or is not racist, nor is it looking to excuse comedians and comedy from critical scrutiny. Just the opposite, actually. What is being asserted is the need to critically attend to how these discussions are framed, what are the implications of these judgments, how they help further a critical interrogation of oppressive social structures, and what are their effects. Tragedy, as a mode of engagement, is flawed for the ways it not only wholly demonizes and demands punishment (for the "bad"), but also in the manner by which it exonerates and removes responsibility (from the "good" or the victim). Yet we live in a culture where the experience of offense is often quickly collapsed into tragic violation, and apology is required. Speaking to the current climate of how triggers and offense operate in contemporary culture, Lukianoff and Haidt elaborate, "A claim that someone's words are 'offensive' is not just an expression of one's own subjective feeling of offensiveness. It is, rather, a public charge that the speaker has done something objectively wrong. It is a demand that the speaker apologize or be punished by some authority for committing an offense" (46). Framed in Burkean terms, the indictment of offense and judgment works to produce the tragic motive—a framing of events that seeks to produce a simplified and punishing outcome. Furthermore, in the speaking of the offense—the "call out"—the person being called out is set aside for scrutiny and interrogation. While not unprecedented, how often in a public "call out" has the accusing voice situated their own complicity in a range of oppressive systems as they so willingly judge another? There, surely, are those who could take issue with Aoki (a man), using a recent hate crime in California as a *soundbite* to "put her away," "to just nail her [Silverman]." When framed this way, Aoki, himself, seems to speak in a way that draws some concern.

Tragedy works to not only simplify, but obscure and protect various investments and complicities. In this media event, Silverman could only be the bigot or innocent, and Aoki could only win or lose—thus setting forth a motive where, in the matching up of "Sarah vs. Guy," someone needs to lose. In addition, within the tragic frame, there is the risk and opportunity for hegemonic power to protect its own investments. Consider one of the most notorious indictments in recent history, that, through some rhetorical reframing, is one of the often mis-remembered moments in recent history. Kanye West stood with Mike Myers during the NBC Concert for Hurricane Relief and delivered an affectively charged, hurried, and emotional monologue. He called out the conditions on the ground in New Orleans following Katrina and our nation's (including his own) failure to act quickly. He delivers this monologue with hard breaths at the end of each phrase, holding back but leaking out an intense emotional affect. His breaths were contrasted with his seemingly tensed physicality, as his hands stay in his pockets, stilled, uneasy. Next to him, Myers' body shifts awkwardly. West says:

> I hate the way they portray us in the media. If you see a Black family, it says they're looting. See a white family, it says they're looking for food. And you know that it's been five days, because most of the people are Black. And even for me to complain about it, I would be a hypocrite because I've tried to turn away from the TV, because it's too hard to watch. We already realize a lot of people that could help are at war right now, fighting another way, and they have given them permission to go down and shoot us.

Mike Myers, awkwardly, follows West, fully shifting the tone of the address back to a crisp, scripted, and rational delivery. Myers states, in a disembodied line read from the teleprompter, "The destruction of the spirit of the people of Southern Louisiana and Mississippi may end up being the most tragic loss of all." It is after this delivery from Myers, this clear evacuation of emotion that neutralizes the affective intensity of West, that West resists his silencing. West interjects "George Bush does not care about Black people." It is this moment, not necessarily this piece of text, that opened up a huge, and continually misquoted controversy. In cultural memory and cultural debate, this event has been re-membered as the time West called George Bush a "racist" and said George Bush "hates Black people." The line, which is easily verifiable, is "George Bush does not care about Black people," but the implication, tone, and charge of the statement altered its reception and the text of the incident moving forward. When interviewed, Bush falsely insisted that West "called me a racist. I am *not* a racist." The media picked up this framing as well, and soon it became the popular understanding of the discussion. Was George Bush "racist" and who is Kanye West to make this claim? While stating Bush does not care about Black people is an indictment, it does not carry the tragic and dichotomous implications of being (or not being) a *racist*. It obscured the ways West also implicated himself in his narration, filing down and dichotomizing his position. It reframed a layered and frustrated expression into a far less complicated discussion. To be or not to be racist became the question, and this tragic shifting of the story worked to produce Bush as the victim and West as his attacker. In turn, any complex investigations of race, class, government, and the devastatingly delayed response to New Orleans were obscured in the tragic media controversy.

Does George Bush care about Black people? Is George Bush racist? One statement centralizes an action—to care—and the other speaks to the essence of the person—what he is. One statement indicts his actions (is he demonstrating care, is he caring?) and one speaks to his selfhood, the de cardio reading of his heart. One potentially opens up a space for self-reflection (do I care? How do I care? What does that mean?) and one forecloses this work through explicit judgment. I hover on the West/Bush exchange not to belabor the point, but to mark how moving a discussion to the is/is not racist tragedy actually worked as a rhetorical device to exonerate Bush and demonize West. Suddenly West's emotionally loaded, and self-reflexive monologue about systemic racism, which was then affectively undercut by Myers' scripted calm, becomes about the "race card." It went from a unique, important, and necessary indictment to a "same ol'" ritual of attack. If this encounter should offer us anything, it's that calling out someone or some thing as "racist," in a space of ambiguity, ought to be a questionable strategy for any form of complicated dialogue. Tragedy, as a frame, fails us all. Within these ongoing controversies and Internet moments of outrage, the role of comedians and comedy occupies a recurrent space of discussion. From Jackson's project and the *End of the Discussion*, comedy is often at the eye of the storm of these controversies of speech, political correctness, and cultural paranoia.

Those "PC" college kids vs. that cranky white cis guy Jerry Seinfeld

The weekly comic outrages popping up on various blog sites—arguably manufactured or blown out of proportion because blogs need to have something to attract "clicks"—seemed to come to a peak moment when Jerry Seinfeld made a headline grabbing comment on Colin Cowherd's ESPN radio show. "I don't play colleges, but I hear a lot of people tell me, 'Don't go near colleges. They're so PC' … They just want to use these words: 'That's racist'; 'That's sexist'; 'That's prejudice.' They don't know what they're talking about." This position was sharply challenged by San Diego State University student Anthony Berteaux, the assistant editor of the Op-ed section of his campus newspaper, whose open letter to Seinfeld went viral. The letter made some strong points about how the role of comedy is changing in a (seemingly) more progressive culture, and cited Amy Schumer and Louis C.K. as two comedians who "have a message and [can] be hilarious at the same time." He rephrases this a bit more colloquially towards the end of letter, stating "Offend the fuck out of college students. Provoke the fuck out of me. We'll thank you for it later." However, he also stated, "So, yes, Mr. Seinfeld, we college students are politically correct. We will call out sexism and racism if we hear it." He concluded, citing Todd Glass's argument, "Fuck offending people. Offend the right fucking people."

It's in these clumsy exchanges where the spirit of Berteaux's letter and the frustration in Seinfeld's declaration both carry legitimacy and limitations. First and foremost, who are "the right people" to offend? What if the racism and the sexism you "hear" and so you "call out" is part of a more complicated discussion, joke, engagement, or comedic process? What if you don't like the way you are being offended or challenged? It's easy to say offend the right people as long as you agree who that person is (and that person is not you). Often the expression "punching down" is used to mark humor that goes after or works at the expense of the culturally disenfranchised, but this assessment still relies on one's perception. Would Berteaux in 2015 agree with Aoki in 2001 about the inherent racism of Silverman's *Conan* joke? Berteaux cites Schumer and Louis C.K. as comedians who both have a message and can be hilarious, yet both comedians have faced their own public rituals of call out and apology. Additionally, how is being "PC" equated with "having a message" in this discussion? The tragedy continues, wherein Berteaux or Guy Aoki get to claim a position of authority to determine what "good" comedy or satire is. On the other side, Silverman and Seinfeld become victims to a "PC" machine—the tragic cautionary tales of the right wings' end of discussion.

I want to approach these comedians as artists and professionals, and offer the possibility that there is a sophistication and process to their work that may not be so easily tracked down in isolating words. I want to hesitantly inch closer to Bill Maher on this one, where he takes Berteaux's letter to task for so arrogantly trying to school Jerry Seinfeld on what makes good comedy. In his "explaining jokes to idiots" segment, Maher speaks with the audience at his target of ridicule (Berteaux) with eye rolling condescension. His tone is steady and absolute, in his trademark delivery of white masculine rationality. His sarcasm is abrasive and he leaves little room for any other opinion besides the "logical" one (which is always his own):

> Now, I sure wouldn't want to be judged by what I wrote at 20, but stupid though I was in 1976, I wouldn't have presumed to lecture George Carlin on comedy, though I sure wish George was around today to write a letter back to this kid as only he could. But since he can't, allow me. "Dear you little shit, I'm sure you're busy with your new letter explaining astrophysics to Stephen Hawking and giving jump shot pointers to Steph Curry, but try to get a clue."

Yes, I want to side with Maher here, who works to express how comics have a sophistication and craft and aesthetic. I, also, can see how it is easy to take pleasure in listening to him cleverly, yet somewhat tragically, tear down this not-all-wrong but seemingly pompous college paper editor. But, I can't because in the same monologue, he discredits Berteaux and simultaneously demonstrates the value of Berteaux's critique—at least from my perspective. There is both a backlash in this monologue that is strong and powerful, but also careless and lazy (jokes about Kim Kardashian's stepfather's "tits"). However, the worst possible response to someone like Maher, who is literally baiting a response that he is being transphobic or sexist, is to attempt a different kind of discussion all together. In Maher's monologue, there is a position he offers that deserves greater attention. Maher begins the Seinfeld/Berteaux issue by discussing a joke that was cut from a Spike TV benefit, that was to be performed by Clint Eastwood. The joke stated, "Dwayne 'The Rock' Johnson is not the first athlete that has gone into acting. There is also Jim Brown and Caitlyn somebody." The cutting of this line is, to Maher, the last straw. He asks, "Why? is 'Caitlyn' the new c-word? We can't even say it in a joke? … What is so worrisome about this new brand of censorship is, it doesn't care if something is *actually* offensive. That joke was not an insult. Not in any way was it a remark that demeans Caitlyn's journey or would make her Adam's apple grow back. It's just certain words that set people off."

Maher makes an important point that the joke, as it was written, seems to be an ironic commentary on Caitlyn Jenner's extreme fame, rather than mocking or belittling her gender identity. He seeks to call out a pattern of critique that actually resists engaging the comedy with complexity, and rather is instantly triggered to offense by the mere mention of a name, a word, or a reference (as with Aoki). His point works to call attention to an overly anxious form of audiencing that seems to be pervasive in contemporary culture, which Seinfeld, Chris Rock, Maher, and *The Atlantic*'s Caitlin Flanagan seem to rather recklessly equate with and attribute to "PC college students." Caitlyn, as the "new C-word" works to question whether one can tell a joke about Caitlyn Jenner, or even reference Caitlyn Jenner in a joke, without being labeled "transphobic." Can a joke about Caitlyn Jenner ever not be "punching down?" Note, even the expression "punching down" automatically enacts a form of judgment by equating the joke as an act of violence (and a simplified linear act) from the outset. Considering the initial Jenner joke, as it was presented ("Caitlyn somebody?"), I agree with Maher. It is hard to locate any overt or unquestioned transphobia in the words, themselves. Could this have potentially been delivered in a way that was more explicitly coaching transphobia, through gesture, voice, pause, expression? Yes, of course, but here we only have the transcript. If this was to be judged as transphobic, based on the information we have (and don't have), Jerry Seinfeld's initial comments start to become instructive. He complained, "They just want to use these words: 'That's racist'; 'That's sexist'; 'That's prejudice,'" he said. "They don't know what the hell they're talking about." Yes, in the lived and material reality of trans murders and the explicit and ongoing violence faced by many in the trans community, the confident judgment of this joke as "transphobic" is, arguably, out of touch. Maher sets forth an important point. But, to prove his point, Maher slips in a joke that exemplifies this *very* form of transphobic mockery ("tits," Adam's apples). When he mentions "Caitlyn's journey" he performs a pronounced eye roll and vocal mockery that carries the same "PC backlash" irreverence of Trump. Does it help demonstrate what the other joke, the censured joke, was NOT doing? Yes, but it also uses this as cover to slip in jokes that simply trade on the audiences' expectation to laugh at and demean trans women.

Across all of these controversies, as well as the "PC" attacks, the "PC" attackers, and the rigid and patterned cycle that continues to play out and repeat itself, is an unexamined space of performative complexity. Uncomplicated positions of "freedom of speech," "It's just a joke," and the "vindictive protectiveness" of PC college kids clash with judgments of bigotry, oppression, and hair trigger outrage. What is sacrificed is critical attention to the ways these "dialogues," themselves, are regimented and patterned performances. What is dismissed is artistry, timing, context, intentional provocation, aesthetics, and the always-present complexity of comedy. What is obscured is the outrage and/or defense we feel for a particular joke, is, at least partially about us, the audience. Enlisting a performative lens and performative vocabularies to interrogate these controversies, this project goes deeper than the ritualized "call out," pushing past tragedy and judgment to disrupt the rigid and predictive optics we, as a culture, have come to use in navigating the comic controversy.

Doings of sexism, racism, homophobia: Citation and the processing of comedy

> Political correctness has cleaned up our conversations, but there's a catch.
> (Jackson 21)

At the heart of these controversies sits a series of tacit considerations and assumptions. Whereas some will defend a particular joke or comment based upon intent or perceived intent, commonly the offended person would dismiss intent in a larger commitment to effect (offense, and/or trigger). Silverman's explanation of how and why she was enlisting irony was dismissed, where Aoki chose to focus on the harm of the slur. One of the unintended effects of more "politically correct" discussions around race is the confusing tension between what is being said and what is meant (87). The distrust of words to line up with intention in a "politically correct" culture produces an ironic tension between language and effect. Jackson discusses this complication of de cardio racism in relation to the reading of jokes (xi). Jackson introduces his project through the example of comedian Dave Chappelle, who famously walked off the set of his successful show one day and never came back. Reportedly, Chappelle was performing a skit when he had an adverse reaction to the laughter of one of his crew. The white male crew member was laughing at the skit, which was the intention of the comedy sketch, yet how he was laughing registered something different, something that worked in opposition to Chappelle's comedic intentions (xiv). He was laughing *at*, not with (xiv).

However, he lacked the words to explain it. It wasn't about language, and words failed to explain what had unsettled Chappelle to the extent that he walked off the show. Why Jackson seized upon this example and positioned it so centrally in his book is its demonstration of how the project of stripping away racist language from accepted speech has not eradicated racism and that comedy occupies a unique and important space in this discussion. The focus of "PC" language, and the belief that changing language will change culture presents a "narrow focus on one relatively small part of this pervasive process of cultural and discursive intervention" (Fairclough 20). The "language turn" of political correctness sought to "change discourses on the assumption that changing discourses will, or may, lead to changes in other elements of social practices" (22). Whether or not "PC" has made cultural changes is beyond the reach of this chapter or project, but the ironic tensions that exist between language and action in a more "PC" culture—whether that be Chappelle's perception of the crew member or the ironic persona of Silverman—calls for a reconsideration of how we think about the relationships of comedy and language.

In terms of communication, the comedic controversy often plays out on the level of the *essence* of the joke, rather than the *process* of the joke. By essence, I am referring to statements about the inherent character or "truth" of the joke. This would be what Silverman charges as "the buzzword" and Maher mocks as "the C-word." We say a joke "is" racist or "is" transphobic, and this choice of wording attempts to map and argue the joke, at its core, enacts violence and is oppressive. As with the Bush and Kanye West example, the is/is not frame reduces us to a discussion of either guilt or innocence—an essence of only oppressive or not oppressive. This section seeks to propose an alternative form of engagement and framework for approach, advocating a "performative turn" to enact what Burke (1984) refers to as a comic frame or comic corrective to tragedy. Wherein the tragic frame is one of evil and punishment, a story of good and bad, the comic frame is a rhetorical mode of dialogue and mistakenness. The comic frame, for Burke, is not necessarily funny, but is a rhetorical frame that allows for error, learning, education, and mishaps. In the comic frame, the rhetorical motive of punishment is replaced with a rhetorical coaching of dialogue and education. Where tragedy is focused on a fixed judgment (this joke is or is not sexist), a comedic frame opens up a space to discuss and explore a broader range of interpretations, understandings, and effects.

A shift from the essential (singular truth or meaning) to the processual move resists this tragic frame in favor of the comic frame, opening up a broader discussion of what the joke *does* (rather than what it is). This move to a performative approach, adapting performative language of doing (rather than being) opens up a space to challenge the faulty myth that a joke should be read in a way that is fixed or correct (Gournelos and Greene, xxv). Wherein the "language turn"—exemplified in the "PC" shift—emphasizes the relationship between words and cultural discourses (Fairclough), a "performative turn" situates language in a broadened context of bodies, relations, affects, and contexts that shape discursive systems. Such an analysis attends to the positioning of the punchline, the audience cue, the referent of the joke, the positioning of the comedian, and the role of persona. This move does not excuse humor through a defense of genre (i.e. "it's comedy," "it's satire," "it's parody") as a plea for innocence (i.e. "it is just a joke"). Rather, it examines how it *does* comedy, satire, and parody and to what (potential) effects?

As demonstrated in Chapter 1, attending to the spoken text erases a wealth of information that shapes meaning. Where Schumer's words enlist and cite cultural discourses, so does her body, her affect, and the relationships she navigates in the communicative moment. To isolate a single word or phrase from Schumer, decontextualize it from the broad range of co-existent information, and then enact judgment on its essential meaning is a limited and tragic engagement. Perhaps there is no clearer way to say this than to simply mark that comedy (the art of telling jokes) is comic (a dialogic process of mishaps and complexity).

A performative turn—with its eye on the processual—resists reproducing a ritualized pattern of textualization, offense, and indictment through a comic corrective. Calling for a shift in the language from tragic judgment (this joke or comedian is racist, sexist, misogynist, ablest, etc.), a performative approach coaches a dialogic engagement with how racism, sexism, misogyny, ableism (etc.) is being *done*. A shift to the comic performative, when engaging comedic work, centralizes the processes of doing and becoming, opening up a critical space of discussion where a range of aesthetic channels, content, and audience are co-conspirators in the production of meanings.

To help demonstrate and ground this approach with concrete conceptual tools, I will be working with two key metaphors. The first is the citation, as in the academic citation—something the reader of this text is surely familiar with. When one cites an author (or authors), it functions in a few specific ways. One, it tells a story, crafting a narrative of key thinkers and concepts that have shaped one's own thinking. Second, it references previous work on an existing topic, tracing a lineage of research and writings. Citational references comprising a review of literature are always incomplete. They are always partial. There are always blindspots, as you simply cannot cite everyone who ever wrote everything touching a shared subject. But, most importantly, citation does not mean agreement or necessary endorsement. You might be building upon a previous idea, or you might be complicating it (or both). You may be completely refuting the claim. Even then, you are citing it. It's mere presence only means one thing—that you are taking this previous work up in discussion.

The academic citation, for many reasons, becomes an instructive metaphor when thinking about the role of language (particularly loaded or controversial language or slurs) in communication. It works to insist upon a more critical space between the citing of an oppressive discourse and the supporting of that discourse. At the center of the Aoki/Silverman controversy is a term that carries the weight and intensity of racist history. Many would argue the word is racist, at its essence is racist, and this position opens up an important place for discussion. Magritte famously challenged representational equation with essence when he playfully declared "this is not a pipe." The painting of a pipe is not a pipe, nor is a word the thing (or many things) it signifies. Yet, to simply argue the word is a symbol, and not the thing, is as dismissive as arguing "it's just a joke." Afterall, a violent painting of lynching is not an actual lynching, but it still cites and carries pain, violence, and connections to histories of trauma. It's never "just a joke" and some words are more than simple symbols that have acquired agreed upon cultural interpretation. Words have weight, words can carry trauma and wound, and words can do things. Words can perform on an audience in a way that carries affect and energy. We don't only think words when we encounter symbols, but we feel them. Words, quite simply, can hurt.

When Silverman reflects upon her choice to use the word "Chink" on *Conan*, she writes that she originally was going to say the unedited "n-word." The producer said she couldn't. He told her she could say, "N-Word," but not the actual word, and she said "that wouldn't work. It has to be brutal" (144). He then suggested "dirty Jew," which Sarah rejected because her being Jewish diluted the humor. "It makes it too soft." She then suggests "chink" and he counters with "spic." She is unsure why she can say one instead of the other, she chooses "chink," and the rest is history. The walking through this process of selection and crafting of the joke helps to demonstrate what Silverman is seeking to cite in her choice of the slur "chink." The primary criteria was brutality—a word that cites racism definitively *and* affectively. Saying "N-word" cites it, just as the word "racism," but it is not "brutal" in the affective sense. Performatively it does something quite different.

There is an important flip happening here that is central to the ironic workings of Silverman's comedy. Where Jackson is arguing that absence of slurs and explicitly prejudicial language does not erase the existence of these oppressive systems and meanings, Silverman is arguing that their presence does not automatically concretize how they function (and what she is doing with them). The words do not fully author meaning. As seen in Chapter 1, our bodies and gestures also cite discourses. Similar to the example of Chappelle in Jackson's book, racisms can be cited in a laugh, a nod, and/or a mode of delivery that works in opposition or in incongruous tension with whatever is being spoken. Yes, Silverman is citing brutal racism, not accidentally, but intentionally. The citation, as with the academic citation, brings it explicitly and intentionally into the narrative, into the discussion, in order to engage it (though not necessarily to support it). This first metaphor works to help us set up the range of ways a discourse can be cited and engaged.

The second metaphor, returning to performance scholar D. Soyini Madison, contemplates this process of engaging violent discourses through the metaphor of the mirror and the hammer. The mirror is "a violent historical wound mocked and scorned without correction, impunity, accountability, or question" (2014: 112.) This was how Aoki engaged Silverman's joke—a lazy reproduction of racism at the expense of Asian persons. However, Madison discusses the hammer as a performative device that both reflects the historical wound, but works to disrupt its reflection, shatter its stability—to bring a hammer to the mirror. In order for the discourse Silverman was seeking to be cited, to be reflected, it needed to be brutal, and yet her joke did more than merely reflect.

One of the more compelling moments in Silverman's negotiation when selecting the word was her rejection of "dirty Jew" for diluting the humor. Intuitively, we understand that we have cultural rules that dictate who can say what, based upon their identity (I'm gay, so I can say this). For me as a gay male, to say "faggot," it mirrors differently, it does something different, it conjures affective discourses, and relational/contextual meanings in different ways that dilute the brutality of the slur. So, why cite such a brutal discourse? What is she looking to do? If not being racist, what is she doing with racism. What is being hammered? Returning to the 2001 *Conan* interview, Silverman adopts her childlike persona from the top of the interview, saying there is nothing funny about jury duty "except for the obvious, the uh duty part," and as the audience laughs at the joke she speaks through the laughter and continues, resisting recognition of her juvenile persona. She walks us through her logic of wanting to get out of jury duty, considers the "I hate chinks" strategy, but then says very clearly, she doesn't want people to think she is racist. By not wanting to seem racist, and in saying so, Silverman sets up the joke. She becomes the ironic fool who so clearly is racist. Her solution of writing "I *love* chinks" is followed by an ironically over satisfied sense of accomplishment, as if to suggest "I nailed it, right?" Her delivery of the line, "I don't want people to think I'm racist" is the final set up, and the punchline, "I love chinks," is the joke (a joke that poses a question to the audience to process). She is the idiot who doesn't understand the word, that word, in all its brutality, is a marker of racism, not her expressions of love or hate. As they laugh at her idiocy, her blindness to the word, placed next to an expression of "love," makes no sense. Clearly, her persona is the fool, unaware of what the word means or does. She is, as she explains, the ignoramus—the white person blind to white violence. She smiles blankly. The person being degraded, in the context of the joke is Silverman, who stands in for a broader system of white racism, white ignorance, and blindness to oppressive whiteness. The word, according to Silverman, punctuates and ironically interrogates white cluelessness (rather than, as Aoki seems to claim, merely enacts it). To play off Maher's critique earlier, "chink" is another "C-word" that simply, regardless of context, frame, or usage, should never be spoken. As with the Caitlyn Jenner joke, nothing about this joke was in any direct way critiquing or "about" Asian Americans (except within their relation to white ignorance). Saying Caitlyn, itself, was not doing transphobia, yet any time the name Caitlyn Jenner is invoked in humorous discourse, the risk and weight and ever-presence of transphobia lingers in the air. The reason for this is that transphobia is everywhere, and when the name is dropped by a comedian on stage, that presence is heightened, felt, and in some ways activated. We are forced to feel its weight. Obviously arguing Caitlyn was a new "c-word" was hyperbole to make his point, but the argument carries over for the slur "chink." Is this another "c-word" and does this mean that only those who both identify and signify Asian descent are culturally sanctioned to speak it? As a symbol, it has power and the possibility to offend in its conjuring, but also reference the existence of anti-Asian racism. It makes racism present, felt, in the room, real, and dangerous. Is it underscored and brought to light, or belittled and made funny?

One strategy for examining what the joke and the comic are performatively doing is attending to where the laughter comes from and where it is pointed to (by the comic). As Maher was indicting the political correctness of "the new c-word," his joke was doing more than arguing this point. In his monologue, he would cue and allow laughs with key moments of emphasis, such as on the word "tits." He argues, "Not in any way was it [the Jenner joke that was cut] a remark that demeans Caitlyn's journey or would make her Adam's apple grow back." Maher rolls his eyes on the delivery of "journey" and takes too much pleasure in his "Adam's apple" comment. These were the moments we were cued and accommodated with pause for laughter—jokes about male biology on a woman and the incongruity of a father who has breasts. He is enacting what French marks as "the comic impulse behind sick jokes … 'a little demon, working mischief in forbidden areas' and obeying a populist imperative by providing a way of fighting back against government or media-induced conformity" (cited in Littlewood and Pickering 292). His tone is outrage, with an aggressive rant that straddles the tone of "this is ridiculous" and "I can say it if I want." It's a slightly temperamental form of masculinity that does not dip far enough to exceed a literal read. The system he is interrogating is censorship, and he is mirroring (but not hammering) transphobic discourses in the process. He is doing transphobia in ways that appear wholly un-complicating—not unlike Shatner at the Sheen roast discussed in Chapter 1. We are called to identify and agree, rather than disidentify and observe. We were invited/called upon to laugh at trans bodies, as opposed to critically laughing at the culture's bigoted perception of trans bodies. There was also a removal of Maher as the speaker and voice of the joke, enlisting a third person perspective, where the joke is not about how Maher sees the world but a general statement of authority regarding how the world is. This differs from Silverman who emphasizes the word "love" in the "chink" joke, and owns the statement as a first person "I." In other words, the joke is invited in and directed at Silverman, Silverman's faulty logic, and the white privileged body that is being inhabited and interrogated. Beyond the slur itself, there is no trace of the joke working to demean outside the comedian, and the slur operates to signify racism, but not to enact racism in any overt manner. With both Maher and Silverman, we are invited in both cases to laugh at a referent of the joke, but these are very different. For one, it is the speaker who does not understand the privileged idiocy of saying "I love chinks" and for the other, it is the transgender celebrity whose body is currently in transition.

Silverman, in her *Conan* appearance, explicitly cites racist discourses, yet is not so clearly "racist" herself so much as she is working with racisms. Her body, the traditionally unraced white body, is explicitly raced in her work. She calls upon and hails the white body, the historically racist body into the joke. By doing so, she attempts to mobilize and engage the distinct and differing ways the white body can do unique work to engage and intervene in racist discourse. There is no doubt this is complicated and contestable work, and material that we—as a culture—monitor and carefully step around. Like Schumer, and Muñoz's study (1999) of Carmelita Tropicana, Silverman's body and her multiple subjectivities as a young, Jewish female, afford a distinct opportunity for cultural intervention and critique to subvert dominant images and understandings of whiteness. Her body can performatively *do* different things. Discourses of race often work to render the white body invisible, unraced, and normative (Crenshaw). It is perhaps one of the key reasons why, when a white body speaks about race, in the abstract, it is seen as remarkable and noble. Yes, this is important, and significant, but also suspiciously safe. It fails to tap into the unconscious that Silverman is looking to explore—that ironic space of racial paranoia that sits underneath everyone saying the right things, but where the whispers of racism remain (Jackson 10). This was one of the reasons why the choice to say "dirty Jew" is too soft, because, as Silverman states, "I *am* a dirty Jew" (144). It is why the use of the softened "N-word" completely misses the working of the ironic humor. Silverman is not speaking about race in the abstract, standing on a soapbox pointing out the flaws of "those" racists, not performing noble self-flagellating white guilt—those distanced and noble postures of the "white savior" that are somehow elevated beyond racist logics. She is interested in exploring the brutal, the affective, shit and grit, rather than the smoothed over workings of racism that are too often made palatable, made noble, made correct, or abstract in contemporary discourse.

Silverman's work is ugly, carries ugliness, cites and seeks to tap into ugliness with an honesty that so much of our softened discourse around race has sought to exorcise, but has fallen short. Yet, the presence of racism and affective citations of racism set off our alarms and trigger our tendencies towards tragedy. As Jackson notes, there is catharsis in this tragic ritual. The irony is, Silverman was intentionally already screaming "racist" when she chose the intentionally brutal slur—resisting the coded and plausible deniability (70) that permeates in a culture of racial paranoia. She explicitly and clearly cited "racism" and the response was to call her a racist. The invocation of racist stereotypes ("I Love chinks!"), through the lens of ironic performativity, is more than an untroubled recitation of racism. Where Maher's crude "tits" and "journey" jokes allow the audience to slide on a steady and uninterrupted reiteration of transphobic performativity, Silverman's racist invocation works to cue an audience otherwise. She is not whispering uncomfortable and coded racisms, that slowly seep in and complicate the cool neo-liberal glide of a joke that on the surface says all the right things, but somewhere, in the gut, feels troubling. She is spray painting racist discourse, and the performance of white innocence (i.e. "I didn't want people to think I was racist, so …) onto her body and saying, it's right here, in front of us, so let's deal with this for a moment. Through irony, she searches and experiments with ways to turn away from existing meanings.

While it is possible to argue Silverman is "racist" (a tragic indictment which seems to imply she is exceptional in a primarily non racist culture), I argue we are better served by attending to the ways she is engaging, exploring, and interrogating (i.e. hammering) racisms. The white body speaking about—and against—racism does one thing, but the white body citing a brutal racist discourse to tap into its affective dimensions does something else. The question is, what is she doing with that affective citation? How is this volatile ugliness attended to? Is it traded on for a cheap laugh? Is it turned back onto the audience in a moment of self-interrogation? Does the laugh turn uneasy, forcing us to reconcile something beneath the surface? These are nuances to the doings of racism that, when given more space, time, and performative attention, allow comedy to do significant and unique critical/cultural work. It is, as Trevor Noah says, "sometimes the only place we can have a conversation."

Conclusion: Different bodies, different discourses, different doings

> But the change in identity and role produces a more telling change in the context in which humor is conveyed and received than would be brought about by a white male heterosexual comedian adhering to an anti-racist, anti-sexist, anti-homophobic, "correct" line.
>
> (Littlewood and Pickering 308)

> We need new ways of thinking about these issues, new ways of talking about race's subtler dynamic, and new ways of spying racial conflict in the twenty first century.
>
> (Jackson 86)

In April 2012, the NBC sitcom *30 Rock*, for the third time in its run, enlisted blackface—the "third rail of the American stage" (Toure Dec 11, 2010)—as a centerpiece to a joke on the episode. The second time the show used the device, Jenna (played by white actress Jane Krakowski), wore blackface and a football uniform, dressing up as athlete Lynn Swann. On the show, Jenna's cross dressing boyfriend, dresses up as Natalie Portman in her Academy Award winning role. Together, they arrive as "two Black Swans." Toure argues:

> One of the reasons it succeeded is because it was placed in a situation that was completely ridiculous … Fey's not using blackface as a simplistic visual way of turning a white person Black but as a complex tool that makes a multi-layered joke at the character's expense. Jenna is a dimwit and the audience knows that for her to think blackening up is ok adds to the perception that she's simpleminded.

The next time *30 Rock* enlisted blackface was in a faux "history of NBC television" episode, where Kenneth introduces an Amos & Andy-like TV show. He narrates, "NBC had the first two Black characters on TV, sort of. For Alfie and Abner, NBC hired one African American and one Caucasian because they thought two Black people on the same show would make the audience nervous. A rule NBC still uses today." The "show" has Tracy Morgan playing Alfie, an African American actor who is annoyed to be cast opposite Abner, played by Jon Hamm in blackface. Hamm overplays every awful dehumanizing moronic stereotype of the minstrel era, as the bubbly, silly, fun-loving simpleton. Morgan, as Alfie, grows increasingly furious at Abner's racist and offensive portrayal, pleading with him to stop speaking like an imbecile. Neither blackface representation on *30 Rock* escaped some backlash, yet both received a fair amount of support and appreciation for their efforts, as well. Most notably, both moments enlist a clear performative practice of racism that is loaded, dangerous, and risky, but is executed with a clearly ironic critical framework. Alongside Hamm's blackfaced role, there was the present and immediate critique of Morgan, explicitly commenting on the portrayal that degrades him. For Jenna, her idiocy and cluelessness are established through the narrative, and so there is a shared pretense that her actions are exposing and critiquing ignorance and bias, not merely regurgitating them. Additionally, she is clearly a character and her persona is established as distinct from Krakowski—a delineation that is more easily pronounced for most audiences than Silverman's ironic stage persona.

I mark these two moments because they identify two recent comedic efforts that enlisted an extremely volatile racist discourse, with explicit critical frames, and still received mixed reactions. Critical attention to the doings of ironic and political comedy force us to deal with gray areas, or what Trevor Noah calls, "Nuance – that thing we all hate" (Pop Culture Happy Hour). There is generally an accepted cultural understanding that humor, when engaging in the examination of identity and privilege, is easiest to swallow when the comedian is joking up the social ladder. It is why Amy Schumer's comedic interventions around gender, body image, and sexism have made her a cultural phenomenon, yet there is more doubt and skepticism in her race-themed humor (Jung)—a theme in her work that has become less prevalent as she rises to the top of the comedy world. As a culture, we feel a greater ease in comedians of color examining race, and queer comedians talking about sexuality. On the Netflix series *Orange is the New Black*, when Taystee and Poussey, played by two African American female actresses, parody "white people politics" Taystee, in a slightly southern stereotypically waspy delivery, jokes, "Did you see that new documentary about the best sushi in the world? Of course, now that I am vegan, I didn't enjoy it as much as I might have." Poussey, adopting a similar sanitized snootiness playfully replies, "You know, I just don't have the time. Tad and I have our Yoga workshop, and then our wine tasting class. And then, we have to have very quiet sex. Every night. At nine." The parody is a hilarious indictment of classist and affectively impoverished whiteness. Yet, had two white actresses adopted stereotypically Black accents and performed a similar dialogue, it would be watched with far greater concern, if not outrage—and rightfully so. Where the bodies of persons of color are always, already coded with race, the white body is constructed in discourse as raceless, without race, and neutral. Thus, when the body of a person of color invokes race and racism, it is already ever present, performatively present prior to an utterance, and always subjugated to the norms and disciplining of whiteness. However, the "neutral" and "raceless" white body is only harkened into discourses of race through citation, and in that citation, the white body becomes visible, suspect, and under interrogation—for the white body carries and cites legacies of violence and oppression just beneath its "raceless" exterior.

This exact tension came to a head in the public falling out between Jon Stewart and Wyatt Cenac over Stewart's *Daily Show* impressions of 2012 Republican primary candidate, Herman Cain—an impression that made Cenac "cringe" as it reminded him of Kingfish on *Amos & Andy.* Reportedly, Stewart and Cenac had a major blowup, where Stewart questioned his offense of this impression, yet was untroubled by many of the other impressions Stewart does on the show (including his very stereotypical Jewish voice for Chuck Schumer). To refer back to Silverman, because Stewart is also Jewish, it's softer and less brutal. Stewart doing an impression of Cain does not exist in a vacuum, as the white male body adopting a Black male voice in a parodic way that questions his intelligence is an act that happens in the present, yet cites and extracts a complex and ugly lineage of violence, degradation, and pain. It is, to paraphrase Aoki, playing with fire.

Histories of violence, alongside contemporary contexts of power, privilege, and systemic racism means it is different for bodies of color to mock whiteness than for white bodies to mock blackness. The question I want to examine at the close of this chapter is not if this is the case (it is) or if it should be the case (I believe it should), but the assumptions, implications and effects of this cultural understanding. Aoki makes the claim that he likes satire, but Silverman is not doing good satire. Similarly, Berteaux writes in his open letter to Seinfeld:

> I can say with confidence that most college students can distinguish the boundaries of what's considered appropriately sexist or not … it's that comedy in our progressive society today can no longer afford to be crass, or provocative for the sake of being offensive. Sexist humor and racist humor can no longer exist in comedy because these concepts are based on archaic ideals that have perpetrated injustice against minorities in the past. Provocative humor, such as ones dealing with topics of race and gender politics, can be crass and vulgar, but underlying it must be a context that spurs social dialogue about these respective issues.

What Berteaux seems to be referring to is a refusal to tolerate what can be referred to as "the sick joke." "By definition, sick jokes flaunt their bad taste, their callous insensitivity to human tragedy and suffering ... Such jokes fly in the face of compassion, grief, and outrage" (Littlewood and Pickerling 292). This type of humor is more focused on disrupting or interrogating the lines of good taste and censorship, than the loaded discourses they are citing. Thus, even though Shatner is citing discourses of racism and Maher is citing discourses of transphobia, these discourses are cited to push boundaries of what a comedian can say, not interrogate oppressive systems of race and gender. They are not using transphobia or racism to disrupt their own faulty assumptions, but as tools for other ends. However, there are ways to challenge, question, and speak back to work that avoids the trappings of tragedy.

If the Aoki and Silverman controversy has taught us anything, it is that the determination of whether or not a joke or a comedian is "appropriately sexist" or "appropriately racist" or "appropriately offensive" is not as simple or agreed upon as it may sound. I do not think Berteaux is capable of speaking for "most college students" in the same way that I don't think Bill Maher could speak for most comedians. "Appropriateness," as a measure, should make us all uneasy. Appropriate leads us to a place where only comedians of color talk about race in complicated ways, and comedians like Silverman and Schumer and Louis C.K. steer clear of racial discourses, altogether, or only reify the do-gooder self-flagellating white liberal guilt postures (which are unpacked more closely in Chapter 5). Comedy pushes, probes, and interrogates in ways that are not purely intellectual, but are affective, uneasy, and sometimes vitally ugly. Appropriateness, as a measure, seems to foster a climate where white bodies are celebrated for discussing racism out there, pointing fingers elsewhere in judgment—yet will resist the ugly work, the brutal work, the work that deals with discomfort, and accountability, and ownership of the racist (and sexist, and homophobic, and classist, and anti-Muslim, and ableist) culture we all exist in and contribute to on a range of levels. Yes, Chris Rock, Wanda Sykes, Kevin Hart, Tracy Morgan, and Margaret Cho (to name a few) have hilariously complicated interventions into discourses of race and identity, but just like the students of color in the classroom, it is not their sole job or responsibility to carry on and lead the class dialogue around racism. Yes, there are more pitfalls when the white body (which cites legacies of racial violence) engages in humor around racism. Yes, it is much more dangerous when the male body (which cites masculine authority and discourses of patriarchy) works to explore gender violence in comedy. Yes, the cisgendered body (citing and reifying normative gender systems and legacies of transphobia and erasure) needs to tread comedic interventions into gender performance with greater caution. But, as Silverman helps us to see, the white body can also do distinct work, cite different discourses, and engage the ugly brutalities of our culture in unique and potentially valuable ways. Yes there are risks, but "the job of the comedian is to delve into these spaces" (Trevor Noah).

In an interesting and unexpected turn, following the Internet debate surrounding Seinfeld's "PC college" comments and Berteaux's response, Sarah Silverman chimed into this dialogue during a *Vanity Fair* interview. The *salon.com* headline reads "Sarah Silverman Pushes Back Against 'Creepy PC Culture' Backlash: 'You Have to Listen to the College-Aged, Because They lead the Revolution'" (quoted in Silman). In the interview, her positions were far more tempered. She remarks that "everyone's always going to be offended by something," yet argues that it's important to "change with new information … I think it's a sign of being old when you're put off by that." The example she chooses to help narrate her own evolution is her past use of the word "gay" pejoratively and how she used to defend that choice. She narrates, "Then I stopped myself and said, 'what am I fighting?'" Although she adopts a strong both/and approach to the "PC" debate, marking offense as inevitable in comedy, she poses the question to her comedic choices in processual terms—"what am I fighting?" Why am I doing this, what are the effects of this position, and who am I aligning myself with, and positioning myself against. Notably absent, however, was any mention of Aoki and her infamous 2001 debate, opting to enlist an example of her use of "gay" that (rather curiously) side-stepped the discussion of irony altogether. She, reminiscent of her letter to Aoki, attempted to honestly reflect on her comedic process, the critical work she is committed to doing, and the implications of her choices. Still the headlines found a way to turn her comic frame into a tragedy, implying she was strongly judging Seinfeld and Maher. My guess would be, fifteen years later, she has grown somewhat accustomed to the ritual.

Notes

1 This title, "Sarah Silverman: Funny Women or Foul Mouthed Racist?" was the title of a 2011 article by Sturges in the *Independent*.

2 Silverman, in her book *Bedwetter*, reflects on the email she sent to Aoki and admits, "Reading this now, I wince at how my self-righteousness seems to match his."

3 The joke is on YOU

Audience contexts, criticisms, and investments

> Where is the joke?
>
> (Anne-Marie Johnson)

> Offense is taken, not given.
>
> (Gervais qtd. in BytesMaster)

> Live audiences represent a magnified series of intimate relations and emotional expressions including love and hate.
>
> (Batalion 3)

> Because every audience is completely different – a completely different group of people with a completely different personality.
>
> (Seinfeld qtd. in Apatow 33)

On HBO's *Talking Funny* (dir. Jones), an informal dialogue about what it means to be a comedian, Louis C.K. shares "the funniest thing he's ever heard in his entire life" with fellow comedians Jerry Seinfeld, Ricky Gervais, and Chris Rock. C.K. recounts his memory of a comic on stage, "bombing," while strumming his guitar, singing the song, "Sitting on a cock cause I'm gay" (to the tune of "Sitting on The Dock of the Bay"). Upon hearing C.K. tell the story, Gervais explodes into laughter, assuming it is funny because it wasn't. He explains, "I laughed ironically at you setting up this guy struggling," but Louis C.K. disagrees with Gervais's interpretation of the joke. Gervais insists C.K. *must* be laughing ironically, but C.K. holds firm that his amusement is not ironic. Gervais disagrees, "No, it's true, you are *not* laughing because it's a clever funny line, you are laughing at the context." C.K. playfully taunts Gervais, "why are you so upset, it's *just* funny" (as C.K. laughs at the joke again). Gervais insists C.K. is either wrong or joking, when Seinfeld cuts in halfheartedly, "No, that's a pretty good joke." C.K. adds on, fueling the fire, "I respect 'sitting on a cock cause I'm gay.'" Gervais is losing his mind, his voice is rising, getting squeakier, as this dialogue has become absurd to him. He argues, "You can only laugh at that because we are intelligent, educated people knowing you shouldn't go out, and go 'sitting on a cock cause I'm gay!'" Rock asks himself, "Would I be upset if Jerry Seinfeld did that? No, I'd probably laugh." The four of them are rolling, trying to make sense out of how meaning, and specifically humor, is being constructed here. Was it a clever parody? Gervais mocks this claim, laughing, "Some parody. Fucking genius! Oscar Wilde!" C.K. resists an ironic read and continues to giggle at his memory of the sad, bombing comic. Gervais refuses the joke, itself, is at all funny, firmly insisting "We built in the irony," rather than the sad strumming comic. "We put irony onto it." What emerges in this dialogue is four comedians, recognized as masters of their craft, who are unable to mark or determine if and why that joke is or is not funny, as well as what that comedian is doing (or trying to do). They tap into a core complexity of comedic reception that frustrates and upsets any clear designation of whether a joke is funny or what a joke a means—the elusive and often falsely homogenized issue of audience.

This dialogue encapsulates the subjectivity of audiencing humor and how context and the audience produce meanings—the "you had to be there" and the understanding that "you" will determine much of the joke. Was this joke (or comedian) homophobic? Was it parody? Was it ironic and did it work to coach ironic reads? Is it more homophobic because C.K. is the one retelling the joke and is oddly, yet deeply, amused by the joke? Seinfeld admits, it was "a lame gay joke." Rock quips, "Anderson Cooper is going to beat our ass" for laughing at it. Hypothetically, what if the openly bisexual, LGBTQ advocate, and Korean-American comedian Margaret Cho performed the joke (or the bawdy Rosanne Barr or a gay male comedian who is a proud self-identified bottom)? Hearing C.K. recount the joke, I, as a white gay male, laughed. I, personally, didn't read C.K. as "homophobic," but I'd argue the unnamed comedian, his joke, and C.K.'s interpretive response were *doing something* with and through homophobia, painful comedic failure, and bad parody. Gervais, Rock, and Seinfeld laughed, but seemed to derive humor from a diversity of positions, including the base awfulness of the joke, Gervais's frustration with the joke, and the peculiar degree that C.K. found this crappy joke so hilarious. Everyone was laughing, yet there remained disagreement about what was funny, what (or who) was being laughed at, and what this comedian was doing (both in terms of intention, but also discursive effect). Furthermore, their discussion assumes a shared text of analysis when, actually, C.K.'s embodied experience in the comedy club frames his response, while C.K.'s narrative creates the text for the panelists. So where does the meaning of the joke reside? As we have explored in previous chapters, you cannot simply textualize and capture the truth of the joke. To merely transcribe the words of a live joke onto the page should usher in a wave of questions about context, delivery, and embodiment that ought to be central to production/reception, for the humor is not *in* those words, themselves, but in a variety of intermeshed communicative factors. Through a performance frame where meanings are multiple, negotiated, and contextual, the overall determination of meaning resides in the audience—an interpretive landscape that requires its own critical analysis and self-reflexive investigation.

The following chapter builds upon aesthetic complexities and naming practices discussed in previous chapters to map and more closely examine the role of audiencing processes within a comic controversy. Phrased in a more colloquial manner, this chapter argues that the way audiences read ironic performativity is as much (if not more) about that specific audience (or audience member) as it is about the speaker/performer/comedian. Up until recently, there has been a lack of attention to the comedic audience (Batalion 7), wherein the audience has been commonly treated as a false collective projection of the critic (Rayner 28). There has been less attention to "How powerful the audience is, how it is both a homogenous force, and yet a heterogeneous mix" (Batalion 6). Whether an audience assigns offense, subversion, or hope to a joke (or some combination) has as much to do with the specific audience member and the context, as the content of the joke, itself. The following pages examine how audience social positions and investments inevitably co-author the interpretive production of meanings and "understanding" of ironic performativities—centralizing the importance of critical self-reflexivity in the audiencing of this work.

The analysis looks to the role of audiencing in the comic controversy, examining discussions of *Talking Funny*'s "bombing" comic, as well as Rebel Wilson at the 2016 BAFTA awards, Ricky Gervais' 2016 Golden Globe introduction, Amy Schumer's "Ryan Dunn" joke and comedians Eddie Murphy, Chris Rock, and Whitney Cummings. Tracing the expanding contexts and critical patterns that define the contemporary comic controversy, this chapter turns to the experience of offense as a resource for self-reflexivity. By critical self-reflexivity, I am referring to an ongoing work and practice of "interrogating how our social location within multiple subjectivities is a fundamental factor in how we see the world, shape understandings, and create knowledge" (Goltz 2011: 391). Thus, where we find and assign offense, humor, or pleasure presents an important site for critical self-reflexivity, as our experience with a joke is tied to our identity and experiences. Context, timing, audience, and our own investments in hegemonic systems of power and privilege enable and goad our laughs, and—as shown by how we make sense of specific moments—our offense. Our own values, beliefs, and expectations dictate reception. Thus, jokes that have crossed the culturally constructed lines of "too much" or "too soon"—often marked as failures or missteps—provide important insights as tools of cultural investigation. These moments of culturally perceived transgression work to underscore and render visible our cultural avoidances, fears, and anxieties as well as our comforts and commitments. As ironic performativity is never stable enough to eliminate any potential ambiguity, there is reason to believe we can easily see what we want to see, what we choose to see, or what our positionality allows us to see (or not see). Ironic performativity requires that we, as audience, accept and examine our role, our commitments, and our complicities.

So how do we make sense of the humor derived from this failing comic on stage, performing a weak parody of "Sitting on the Dock of the Bay?" The chapter works to map a broad range of factors shaping the heterogeneous, shifting, and networked dimensions of the contemporary audience in a comic controversy, troubling seemingly stable notions of context, criticism, and authorship. The analysis begins with a discussion of shared pretense in the audiences' production of meaning, enlisting the Burkean concept of perspective by incongruity to examine the role of identity in the workings of ironic performativity. This section examines how fixed interpretations of what a joke "means" are reliant upon the faulty assumption of a shared interpretive audience. Next, the chapter troubles stable understandings of the traditional comedic audience. As comedic events move from physical spaces of the *primary* audience (the live comedic room) to *mediated* audiences (the recorded comedy set) and to edited and *networked* audiences (clips and textualizations of single jokes via Twitter and blogs), the ongoing (re)contextualization of a controversial joke actively reshapes and reframes its potential meanings. Moving forward, the chapter considers the rhetorical workings of audience criticism, arguing that critics of comedy actively assert counter narratives about a joke/comedian that produce the comic controversy which also demand critical analysis. The critic of a joke is *also* constructing a narrative, rhetorically producing a story about the meaning/effect of the joke that has implications and limitations. Herein the investigation of audience considers the patterned and performative trappings of criticism through the concepts of paranoid readings and the critical-norm. The analysis explores how paranoid and patterned modes of audiencing become routinized and predictable, undercutting a range of potential ways to engage and experience a text, and often leading to negative effects and findings. Finally, the chapter provides a close study of Amy Schumer's controversial "Ryan Dunn Joke," to locate, interrogate, and process our own personal investments and blind spots through the various ways we understand ironic performativity, find humor, take offense, and position ourselves within and across comic controversies. In other words, when considering the "understanding" of ironic performativity (or the "bombing comic" performing a weak song parody) the effect and intelligence of a comedian can only be as layered, subversive, or critical as their specific audience allows or enables.

Shared pretense: Whose page are we on?

> If our founding fathers wanted us to care about the rest of the world, they wouldn't have declared their independence from it.
>
> (A quote by Stephen Colbert)

> Holocaust? Ninety million Indians? Only four million left? They all have casinos – what's to complain about?
>
> (Rush Limbaugh qtd. in Maloy)

In a class on the performance of humor, I pass out a handout that mixes up a range of quotes from Steven Colbert delivered on *The Colbert Report* with quotes by Rush Limbaugh from his conservative radio program. I ask students to try and determine the original author (and thus, the intention) of each quote as a class activity. It is not as easy as one might think. Limbaugh's brash and extreme conservatism, when placed next to Colbert's ironic conservatism, can look quite similar when the quote is divorced from a body, a persona, an audience, and the aesthetic dimensions of Colbert's performance. The presence of these (now removed) elements work to produce a shared pretense with the audience that are imperative to the ironic operations of Colbert's message. For an audience to escape the naïve read of the text, assuming the person speaking is to be taken at face value, there needs to be an audience understanding about the values and beliefs of the speaker (Kreuz and Roberts 102). Colbert's irony requires "the element of pretense ... the pretension of ignorance is used to enlighten" (101). Irony, as a strategy, operates to communicate contempt or resistance, yet "to be ironical, is, among other things, to pretend (as the etymology suggests), and while one wants the pretense to be recognized as such, to announce it as pretense would spoil the effect" (Grice quoted in Clark and Gerrig 121). Herein lies the crucial role of audience in the reception of irony, as the pretense of ironic messages will always risk the faithful audience—those victims of irony—who may miss (or choose to look away from) the tones, exaggerations, and affects of the ironist and accept their ironic statement with uncritical belief (Clark and Gerrig 122). "A listener's understanding of an ironic utterance depends crucially on the common ground he or she believes is shared by the ironist and the audience – their mutual beliefs, mutual knowledge, and mutual suppositions" (122, see also Clark and Clarkson 1981; Clark and Marshall 1981).

The assumption of shared interests is one of the reasons the signified/assumed identity of the comedian becomes central to audiencing ironic humor. Assumed/signified identity becomes a core premise that audiences will use to produce meanings. For an out and proud gay male, such as Neil Patrick Harris, to perform "Sitting on a cock cause I'm gay" the effort would intuitively coach a stronger pretense with the audience. Put differently, it is more likely for an audience to think, "Hmmm, he must be pretending or being sarcastic, here. Perhaps Harris is playing with the reductive stereotypes we place on gay men?" However, if a cis heterosexual male, such as Dane Cook, were to sing that ridiculous song parody, his motives, and the risk of homophobic reads, would be heightened. For Cook, there is not a necessary tension, an incongruity, an ironic coaching intrinsic in the effort. In short, there is a larger question if Cook means or is aligned with the homophobic positions he is citing. This default logic is somewhat boxy and limited, yet much of our understandings of identity, social position, and meanings are reduced to essentialized and reductive logics. In other words, we just say, "He can't tell that joke."

Central to much comedy is the core presence and activation of incongruity (Weaver). The juxtaposition produced from Neil Patrick Harris singing the song in this imagined scenario (alongside the meanings cited through his identity) creates a tension, a paradoxical collision that can be understood through the Burkean concept *perspective by incongruity*. As discussed previously, perspective by incongruity is "verbal 'atom cracking'" (Burke 308)—the moral methodology of democratizing ideas and freeing them from the entrapment of limited constitution (309). Intentional incongruity works to position two seemingly opposing ideas or frameworks of thought in tension with one another in order to liberate and extend the rigidity of their understandings. For Burke, perspective by incongruity is an effective critical tool for dismantling rigid, tragic, and dichotomous meanings. It provides a means for troubling restrictive orientations through the work of "metaphorical extension" (309). For Harris to perform that seemingly base and offensive song positions a gay male body in juxtaposition with this daft and un-clever parody. Two fixed meanings are paradoxically placed into tension (crass, seemingly stereotypical text spoken from seemingly proud gay male body). Perspective by incongruity, through ironic performativity, is more easily coached for an audience in this scenario. The audience is asked to work harder, negotiate multiple contesting meanings (proud gay man parodying gayness), and allow a space for new meanings to emerge. "Hmmmm, Harris must be critiquing the parody, perhaps calling upon us to reflect on what it does. Wait, why am I laughing?" However, because Harris is who he is, the joke is allowed to be approached "in good fun" and "from a sense of playfulness" (Wilson 278). The audience is freed to "take up the joke in our own way, to connect the dots as we wish, and to the purpose we wish – to play with it" (278).

So, for Neil Patrick Harris, ironic work around gayness is more easily facilitated. It is one of the reasons his hyper-hetero-masculine "bro" performances on *How I Met your Mother* or the *Harold and Kumar* films were so successful. As a gay male performing exaggerated extremes of the crude and womanizing masculinist pig, the ironic performativity of his gay identity (alongside his real life "good guy" image and the sweet *Doogie Howser M.D.* child star persona) affords a critique of hegemonic masculinity and female objectification, rather than a mere reiteration. Occupying a body coded with gay maleness (and all the assumptions this carries), Harris can accomplish distinct work with signified gay male sexual identity, just as Schumer can in the discourse of gender and (white) femininity (as discussed in Chapter 1). But if Harris were to move his ironic efforts to examine discourses of race and whiteness, different obstacles and limitations are presented (as are different potentials, as discussed with Silverman and C.K. in Chapter 5). Imagine Harris performing some of the critical and ironic texts of Dave Chappelle around blackness, such as Chappelle's infamous "Black Bush" sketches? In this recurring sketch from *The Dave Chappelle Show*, Chappelle mixes actual footage and transcripts with his own interpretive performance as a Black President Bush. For example:

BUSH (CHAPPELLE): After careful examination of the region, me and my cabinet agree that that area is definitely ripe for regime change …

CABINET MEMBER #1 (AFRICAN AMERICAN MALE): *(affirmation)* … Alright …
BUSH: … But if I can be real about it …
CABINET MEMBER #1: … Be real son …
BUSH: … Real?
CABINET MEMBER #1: … Be real real son
BUSH: He tried to kill my father, man.
CABINET MEMBERS: … What? …
BUSH: … Don't play that shit …
CABINET MEMBER: Yo say word he tried to kill your father, son …
BUSH: (grabs press mic and hollers): The Man tried to kill my FATHER!
(Comedy Central)

The back and forth between Black Bush and his cabinet, their phrasings, and their linguistic (Scott) and affective (Muñoz 2000) performative cues of Blackness—produced through the Black male body in the role of Bush—disrupt and call attention to layers of normative whiteness. Irony is coached and perspective by incongruity is mobilized. However, for Harris to adopt these phrasings, perform this affect, and attempt to replicate Chappelle's "Black Bush" (without even touching the absolutely problematic territory of hair or makeup alteration), dis-ease and discomfort abounds. Harris's body does not carry the meanings to coach and conjure perspective by incongruity, which is encapsulated in the very name "Black Bush." The collision and extension of meaning occurs because Blackness is incongruous with Bush—a fixed marker and signifier of whiteness. This inability for Harris to do this work is significant for a range of ways that this project will explore, but most immediately, it seeks to theorize why "he can't say that joke." It is not merely who he is, as a white cis gay male, but more so what his white cis male body *does*—the discourses his body cites and negotiates.

When ironic critique is being enlisted by someone from a dominant/normative position, for example Colbert, explicit pretense is needed to coach an audience away from simply reading the joke as "punching down." In other words, it is imperative that Harris establish he is pretending, he is playing the fool, and still, with all that established, it is key to understand that his ability to critique discourses of race still emerges from and through HIS body. He cannot parody Blackness, as when performed through the white body, it too powerfully cites a legacy of white supremacy and Black degradation. In other words, it is not that he can't say that joke (as in, cultural norms forbid it—although they do) but rather he literally can't do that joke (his body does not permit him to override the performative citation of whiteness that will drive and restrict the doings of his comedy). Herein, pretense and performativity work in concert, yet also mark the limits of what a specific comic can do in relation to hegemonic discourse. Bodies set and enable distinct *opportunities and limitations* for how, and if, and to what degree a comic can do certain types of critical work.

Revisiting the TV series *30 Rock*, their risky and always questionable choice to put the character of Jenna in blackface relies upon a shared and established pretense with the audience Jenna is shallow, ignorant, and not paralleled to the politics and beliefs of the larger show. She is a foolish character, played by the actress Jane Krakowski, who pretends ignorance for ironic effect—the mirroring and critical hammering of white ignorance. If there was not this established pretense, then there is the risk of Krakowski and the larger show being read as faithful to the racisms they cite, thus endorsing a degrading historical lineage of Black stereotype and dehumanization. Without an iron-clad pretense, Jenna's performance of blackface would resist an ironic read and could easily be seen to merely coach laughter through dominant white supremacist meanings. With stakes and risks this elevated, it is commonly argued that comedians, especially white comedians, should simply stay away. Given the limitations of their bodies and the violence and pain of these discourses, there are extremely convincing arguments for laying down this line. This chapter, and this larger project, aim to unpack and complicate this position, challenging its universal applicability, in order to continue carving out and examining the stakes, the risks, and the potential opportunities for this type of comedic work.

So, if Jenna fails to coach an ironic audience read, and worse, brings forth un-ironic and non-reflexive laughter, there is no breaking or disruption of meanings. There is no perspective opened up, no "atom cracked" through incongruity. There is no intervention, and thus her use of blackface merely reiterates and further constitutes fixed racist meanings and significations. Discourse remains unchallenged, and meanings reside in the audience member's constituted orientation. As symbol using animals in a Burkean framework, a person's orientation dictates and also constrains how life is experienced or understood ("Attitudes"). For Burke, orientation reflects how our realities are produced, defined, and confined. This can be extended to our understandings of race, gender, sexuality, nation, and the broadest ways that our identities, affinities, and hierarchal relations are organized within our symbolic systems. However, our orientations become problematic in how they foreclose and resist additional understandings, when they fail to account for a given situation, or resist relationships outside symbolic structures. This is because orientations are always limited. As one adopts a perspective, a way of understanding and seeing the world, this reduces one's capacity to think, experience, or assign understanding beyond this orientation. As a person's orientation is formed and solidified, others will be rejected, resulting in necessary reduction. Burke argues that our inability to think, understand, sense-make or process information beyond our orientations presents a trained incapacity (Burke 1984: 7). Perspective by incongruity, through ironic disruption, is the "verbal 'atom cracking'" that seeks to intervene in these trained incapacities, and challenge the limitations of reductive (and violent, and dehumanizing) orientations. Thus, in its most ideal read, the choice to put Jenna in blackface does not reiterate the dehumanization of Blackness, but rather interrogates our tacit commitments and affinities to whiteness. Jenna's white ignorance is NOT white innocence, but IS white supremacy. White ignorance IS violent and dehumanizing. Why are you laughing? With whom and with what commitments are you laughing?

Much like the Limbaugh and Colbert quotes, if Krakowski's actions or statements are decontextualized from this persona, they can easily be read as vile and degrading (with the assumption Krakowski means the things she says). Where Colbert is citing existing systems of meaning and discourses—what can be called "echoing" previous utterances for critical effect upon the logic of that utterance (Clark and Gerrig 125)—Limbaugh is asserting the claims as logical, literal, and direct. So, pretense and an understanding of pretense is central to audiencing irony. Yet, even under the banner of irony, Colbert and Krakowski are limited in what their comedy can do. They can use (with risk) white performativities, cited through their bodies, to coach a critical reflection upon white ignorance, white innocence, and white supremacy. However, any effort to embody Blackness *as* a critique of whiteness or Blackness is always in resistance to the bodily discourses of the white body that cite white dominance and Black degradation.

Many of the comic controversies that dominate the contemporary media landscape emerge when an audience perceives the comedian on stage may not share the same, "mutual beliefs, mutual knowledge, and mutual suppositions" (Clark and Gerrig 124). There is no shared pretense, the doings of the joke become unclear, and the comedian's objectives are questioned. It becomes a form of *de cardio* (Jackson) audiencing, an attempt by the audience to interpret and read the heart and unstated intentions of the comedian through a range of contextual cues. Two key variables in the previous sentence, however, work to assume stability where there is none. Which "context" is "the audience" using to draw contextual cues, and which "audience" are we talking about?

The audience has left the building

> Jokes are complicated, context is hard. Rage is easy.
>
> (Biddle qtd. in Ham and Benson 50)

In order to interrogate the workings of the contemporary comic controversy, it becomes necessary to consider all the ways the audience is radically reconfigured in the new media landscape. In terms of the primary audience, the physical audience in the room of a stand up comedy event, it is important to mark the heterogeneity of this primary site before looking to secondary forms of audiences. In the live stand up event, audiences are not merely receivers of meaning, but present a heterogeneous and shifting network of relations who are co-producers of the event (Batalion; Harbidge; Krefting; Rayner) "The stand-up gig not only promotes but positively thrives on a complex nexus of intra-audience relations" (Harbidge 129). In performance studies, it is commonplace to discuss *audiencing* (Park-Fuller) as a verb, as an active meaning making process. In comedic studies, Harbidge refers to "audienceship" to mark a "sustained focus on intra-audience bonding" (129). Pushing beyond simplified notions of collective audience, Harbidge argues that an audience is not merely passive to the event, but is a vital force where power between audience members and the comedian on stage are in constant flux and ever-changing (132). For example, he identifies the moments of non-laughter as "telling signifiers of intra-audience dynamics" (130), wherein meanings are being processed and negotiated in community, context, and relation. In addition, even in moments of laughter, there are ranges of different types of laughter which carry very different meanings, agreements, and negotiations between audience members (both between one another and with the comedian). As one concrete example of this, Harbidge looks to the stand up of Steve Martin to mark a distinction between the audiences who are and are not initiated to Martin's unique form of humor (135). Thus, even the primary audience, the audience in the physical presence of the comedian, plays an active role in the production of meanings which are negotiated, unfixed or never stable. In this sense, the primary audience becomes co-author for the secondary audiences. So, when the discussion extends outside the room, introducing the expansive range and possibilities for secondary audiences afforded by media (who also take on an interpretive authorship role), the very notion of context paradigmatically shifts in the contemporary comic controversy.

There was a time when the comedic audience, the recipients of the joke, were only those primary audiences "in the room." For decades, this has been expanding, when considering the live comedy concert being recorded on LP records, being filmed for television, the coveted HBO comedy special, televised award shows, late night talk shows, and a range of mediated forms where the audience extends outside the physical confines of the immediate space. In this move beyond the primary audience to the mediated audience, it can be argued "the act loses this living quality and presumably much of the audience's power to shape it" (Wilson 283). However, this power is only limited in the mediated audience's ability to influence through audienceship—that power of the live audience to actively shape and impact the moment by moment malleable and adaptive comedic exchange (Wilson 283). However, while the text of the mediated event may now be distributed in a form that appears more static and fixed, it is encountering an expanding network of mediated audiences that are actively negotiating and reproducing meanings in participatory and geographically unrestricted ways and exponential contexts.

With the advent of the Internet and social media, the very notion of context has seismically shifted in ever-increasing ways. Take the live HBO comedy concert recorded in the 1980s or 1990s, understood to be mediated through television, yet with the expectation of a larger context of the full comedic set, a warm up, time to establish pretense, and a chance to create relation and understanding with audience (primary or mediated) before the next joke. Now, in a time when media is severed into four- and five-minute (or less) snippets on YouTube, the very notion of context, as it was ever understood, operates differently. In 2016, rather than a joke within a comic set being framed with twenty minutes of set up, and an additional thirty minutes of follow up, a singular joke can be isolated in a tiny edited clip and decontextualized in a BuzzFeed article. Furthermore, this one little snippet can be reframed in whatever manner the blog author interprets and writes the utterance (Ex. "Chelsea Handler's Racist Jokes Land Her in Hot Water"). Thus, context is less something negotiated in space and time when it comes to mediated audiencing of comedy, and more something that can be primarily written, rewritten, and reframed by any number of audience members with a computer. In this critical forum where the joke is now re-contextualized within a critical frame, the joke is "then (re)presented to a new audience with different expectations" (Wilson 283). The audience is constructed differently and constituted differently through the framing and headline. "In this temporal context and in this space, no longer are we dealing with people expecting to see stand up, willing to approach the act as humour and grant some leniency to the speaker on points with which they disagree" (Wilson 282).

Couple this shifting context with the shifting logics for which people audience comedy in the contemporary culture. Often, audiences in a comedy show would attend an event because there was an interest, willingness, or favorable connection to a comedian (or in comedy). Nowadays, the audience is not only those showing up or tuning in, but a newly courted and constituted audience hailed through their Facebook and Twitter feeds, even if they have no interest in comedy and never considered audiencing the work (before encountering the re-contextualized critique of the work). Furthermore, even for those intentionally "tuning in," antagonistic and oppositional viewing is now an accepted and culturally rewarded practice. While "hatewatching" television has become an accepted cultural process and performance, various award shows, comedy concerts, and televised cultural events are now engaged through the practice/performance of "live tweeting." Moment by moment, utterance by utterance, the tweeters are at the ready with commentary, witticisms, support and/or critique joke-by-joke, comment-by-comment. Herein, the temporal unworkings of a joke, the process and evolutions of negotiated meanings is clipped and undercut, coaching an audience to hear/respond in a manner that favors rapid reaction and instant commentary in a "play by play" format that is likened to sport commentators. In this context, "we value what grabs public attention – the ideology of publicity"—there are rewards for presenting self in an "easily-consumed public way using tropes of consumer culture" (Jodi Dean cited in Marwick and Boyd 6)

Live tweeting is now an event, a fragmented and alternative constitution of audience that shifts away from the live or mediated event, and produces a parallel, alternative and splintered audience context established through shared interests, like-minded opinions, and mediated networks. This is a significant shift from live stand up engagements, where live audiences and the comedian in the room work out and negotiate meanings. In live stand up, "the audience is not just a preexisting condition but also a consequence arising from the very gap in the fabric of thought and perception identified by the joke, making the joke itself a generative tool for creating audience" (Rayner

33). Jokes, as do tweets and critiques about jokes, constitute audience within the realm of social media. Herein, a (re-contextualized) joke, or a critique of a joke, is distributed across a fragmented network of momentary communities that are produced via similarities in reception, interpretation, dialogue, and commentary—what can be referred to as one's "tribe" or imagined/like-minded audience (Marwick and Boyd 7). Live telecasts seem to be both aware of this shifting audience, and use this as a marketing tool. Beyond the "OMG" moments that trend from Shondaland every Thursday night following *Scandal* and *How to Get Away with Murder*, live musical telecasts, award shows, political debates, and a range of live televised events are now structured around "live tweeting." *The 2016 Golden Globe Awards*, hosted by Ricky Gervais for the third time, worked to capitalize on his controversial humor and "take no prisoners" approach to comedy to advertise and promote the awards show. The copy, "Hold onto your globes, he's back" promised a night of Twitter outrage and offense, as Gervais himself, the morning of the show, tweeted a shirtless photo with the words "Better get dressed and offend some humourless cunts I suppose." Audiences were not only prepped to be offended but were ready to tweet about each offense, as it occurred, in real time.

There is no question the broadcast networks understand the promotion of live tweeting as an important and effective strategy for ratings, specifically for a younger demographic that is less committed to the practice of the live televised events of yesteryear. It is hardly news that controversy is good ratings business (is it even necessary to provide examples anymore? Please just insert your favorite). Yet, in the new media climate this extends beyond network television. Internet sites and search engines make large profits off of controversy, even if on the back of an individual's public shaming and professional ruin. Author Jon Ronson, enlisting the help of economist Johnathon Hersh, attempted to estimate how much money Google made off the Justine Sacco web searches because of her Twitter controversy. His estimate was $120,000 with the likelihood this figure was highly conservative (Ronson 277). Controversy is big business, yet the contours and effects of its workings are more complicated and impactful than dollars and cents.

There is no doubt there are a range of ways this shift to social media opens up incredible opportunity for democritization of audience voice, resistance to dominant messages, and the forging of multiple critical communities that strategize and undermine hegemonic systems. There are, surely, a broad range of democratic and resistant potentials to celebrate. Returning to our early example of a live comedy show, where a primary audience sits in a room and negotiates meanings with a stand up comedian, it is highly simplistic to assume everyone in that room is on the same page. Furthermore, it is a foolish assumption that if, in that space, a singular audience member (or a scattered minority of audience members) felt uneasy with a joke, that these individuals would feel empowered and safe to voice dissent, contest, or resistance. In this instance, the power of social media to voice critique, enact counter narratives and minoritarian positions is deeply powerful. However, with this power and capacity to publicly assert a counter narrative, there are a range of critical considerations and questions introduced in this capability.

Critical audience as storyteller

> The storyteller … "takes" from experience in order to "make" experience for the audience.
>
> (Langellier and Peterson 2004, 163)

As previously discussed, much discussion of audience tends to use terms that imply a more passive and static collective—one way receivers of information—oversimplifying the dynamic process of communicative meaning making. Such framing works to obscure audienceship and how immediate feedback from a primary audience works to adapt and shape the message (Langellier and Peterson 164). In other words, it erases the active authorial role the audience has in the process of producing meaning. Looking to the comic controversy, which is mostly staged and performed through social media, the participatory audience is a networked collection of negotiated and rhetorically manufactured selves who "take" the joke in order to "make" their narrative of the joke. From tweets and blogs, to comment threads, Yik Yaks, and Facebook, the controversy plays out across and through a range of manufactured online performances. "The process of self-presentation becomes an ever-evolving cycle through which individual identity is presented, compared, adjusted, or defended against a constellation of social, cultural, economic, or political realities" (Papacharissi 207). Social networks provide "such sites of self-presentation and identity negotiation" (207). Herein, the self is "an information game" (Goffman cited in Papacharissi 207). Through the presence and absence of photos, friend networks, and selected interests, information, and opinion, identity is performed in highly strategic and negotiated fragments of presentation. To produce an online self is a performance, just as to offer a critical response to a comic or a blog post is a performance. To be a critic, regardless of the length or medium, is to be a maker of stories, a producer of a narrative with rhetorical force and implications. Regardless of the amount of information one shares, or chooses not to share, the assertion of a critic is the telling of a story, and thus engages in the construction of a personal narrative.

Consider the short-lived "comic controversy" involving comedic actor Rebel Wilson. "Staff Writer" at news.com.au wrote the short article "BAFTAS[1] 2016: Rebel Wilson Courts Controversy with Transgender Joke" on February 15, 2016 (*Rebel Wilson Makes …*) and the article was picked up by a dozen or so additional outlets. The article narrated, "She [Wilson] told the crowd she had 'been practising my transgender face' in the hopes of winning a gong in the coming years – a reference to actor Eddie Redmayne's acclaimed performance as transgender artist Lili Elbe in *The Danish Girl*." The article reported that the quip "left a sour taste for some," especially coming right after "Ricky Gervais' barrage of trans-related jokes" at the Golden Globes. The article is no more than a paragraph or two long, including two images of Wilson, and an image of Redmayne in *Danish Girl*. At the end of the article are seven screenshots from various tweeters who are upset or generally insulted by, and insulting to, Wilson. For example, "not lupe fiasco" writes "Why is Rebel Wilson still relevant? I thought we agreed she was trash?"

These may seem like simple "just the facts" articles or 140 character opinions, but within the context of the comic controversy, where various audiences blog, tweet, and comment their story of the event, the audience becomes an active storyteller. The critic is not only narrating alongside the comedian, but is also constructing *the* comedian, *the* comic content, and *the* larger audience. The comic controversy is always a collision of competing (personal) narratives. There is a broad range of critical considerations that need to be factored into each of these accounts, most specifically their performative effect. In other words, shifting attention away from what these accounts *say* to what they *do* (in relation to the production of identity, the constitution of audience, and their claim to the truth of an experience). The next section will work to unpack these ideas, using the 2016 Rebel Wilson post as the central example.

The personal narrative is an intervention into cultural discourses, marking a strategic and political struggle over meaning (Langellier 1999). Beginning with the "Staff Writer," the unnamed author of the short article, there remains an unmarked yet constituted "I" that is set forth through this "just the facts" reporting of Wilson. By posting the article in the first place, a story is created, produced, and constructed, rather than merely uncovered or "found." There is the performative co-presence of "taking" the experience and the "making" of the story (Langellier and Peterson 3). The story is produced in and through the telling, as is the identity of the unnamed author. The focus of this form of analysis is not to try and uncover the author's intentions, but rather to trace and analyze how storytelling is the struggle over meanings (20). The story asserts a truth, produces knowledge of what happened, and thus *does* something in the world.

The unnamed writer frames Rebel Wilson's comment with the title, "Rebel Wilson Courts Controversy with Transgender Joke," which, through their word choice, already contextualizes and defines the utterance as controversial. Wilson's primary action in this story is her "courting" of controversy through her "transgender joke." The frame prepares and rhetorically constructs the audience to engage with her statement in a specific way. Already, through the title, meanings are solidified, a focus is determined, and a wealth of possible reads are foreclosed or removed that existed beyond this narrative frame. The joke is reconstructed, and then immediately positioned by "Staff Writer" within a context by paralleling Wilson with Ricky Gervais and his "barrage of trans-related jokes" (as opposed to an infinite number of additional contexts where the joke can be situated to make sense of it). Furthermore, "Staff Writer" asserts "many pointed out" that Wilson has a history of making "questionable awards ceremony jokes." This choice by the author places the joke in very specific company and casts the joke within a controversy, creating a stage and producing a story of outrage.

So what is the story? What is present, absent, assumed, reified and questioned in this telling? Most notably, as discussed at length in earlier chapters, the joke is reduced to words, divorced from any additional performative and aesthetic information. There is no sense of the audience feedback in the space, how the live audience responded, how Wilson navigated those moments preceding or following the joke, or where and how this text was delivered in relation to her statements critiquing the Academy Awards for their lack of diversity. The article "mediates experience even when a factual account is promised" (Langellier 1999: 128). The very limited telling instantly politicizes her joke, a "courting" of controversy, and constitutes the audience as the "Us" (Madison 1998: 282), the necessary jury (with all the necessary information) to formulate our judgment.

In addition, the identity of the teller, even though unnamed is a rhetorical production—this seemingly neutral and "just the facts" staff writer who performs objective innocence yet rhetorically and strategically sets forth their story as evidence for the audience. In the making and assertion of the critic, the author of the critique is casting, creating, and performing a version of themselves for another audience. They are producing a specific identity, even if they avoid the use of first person, who is formed in the telling. Herein lies one of the single largest pitfalls for criticism to emerge into tragedy, for the critic judges the comic (Wilson is transphobic), yet obscures their role *as the storyteller* (I, "Staff Writer," am making the choice to write Wilson as transphobic). The implication of this omission is layered, as it not only reproduces an is/is not transphobic dichotomy around Wilson, but also reproduces an implicit heroism for the critic (the "I" writing this story is *not* transphobic). The unnamed person performs their identity as "a good citizen," rhetorically distanced from any system of oppression or connection to transphobic culture. They rhetorically distance themselves from the act of judgment, arguing the joke left a foul taste "for some" and "many" pointed out her "questionable" past. The author makes no explicit claim to a position, but makes the story through rhetorical indictment. Such an approach is reflective of several claims Donald Trump tweeted during the 2016 Republican primary. He would invoke the "many people" who questioned rival Ted Cruz's citizenship or called Megyn Kelly a "bimbo" in order to assert a narrative without claiming authorship. These storying choices by "Staff Writer" all work to constitute the audience in specific ways, indict Wilson, and obscure the active authorial role of the critic—each driving performance of the comic controversy. After all, others (perhaps many, if not most) may not have been left with a "sour taste" (the author's words, no one else's), and others (perhaps many, if not most) made no links in their mind between Wilson's joke and Gervais. Most, actually, did not know the joke, or the awards show, *even happened*, until this story was produced through the Staff Writer's telling. So who is this unnamed author, subtly positioning themselves as a trans advocate, yet cloaked behind "just the facts" journalism? How else is their identity produccd? Most notably, their identity is constructed through the company they keep. By choosing to surrender their closing argument of the article to the seven Twitter screenshots embedded, put forth "objectively," yet chosen very specifically, they solidify the narrative. Tweeters indict Wilson with a range of insults and outrage. She is called "disgusting," with repeated references to her "police brutality joke" at the VMA's earlier that year (which will be detailed later in this chapter). Zoe S argues "'transgender face' brings up all kinds of garbage feelings about blackface, which Hollywood STILL does, so I'm doubly disgusted." Through the assembly of these tweets into a closing argument, "Staff Writer" is choosing to degrade, criticize, and indict Wilson. These were choices they made, selected and assembled, under the guise of objectivity.

What is obscured here is that Wilson's set, and the controversial joke, was part of a larger set of jokes within the context of racism at the Academy Awards. It is within this context that she makes the "face" joke, which is most immediately poking fun *at* Academy Award winning actor Eddie Redmayne, who is a cis heterosexual white male being widely celebrated for *playing* a trans person. The leap to Wilson being the "disgusting" person, and linking her joke to blackface, is a fairly significant leap (one right over the head of Redmayne). The final tweet "Staff Writer" printed, from @CrimesofGenocide states, "Do you know that more than half of transpeople will attempt suicide at least once in their life, @rebelwilson? Did you know that?"

The assembly of these tweets to complete the account operates to shape the identity of the author of this story, as well as constitute the audience in a way that reifies a tragic indictment of Wilson. She is framed as a transphobic and racist punching bag, who is rapidly and unreflexively tied to the epidemic of trans suicide. How does "Staff Writer" leap so far in such a short narrative? It is important to mark that there is zero indication that any of the seven tweeters embedded at the close of this story were in the audience of the BAFTA's or even watched it in any form. Rather, they appear to be tweets responding to other tweets *about* the joke. Actually, you have to work through many articles and links of responses to this joke to finally locate a recorded video of the joke, itself. It was not coming up under the search terms I expected, such as "transgender," "Wilson" and "joke." Rather, I found the clip on the Guardian website under the title "Rebel Wilson Makes Fun of Oscars Diversity Row in Show-Stealing BAFTA's Speech." At first, I was not sure it was the same event (it was the same event but a very different story). All you have to do is click on the still video image of Idris Elba, Julianne Moore, and Jimmy Kimmel laughing in the audience to see the original footage (*Rebel Wilson Makes …*) In this narrative account, the accompanying text framing the video is as follows: "The Australian actor known for her roles in *Pitch Perfect* and *Bridesmaids* pokes fun at the diversity controversies dominating this year's awards season. Speaking on stage at the BAFTA awards, Wilson says she has 'never been invited to the Oscars, because as you know, they are racists.'" The story, told through this narrative, produces an entirely different account with differing effects. There is no frame of controversy, and the "transgender face" joke is re-contextualized as part of a larger critique of the academy. In one account she is a show-stealing success and in another, she is linked to perpetuating transgender suicide.

As my own critical response, for this book project, continues to narrate and tell a story, there are a few points worth detailing. My choice to use Wilson's joke (and "Staff Writer's" account) as the example is based on a few criteria. One, it's a story that is easy to summarize and demonstrate in a limited amount of space. Two, it demonstrates a counter narrative simply through a differing headline. In addition, it centers around a joke that, personally, I think is not fully formed and I do not think is particularly funny. In truth, I am not a huge Rebel Wilson fan. Like some of the tweeters "Staff Writer" cites, I thought her police brutality joke at the 2015 VMAs trivialized something urgent and important. She walked out on stage, dressed in a police uniform, joking "A lot of people have problems with the police, but I really hate police strippers." She ripped off her shirt to reveal a shirt that read "F – k the stripper police." I remember watching it. I remember groaning with disease. The joke just didn't do good work (for me). But, the extremity of responses about the comedian and about a joke that most people have never seen and will only audience via textualized and narrative account by another (but will indict) demonstrates the power, influence, and impact of "Staff Writer's" accounting of the events. I also do not wish to imply that what "Staff Writer" did is by any means unique, nor do I wish to single this person out. "Staff Writer's" story will always be partial, will always have rhetorical workings and will always mark an intervention into discourses of power (Langellier 1999). This is not escapable. The critic is a storyteller and that story is an account amongst many others. The audience to that account is now the audience of a wholly different event (neither live or mediated, but the critic's), yet they engage the critic's event with a blind faith of transparency—this is "the truth" of what happened. Furthermore, this positions the audience to deliver a judgment, take a side, and speak/comment on the "event." As Williams argues in *Anti-Intellectualism and the Dumbing Down of America*, "In the new media age, everybody is an expert" (Williams). He suggests we are creating an anti-intellectual world made up of people "who feel they have the right, the authority, and the need … to comment on everything." However, too often in the contemporary comic controversy, we comment on a story or a narrative account of an event with the false sense we have experience of the event (rather than an experience of one's story of the event). We confuse the differing experiences of primary, mediated, and networked audiences and their shifting contexts. It is why Louis C.K.'s narrative of the sad comic is not "what happened" but what C.K. produced. Rock, Seinfeld and Gervais will never be audience to the sad comic, only to C.K. Yet, amidst all of these layers of authorship, identity production, audience constitution, and interpretation, we all too commonly engage as if we have a *shared event* to work from.

Audience power and negotiated meanings

> Stand-up comedy is often described as a battle between audience and performer … From a comedian's point of view, an audience can be an intimidating and frightening beast.
>
> (Quirk 219)

Surely, if the new media landscape has shown us anything, it's that the networked audience has the power to author its own interpretations, and through the use of social media, distribute and argue for the mainstream acknowledgment and adoption of their version of events. Stories and accountings of events are fractured and multiplied in a networked audience. However even within the immediate primary audiencing of the comedic event, the audience experience is both collective and heterogeneous (Rayner), filtered through discourse, and a contested site of negotiations and resistances. In the 2016 Golden Globe awards, as Ricky Gervais stood in front of hundreds of celebrities, his efforts at humor were not uniformly or passively received. Playing off of Gervais' history of pushing boundaries and angering members of the audience—a tension that was highly played up in the media prior to the Globes broadcast—Gervais opened with a flurry of antagonistic jokes. He mocked audience talent, arguing that some had it and others just married well. He referred to the Hollywood elite in the room as "disgusting pill popping, sexual deviant scum." He even took a direct shot at the sponsoring network, NBC, saying they would be impartial because they were the only network with zero nominations this year. The audience was responsive, meeting his punchlines with affirming and self-deprecating enjoyment. He continued:

> But as I say, I'm gonna be nice tonight, I've changed. Not as much as Bruce Jenner, obviously, now Caitlyn Jenner, of course. What a year she's had. She became a role model for trans people everywhere, showing great bravery in breaking down barriers, and destroying stereotypes. (pause, an afterthought) She didn't do a lot for women drivers, but … (raises his arms in a "what can you do" gesture).

The mentioning of Bruce at the outset of the joke set up an uneasy tension, as for some the "deadnaming" of Jenner crosses the line that will always be problematic. Additionally, it created a dis-ease in terms of where the joke was headed. He delivered each building movement about Jenner's bravery directly, conversationally, with a simple sincerity that elevated discomforts—where is he going? The punchline, "she didn't do a lot for women drivers" received a large laugh, with the camera cutting to Jamie Lee Curtis, who was also laughing. The joke plays on the high profile and fatal car accident involving Jenner in February of 2015. The camera cut to Queen Latifah during the laugh, who seemed less responsive. Gervais continued playing out the punchline, "You can't have everything, not at the same time." The camera now hovered on Cate Blanchett, who was laughing with a slightly shocked, but amused, reaction. While not uniform, and with levels of negotiation, the tension was somewhat relieved and the joke seemed to land. Following the Caitlyn Jenner joke, however, Gervais segways into a short bit about being "pulled off" by a man from the Hollywood Foreign Press if his jokes get too crass. The audience both groans and offers compromised amusement at how base it has already gone. Gervais, as a meta-commentary, responds, "Yes, yes, that is *the level*. An old man pulling me off." He then leaped, rapidly into a short bit about Jeffrey Tambor, the actor of the groundbreaking TV show *Transparent*:

> At least Jeffrey Tambor did it in a dress. (camera cuts to Tambor who is stone faced) Um, what a year he's had. Oh. What an actor, what a role. (audience applause for Tambor). Every day, he has to put on all that women's clothes and the hair and makeup and let people film it. That takes balls. So, I don't know how he does it. I really don't. I've seen his balls. They are huge and long. I don't know if he tucks them in his bra, or does that thing where he pushes them out the back and lets them hang, like a bulldog? No one knows.

The joke, which was for me, hard to decipher as a joke, fell flat, dragged uncomfortably on, and the audience offered little to no positive reaction. In its completion, the camera cut to the top of Lady Gaga's head, as her head was facing down, shaking her head, smiling, but refusing identification. Gervais was failing, perhaps intentionally, and the audience was speaking his failure. There was no rhetorical exigence here for social media or the networked audience. There was no urgency from the situation[2] calling for a rhetorical response (Bitzer 63), as the response was present and occurring. The audience *was speaking*. It did not take someone jumping to Twitter or writing a post on Salon.com to offer resistance to this failed effort. The audience, in that moment, did this work. Tambor, sitting stonefaced in the audience, was visibly not having it and clearly unimpressed with whatever Gervais was trying to do. As Lowder writes in his Slate article, hearing Gervais, "my cringing at his comedic choice faded into a modicum of relief when it became clear that very few in the room were laughing." The audience, in the theater, resisted what the joke was doing, and in turn, did something else with the joke. It was not merely a narrative being asserted by Gervais, but a countering and negotiated meaning was collectively performed through the audience. However, this did not stop a range of responses the next day responding to a more "contrived exigence" (Bitzer 66), calling out Gervais, with headlines like "Ricky Gervais Unleashes Barrage of Transphobic Jokes at Golden Globes" (Advocate). Yet few of these articles, with the exception of Lowder, offered the live audience any say, agency, or credit in the production of meanings. Their collective resistance was obscured in the accounts, assuming the primary and mediated audiences are naïve and in need of their critiques, and the noble critics were storied as the righteous voices emerging to indict and call out Gervais.

It is understandable why these types of headlines emerge, as manufacturing outrage and spurring controversy through contrived exigence is a business. This helps explain why a handful of idiotic hate-filled tweets, offensive comments, or ignorant claims by any unknown individual can suddenly garner national attention by going viral. But, there is a compulsive assumption that audiences need to call these persons out, publicly come out against Gervais, lest their offensive ideas will be blindly adopted by the public. Particularly when it comes to stand up comedy, live audiences have an active and dialogic role in shaping meanings. The boo, the silence, the uncomfortable laugh is not just a *response* to a meaning, but works to produce and contextualize and negotiate *the meaning* of a joke (Lockyer & Myers; Wilson). As with Gervais the audience can resist. At the same time, the comedian, in turn, works with and through how an audience is assigning meanings. Telling bad jokes is a part of Gervais's, and many comedians, artistry.

For example, in Whitney Cummings's 2016 HBO stand up special *I'm Your Girlfriend* (dir. Calner), Cummings performs a sequence of jokes about the increasingly violent language men are using to talk about having sex with women (ex. "smash that" or "hit her"). She elaborates, "I don't think music is helping. Music has gotten so rude towards women. You guys heard the song *Fight Night*? (a beat of audience silence). No Black people here?" She asides, calling them out, "That's *embarrassing*." She then meta-comments on her audience, sarcastically, "Santa Monica! Hashtag, Santa Monica." The audience is clapping and rolling with her, and she interrupts, "Are you *applauding*? Like some kind of white power rally? Don't *applaud* that!" The audience laughs more, a shift in tone and direction, and the meaning and awareness continues to unfold and produce new understandings through the joke. This type of negotiated laugh between Cummings and her audience emerged in a later joke. She was setting up a story about twenty-five minutes into her set, narrating how when she turned 30 she could no longer use condoms, and this male voice in the audience yelled, "Yaaaaaaa!" She paused, cocked her head, seemingly taken aback, and said, "well, that's really aggressive, um …" Turning an uncomfortable side glance to the rest of the audience. "Troubling," she commented, directly disciplining the reaction, before continuing. In both of these examples, the comedian and the audience are having a dialogue. While both have agency, there is a negotiation taking place moment by moment, whether it is in the form of an aggressive masculine laugh in the audience or an unfunny joke about Jeffrey Tambor from the podium. In the comic controversy, there is a tendency to ignore the primary audience and dismiss one side of this dialogue. Rather, the critic will leap to rapidly respond to a specific utterance, indict the words, obscure the context, and carry out a pattern of judgment that has now become commonplace.

The patterns and performances of Internet outrage

> (Tweet 45/53) As always, and from now on, no matter what the intent, aim, or satirical content (Tweet 46/53) the deepest apology is offered to ANYONE (Tweet 47/53) ANYWHERE (Tweet 48/53) for ANY REASON WHATSOEVER (49/53) Who found any offense in the previous joke.
>
> (Patton Oswalt Twitter rant April 1, 2015)

In a 53 tweet joke/rant, comedian Patton Oswalt took to Twitter to defend the newly announced *Daily Show* host Trevor Noah. Immediately following the March 2015 announcement that Noah was to replace Jon Stewart, Noah faced a series of online criticisms for some tweets he had sent in previous years. Critics went back to mine these tweets and leapt to judgment, referring to Noah as "anti-Semitic," "racist," "ignorant," and "fat-phobic." Oswalt satirizes the culture of offense in his Twitter rant, and closes by saying, "A simple series of clarifying post-joke Tweets like the ones I just sent out will insure EVERYONE a gentle, comforting chuckle." Performatively, what is happening in this rant/tweet chain is a parodic over-clarification of a simple and unfunny joke to ensure, at the level of exhaustion, no possible offense is assigned. In addition, the rant/tweet performatively demonstrated the effort, agency, and willful dimensions of the audience in their experience of offense. This online performance, championed by many, came at a moment when the cultural battle between comedians and "internet outrage" seemed to hit a peak.

In the land of social media, with the never-ending stream of access to information, it is often the absence, or the abstraction, of information that causes a lot of noise. As demonstrated in Oswalt's series of tweets, he is taking to task Noah's critics with a general and sarcastic monologue that is so reasonable and logical due to its level of generalization. Have you ever seen a Facebook post where something incredibly vague and seemingly simplistic is posted, such as "Racist Journal Editors need to be fired?" What about, "Homophobia isn't funny" or "I don't know how anyone can vote for sexism!" Each one of these begs for "likes" and support, due to the seemingly obvious correctness of the statement, but this is only due to its abstraction (and veiled interests). These ambiguous assertions are not situated and contextualized as perceptions coming from a particular person about a particular event. Rather, they are highly abstracted stories seeking audience validation. They obscure the personal and the contextual with abstractions that rhetorically enact judgment, constitute the audience to align themselves with the (obviously just and correct) statement, and produce the author of the message as heroic.

"Homophobia isn't funny" seems like a true enough and noble claim. It seems easy to stand behind, even to "like," unless the claim is complicated by stripping away the abstractions. Replace the generalizing term of "homophobia" with our sad strumming comic singing ("Sitting on …"), and Louis C.K. is likely to strongly disagree. However, the disagreement is not only about whether or not this *is* funny but also, whether or not this *is* homophobia. The move to the abstract (equating the bombing comic singing a poor parody song with homophobia) obscures the complication, contestation, and nuance that requires the audience of the post to *do more work*. It erases specificity, content, body, audience negotiation, and all the things that make comedy, well, funny. Any comedian will tell you, theorizing comedy fails and "science can't deal with comedy" (Rayner 30). When Lewis Black was asked by Wiseman, a social scientist, about the best way to understand comedy, Black replied, "You go tell jokes" (29 cited in Rayner). In other words, comedy is an embodied knowledge, a situational and experiential knowledge and an art that resists abstract generalization. But, this does not stop a recurrent wave of criticizing comedy *through* theory, which is ever present in the new media culture. Revisiting the Jerry Seinfeld debate regarding "Those PC college kids," I want to reconsider and examine whether Seinfeld, is in fact, really talking about "political correctness"—at least in the ways the term has been historically considered. He marks the college kids' rapid, and in his mind unsophisticated, assignment of labels such as "racist" and "sexist" to a particular joke without actually engaging or understanding the joke. While Seinfeld may feel an increasing pressure to use different words or not say certain things because of a cultural refusal of these terms or topics (which he can attribute to what some can label as a trend of "political correctness"), he seems to be making a different point. He is actually calling out the patterns and performances of criticism enacted by the student audience. In the next two sections, these patterns and performances will be theorized by two interrelated concepts; the notion of the *paranoid read* and the process of the *critical-norm*.

Paranoid vs. reparative encounters: Differing modes of approaching a joke

> Michael Che: It was edgy stuff, but it's just not the same climate today. Now it's this whole thing of you are what you tweet. I could know you for twenty-five years, I could have followed your whole career, but if you tweet something I don't like, that means you're just this kind of a person and you should never have a job again.
>
> Judd: Treacherous waters.
>
> Michael: Oh my God.
>
> Judd: At any moment, some joke you make in the middle of the night can end your career. It's a very different time for humor because you have to assume, with any great joke, it's going to anger a certain percentage of the audience – and those people now have a way to communicate their rage. You can unleash the lunatics no matter what side of the issue you are on.
>
> (Apatow 345)

This section introduces Sedgwick's distinction between the paranoid and reparative reading strategy, which is instructive in tracing predictive and interpretive processes that lead to reiterating the patterns of the comic controversy.

Many of the comic controversies emerge from an orientation toward the joke that adopts "the paranoid imperative" (Sedgwick), an engagement toward the text (in this case, the joke) that is singularly attuned to unveiling, exposing, and deciphering (if not anticipating) its absences, violations, and/or failures. The paranoid read is the reading of suspicion, which, consequently resists credit or faith in the comedian. "Paranoia knows some things well and other things poorly" (8). Sedgwick's analysis marks a "Shift to what does knowledge do – the pursuit of it, the having and exposing of it, the receiving again of knowledge of what one already knows?" (4). In other words, she approaches the creation of knowledge performatively, marking the paranoid read as "habitual practices of the same forms of critical theory that have given such broad currency to the formulae themselves" (4). Leading to the production of predictable patterned outcomes, the paranoid read marks our "critical habits" (4) and questions the effects of that knowledge orientation. "In a world where no one need be delusional to find evidence of systemic oppression, to theorize out of anything but a paranoid critical stance has come to seem naïve, pious, complaisant" (4).

Critical paranoia has become an important and increasingly accepted mode of engagement. However, Sedgwick marks a limitation to paranoid reading practices, suggesting they are contagious (6), reductively predictive, and tend to focus on negative effects. It finds what it seeks to find (13), but at the expense of other forms of knowledge. The paranoid read is "to apply a 'hermeneutic of suspicion'" and is "widely understood as a mandatory injunction rather than a possibility among other possibilities" (4). The paranoid read operates under the faithful and perhaps faulty assumption that exposing the presence of a system of domination (Rebel Wilson is transphobic) is productive in itself, as if pointing it out is "a mere hop, skip and a jump away from getting it solved" (16). Furthermore, "The paranoid trust in exposure seemingly depends, in addition, on an infinite reservoir of naiveté in those who make up the audience for these unveilings" (17). It assumes that the audience in the room, the audience at home, and every other person but the noble and paranoid critic is naïve and blind to the offense. It relies on the production of faulty exigency and assumes audience passivity/gullibility.

Thus, if we return to our two earlier examples of Rebel Wilson's BAFTA joke and Gervais's "joke" about Jeffrey Tambor, we can trace the paranoid impulse and the effects of this knowledge production. For Wilson, the paranoid read attended to and interpreted transphobia, and produced the knowledge of this event as evidence of that transphobia (Wilson is transphobic, "Staff Writer" is not, Wilson's joke is tied to trans suicide, etc. ...). In this respect, paranoia is tied to the workings of the tragic frame. Yet, a reparative read (more aligned with the comic frame) might not have dipped so rapidly into that singular interpretation, and bypassed the predictive and negative effects of this paranoid posture. Instead, it would remain open to other possibilities in the joke, where the very mention of "transgender face" does not trip the fuse, but potentializes a larger critique of diversity, The Academy Awards, and the bodies and actors we choose to celebrate. If the paranoid audience does not leap to constructing a paranoid exigence following the Gervais joke about *Transparent*, a different form of knowledge could have been pursued. The story is not one that bothers to indict Gervais, and is also not one of tragic and negative effects. Rather, it is a story about how Tambor resisted being hailed into a joke that was weak and misguided. It is a story about how the audience at the Golden Globes performed resistance, marking a cultural shift in trans discourses (and how audiences pushed back against being constituted into certain chains of meaning). Lowder touched on this in his essay, whereas so many other critics and writers opted for paranoia. This form of reparative work and the knowledge it produces opens up a range of alternative knowledges and ways of reading comedy.

The paranoid imperative provides an instructive frame to explore what has been happening with comedy over the last few years. It works in opposition to a fairly simple yet contested idea—what if we were to allow the comedian some leverage and entertain the possibility that they might know what they are doing, might understand our rapid critiques, and be doing something else than what our paranoia has leapt to in a split second. In 2016, Tina Fey made the bold announcement that she will no longer explain her comedy, feeling the work, labor and considerations she places into the development of her comedy are overrun in this climate of suspicion and outrage (Framke). Schumer argues, "Jokes are like works of art and they take years to figure out" (Apatow 103). In 2015, faced with criticisms about her engagement with race and feminism in her comedy, Schumer took to Twitter to respond to fan criticism about some of her jokes. On Twitter, she joked, "Put down your torches before reading this so you don't catch on fire." In a more detailed response, she wrote, "I ask you to resist the urge to pick me apart. Trust me. I am not a racist. I am a devout feminist and lover of all people. My fight is for all people to be treated equally" (MacDonald). Schumer's request to "trust me" asked for faith and license from the audience. It fell in line with Trevor Noah's claim, that "To reduce my views to a handful of jokes that didn't land is not a true reflection of my character, nor my evolution as a comedian." However, Schumer's "trust me" response was not wholly reparative or comic, either, as it seemed to try and brush off the criticism without fully engaging it. In the end, Schumer's request (what some interpreted as a dismissal) was not met with trust by several of her critics, but additional suspicion, criticism and backlash (Clifton; MacDonald).

Critical-norms of comic controversies: Differing theoretical patterns

Sedgwick's conception of the paranoid (vs. the reparative) read works to draw attention to the performative effects of criticism, what the knowledge that emerges from our critiques *does*. Does it foster suspicion, anticipate negative effects, allow reparative possibilities? At its best, the work of critical theory and critical engagement—the examination of how systems of power and hierarchy are negotiated within a particular text or joke—can open up new, productive, and liberatory understandings. Critical engagement can help us to see, know, and understand our social world in ways that are productive, innovative, motivating, and aesthetically enriched, and assist us in the work of making a better and more just world. This is the critical ideal, yet when paranoia becomes the primary mode of orientation to our objects of study (in this case, humor), the idealized critical project is stalled. We engage in a performative pattern of tragedy, of simplicity, and negativity. Returning to Seinfeld's indictment of "PC" college kids, his critique was less about political correctness, and more about challenging paranoid orientations, and, by extension, their performative effects. By approaching comics with a fixed mode of paranoid suspicion, he suggests the students were quick, predictable, and uncomplicated in their labeling work as "sexist" or "racist." These theoretical terms, abstract in their very nature, assisted in generally demonizing the work without specifically engaging the work—setting a mode of rapid (and abstract) critique in motion that is well-suited for racking up Facebook "likes" and retweets. He is interrogating critical patterns of interpretation. He is "marking the inherently abstract dimensions of theory, and how relationally, contextually, and individually, abstraction fails" (Goltz 2013: 29). Rather than take on the slippery, ever-expanding, and contested scope of "political correctness," I want to reframe Seinfeld's position as attempting to identify a paranoid mode of engagement with comedy that leads to a "*critical-norm*." "The critical-norm [is] a concept to mark and examine the performative dimensions of critical engagement" (2013: 23). The concept seeks to mark how "the many distinct potentials of embodied and aesthetic performance work – the messy, the clumsy, the queer, the elliptical, the dangerous and the contradictory" (23)—get reduced and simplified through the application of theoretical frames of interpretation. Thus, a paranoid orientation towards a text, works to produce and reproduce a critical-norm, where a once layered and complex joke can be quickly and wholly rewritten as homonormative, homophobic, sexist, whitesplaining, or any other critical concept. The critical-norm is not arguing against the extreme value of these concepts, but seeks to mark how they can become strongly patterned in their usage in a way that erases complexity and particularity in aesthetic works of art.

When looking at comic controversies, there is a patterned tendency to leap to theoretical abstractions, enlisting critical concepts and judgment in order to indict the comic. As demonstrated throughout this volume, the comic controversy is not an outlier or a rarity, but has become a recurrent and ongoing performative ritual, fueled by the continual public calling out of comedic work. Seinfeld's frustration is not what can't be said, but the rapid reflex of leaping to abstract judgment, by labeling work as "racist" or "sexist." The critical-norm becomes a useful concept to unpack this pattern, for it examines how critical engagement that was "once challenging to discourse, slowly becomes incorporated into the discourse as a critical-norm, constructing a convention that works to frame (and contain) interpretations" (Goltz 29). In other words, the leap to labeling a joke "sexist" or "racist" (or any other generalized judgment) becomes routinized as a pattern and starts to drive and predict our responses and understandings, rather than unpack and trouble them. The practice does not help us to understand racisms or sexism in new ways, but rather normalizes the indictment of racism and sexism in ways that resist complicated, alternative, or negotiated interpretations.

In socially mediated environments, "patterns of sociality" (Papacharissi 210) emerge through social networks, suggesting "genres of behavior" (213). This tendency is not at all surprising or unique. As human beings, we seek out patterns, assemble information into sequences and relationships, and work to produce accounts of events that help us make sense of our environments. We, as Reyes and evolutionary biology assert, are pattern junkies (Reyes). Whether it's staring at a Jackson Pollock painting or Rebel Wilson making a joke at the BAFTAS, humans like prediction, they collect and assemble information into patterns (Reyes). Thus, when considering the critique of Seinfeld, the critical-norm helps to more specifically name the rapid and reactionary leap to label something "sexist," an abstract and totalizing assessment, rather than deal with the nuance, complexities, and multiple dimensions and meanings at work. He is speaking to a genre of behavior, a ritualized pattern of shared values and commitments in the communicative process, that has come to produce the performance of "the outrage machine." To call this "political correctness" falls into reiterating "PC" as being synonymous with only censorship. Reviewing Seinfeld's argument, he is alluding to how any citation of a system tied to sexism or racism is too quickly reduced to *reifying* racism, and then being labeled as *racist*. Perhaps this tendency can be placed under the expanding umbrella of political correctness, but it is more specifically and productively captured as the workings of critical-normativity.

Willful misreads and audience investments: Questions of identification

In the area of comedy, paranoid reads and the uncomplicated reproduction of critical-norms place the audience at the center of the discussion—their narratives, their investments, their choices, their blindspots, and their performative patterns. When an audience's critical patterns become conventional and naturalized, this facilitates a quick leap to the abstract and theoretical that rewards patterning abilities and obscures the contextual factors that complicate, shape, and differentiate complex comedic processes. What is at stake? Why would a critical voice from the audience rely upon critical-norms to frame the meaning of a joke, a set, or a comedian? Like with all things, there is a not a singular answer, but a spectrum of possibilities to consider. On the far end, the most ill-intentioned range of considerations has to do with extreme suspicion and paranoia—the willful misreading of a joke. In Ronson's *So Now That You've Been Publically Shamed*, he revisits the infamous Justine Sacco tweet and marks how the tweet, with even a little consideration, is clearly an attempt at humor through the performance of white ignorance (73–4). Such a read matches up with a range of tweets Sacco had sent prior to the one that lost Sacco her job and irreparably upset her life. Ronson, in addition, reflects on social media posts he has written that enlist similar humor, require some general pretense of ignorance, and could have, seemingly just as easily, led to his public shaming and demise. He alludes to something in the collective shaming of Sacco that seemed to *willfully not see* the pretense, to choose to ignore it, and make the tweet something that stands in for the foulest demonstration of heartless privilege. The audience chose tragedy, and seemed to resist, reject, or willingly evade shared pretense. As Sandra Bernhard has said "Audiences can turn real vicious sometimes. You know, collectively … They can turn on you. They're very – people are weird, they're like wild animals" (750 in Apatow).

While this is the extreme end, it is likely less common that the audience is viciously and willfully out for blood, when they approach ironic comedy. Yet, we live in a culture where tragedy breeds controversy and controversy makes money. So, even if the initial critic who judges a work and enlists a critical-norm without malice and with the best of intentions, those who then audience the joke are now encountering it in a secondary context (already framed as offensive in a blog post, clipped from its original context, and narrated now in a tale of tragedy via a critical-norm). Such an audience response merely reproduces and further fosters a posture of paranoia.

Extending further down the spectrum from willful misread, there is a large grey space where jokes can deal with difficult subjects, meanings can be very slippery, audiences' investments can be vastly diverse, and certain words, citations, and references can produce a whole range of triggers. Darren Criss, while improvising on stage during his Broadway performance of "Hedwig and the Angry Inch," allegedly said the words, "Man, woman, moman, wan, Bruce Jenner, whatever you are," (Kelley). Although he was playing the character of Hedwig, an outspoken, often offensive and subversive trans glam rocker, the 'deadnaming' of Jenner created a mini social drama. As expected, Criss's public apology had to forefront and reaffirm his shared commitments with the audience. He publicly posted on Facebook, "I want to sincerely apologize to Caitlyn Jenner, all transgender people, and anyone who was offended for my words on stage during Tuesday evening's performance. In no way do the remarks reflect my personal belief system or my support for transgender people." In a similar social media event, RuPaul's use of the term "tranny" also received an attempted public shaming, but RuPaul refused to apologize and resisted the need to reassert her beliefs or commitments. She stated, "My 32-year career speaks for itself," and went so far as to argue that loud voices demanding she apologize are "not the transsexual community. These are fringe people who are looking for story lines to strengthen their identity as victims." RuPaul seems to argue the controversy emerges from the far end of the spectrum, the willful misread of a paranoid audience member. In this characterization, RuPaul is both calling out tragedy, but also reproducing the tragic model.

At the center of these orientations of paranoia, and reproduction of critical-norms, is a slippery and imprecise metric of trust—the very thing Schumer called for from her critics. Much like Jackson's *de cardio racism*, when determining the level of suspicion and paranoia to engage a comic with, audiences are forced to engage in the work of reading the comedian's heart. However, where and how this reading occurs is as much, if not more, about the individual audience member, their investments, their subjectivity, and their identification with the comic. When an audience fails to locate identification, shared pretense, or have faith in mutual commitments with the comedian, paranoia often takes over. For many, it is not enough to simply say, "trust me." This lack of trust, or lack of shared identification, can produce a paranoid exigence and a need to "call out" the comedian. Yet, "offense is taken, not given" (Gervais qtd. in BytesMaster). There is the most literal interpretation of the comic controversy, where the audience firmly and resolutely believes the speaker has, in uncomplicated and unequivocal ways, committed hurt and damage through their actions. Although a problematically linear model, the ritual of "offense-indict-apology-makes-right" is central to this tragedy. It ought to be complicated, negotiated, and allowed space for nuance and multiple interpretations, but more often than not, humor is not allowed such space. The comic controversy simplifies a broad field of meanings (and possible meanings) into a rigid and paranoid configuration of us vs. them. In comic controversies, when a critic creates and sets forth their story, the audience (of the critic) is too often positioned in the role of either suspicious ally or rabid defender. This pattern offers credence to the right wing argument in the *End of Discussion*. There is a firm (although highly questionable) belief that leftist critical patterns are trapped in the "Us-vs-Them" mindset. The authors argue, "Just how blind the 'Us-vs-Them' mindset can make people when they try to process new political information. Once this partisanship mentality kicks in, the brain almost automatically pre-filters facts – even non-controversial ones – that offend our political sensibilities" (Van Bavel qtd. in Ham and Benson). I cite this excerpt because the conservative authors and their audience strongly see this as a problem with the left. Let me be very clear that in my experience, there is no doubt this patterning is not unique to critical progressives. The right has their own paranoid practices and sedimented patterns of engagement. However, the paranoid "Us-vs-Them" mindset does work to trace the effects of paranoid critical-norms that potentially foreclose alternative modes of engaging and identifying.

Somewhere beyond us/them configurations of tragic modes of argument and paranoid critical-norms, is a more complex and reparative mode of audience negotiation. Why must audiences "side" and adamantly defend the simplified positions they do? There are a range of factors that can work to impact how we do or do not assume shared meanings, values, and understandings, and some of them may be invisible and/or insidious. Perhaps some of our paranoid practices should be shifted inwards, posing some questions and skepticism to the identifications and attachments we are willing to trust.

Krefting, when looking specifically at comedy, questions "what are the rewards – material or otherwise – for audience engagement with or identification with comics?" (142). She asserts that while comedy (and I would argue the majority of comic controversies) "rely heavily on affirmation of and identification with the comic" (145), there is problematically less audience reward and cultural incentive for identifying with female comics. While her analysis does not deal directly with irony, and seems to focus on more linear identifications with audience (rather than processing layered messages and pretense), her core argument marks how social systems work to shape and inform who audiences establish (or assume) shared meanings and values with. Who do they willfully see themselves in? In a previously mentioned study of audience meaning making processes watching Steven Colbert's "The Colbert Report," it was found that more liberal audience members would read Colbert as more liberal than the conservative-identified viewers. They assigned different political ideologies to Colbert, reflecting their own, yet both were able to find humor in the messages (Lamarre, Landreville and Beam). This identification, according to Krefting, is likely facilitated by the fact that Colbert occupies and embodies cultural normativity and thus identification with him exudes multiple forms of cultural incentive (white, male, cis, heterosexual, able-bodied). In other words, beyond the establishment of pretense or one's own critical patterns and approaches to a comic is the question of identification—if and how and in what capacity the audience is willing to identify with the comic. What are the stakes and benefits of identification, and what are the risks? Who do audiences identify with and to what effect?

We are at a period of great cultural shift. One need to look no further for evidence than the reactionary outrage of *The End of the Discussion*, Seinfeld's cranky PC attack, and the frustrated complaining of comedians like Gervais and Maher for not being able to say what they want. In this moment, it's important to mark how audiences are changing. As our culture, with much influence from the Internet, fosters a growing vocabulary around various systems of normativity (whiteness, heterosexism, ableism, cis genderism), the very notion of audience identification gets complicated. First, the normative white cis male body, while still mostly resistant to scrutiny and elevated through a range of privileges, has become more scrutinized than historically has been the case. It is a body of power, and one we are learning to read through suspicion. Where identification with Seinfeld or Maher was once assumed to be universal, as they are the white cis male universal subject, these ties are more complex—particularly with all the meanings and discourses their bodies cite within the exchange. Their performative citations carry weight and court paranoia (for some), particularly when they tread into the fraught territory of speaking of society's margins in comedy.

Consider a small but highly successfully comedic moment at the 2016 Golden Globes, when America Ferrera and Eva Longoria walked on stage to present an award. With winning smiles, Longoria began, "Hi, I'm Eva Longoria, not Eva Mendes." Ferrera followed, "And I'm America Ferrera, not Gina Rodriguez." Longoria added, "And neither one of us are Rosario

Dawson." "Well said, Salma," Ferrera stated. "Thank you, Charo," Longoria finished. The joke, which was calling out the Hollywood conflation and confusion of Latina actresses was a success. It was an indictment and mocking of white audiences, and the (primarily white) audience laughed, seemingly with ease and appreciation. There is something in the success of that joke, that ease, which speaks to the complexities of audience identifications and comforts. With the Longoria and Ferrera joke, there is a distance permitted where we do not need to fully identify with white racism, but instead we get to comfortably align ourselves with brown critiques of whiteness. So with Longoria and Ferrera—we laugh, but in a way that does not make us work. It's a bit self-congratulatory but without confronting us. We, as audience, are not forced to identify with the ugliness, but rather through laughter we get to exonerate ourselves and identify with Ferrera and Longoria (rather than navigate the uncomfortable identifications with the white body doing racism). So, we are okay with that, but how okay? Are we too okay with it?

Rather than calling out the abstracted and assumed white audience as fools—where white audiences get to feel identification *with* the two actresses, get to feel *in* on the joke, laugh at racisms *with* the actresses, and simultaneously absolve themselves—an alternative staging of the joke would have very different effects. If Bill Maher and Jerry Seinfeld were to have joined the two Latina actresses on stage and authored the idiocy, taking turns calling Longoria and Ferrera the wrong names (even with established pretense), the joke would not have been so easily digestible. It would confront the same racisms of the first joke, yet in a different way. First, white male bodies would be on stage erasing and depersonalizing two brown female bodies, citing a range of violent histories. Identification with racism would be hailed through identification with the cis white male body. Racisms would be enacted in the body, not merely referenced in the joke. The white audience would then be called to identify with the racist body and negotiate that identification. From an audience position, this would potentialize a far more complex and self-reflexive negotiation. As with a comedian like Silverman or C.K., who does not merely do the performance of white guilt, but actually works to embody the ugliness of racisms in order to explore, interrogate, and dismantle racisms, audience identification is (intentionally and I would argue productively) much more dangerous. It is the mirror before the hammer. It turns the reflection of racisms back on me, the white audience member, in ways that deny the easy laugh. How audiences navigate that mirror, when faced with the messy ugliness of oppressive privilege, has less to do with the comedians as it does with the audience, their commitments, and their investments.

It's messier to have a white body implicated in racism, faced with racism, and called upon to negotiate their relation to racism. As with the paranoid read, simply pointing to racisms (like Ferrera and Longoria) does not take us to addressing it. However, to watch the navigation of racisms being interrogated, embodied, resisted, protected, shrugged off, and defended asks more of the audience. Keep in mind, the tragic and paranoid audience will likely resist this identification, this mirror, and enlist a critical-norm to distance themselves (opting instead for tragically judging Maher as *the* racist and a sexist). If this mirror is engaged, however, then identification is potentially examined. That's an ugliness that seems to have more possibility. The Longoria and Ferrera bit was great, I loved it, and just how much I loved it (and everyone loved it) is the point. Of course we are more at ease with calling out the racism of whiteness than negotiating the embodiment of white racism—it's less real, less scary, less uneasy. These two different approaches to the "same" joke do very different things. They confront systems of racism in different ways by different modes of identification. Aligned with Ferrera and Longoria, pointing outwards at those racists, our laughter is easy, and while this joke is funny, it is uncomplicated. It protects us, and also protects the very oppressive systems it seems to be mocking. This type of joke hides and disguises so much under a well-meaning and self-congratulatory laugh. In this respect, it's the "PC" equivalent of the joke.

Where is the joke?

> Puckrik: You've attracted controversy with your material addressing racism. Do you ever get fans who don't understand the irony?
>
> Sarah Silverman: Oh my God. Horrifying. My old boyfriend used to call it 'mouthful of blood laughs,' people who feel a kinship with me and couldn't be farther off.
>
> (Puckrik)

There is a negotiated line here that needs to be attended to when considering irony, identification, and pretense—is the comedian playing the ignoramus or is the comedian ignorant? Do they pretend to not know better or do they simply not know better? Do we trust them to be ignorant or do we trust them, when they hold up the mirror, to engage our own ignorances, privileges, fears, and blindspots? This presents a responsibility and role for the audience, and these are not always clear cut. These roles and responsibilities rarely work with periods, so much as commas and question marks. In a previous class, I assigned my students to watch segments of Eddie Murphy's *Delirious* and *Raw* comedy specials from the 1980s, and planned on discussing the blatant homophobia and ignorance around HIV transmission that Murphy regurgitated. To me, this work exemplifies the most egregious forms of comic homophobia. Every one of my friends and siblings could recite these concerts by heart when we were kids. Eddie Murphy was it, and growing up in the 1980s, he was also the first person I remember talking about AIDS and was formulative in my understanding of gayness. He tells a joke about being afraid his girlfriend would come home with AIDS on her lips, after hanging out with one of her gay friends. He would incessantly mock and belittle "faggots" in ways that were simply acceptable to the mainstream in the 1980s. I expected students to be appalled. However, I was rather surprised when the bulk of my students read his work as ironic, finding it hilarious and assuming no one could possibly be as ignorant about HIV, nor as cluelessly homophobic. Sure they can. They were, and in the 1980s there was much hatred in those jokes and pain in those laughs. Herein, you see the less common case where the comedian's offense is read more generously. It highlights how, no matter how explicit one thinks a particular joke (and joke's intention) is, meaning always rests in the contextualized audience. The joke is never the possession of the comic and the intended or assumed audience is not always the audience.

In an interview between Judd Apatow and Jon Stewart, Stewart reflects on comedian Dave Chappelle.

> The sense I got from Dave was it wasn't so much the responsibility as he wasn't sure if the show was being received in the way it was intended. I think Dave felt a responsibility, as a black performer, to live up to a responsibility and to not give people—you know, it's sort of what we call the bucket-of-blood laugh. George Carlin and I used to talk about that a little bit because he would do those shows where he'd be like, "You know, we only bomb brown people. We only bomb brown people except when we bombed Germany they were white people and that's because they were going, you know, because they were bombing people and that's our fucking job. That's our fucking job." It's a great bit but you definitely felt, in the audience, that there were some people going, "Yeah, that's our fucking job!" And for George, it created this sense of "Oh they're not taking this in the way that I intended it." And in some ways you have to let that go because it's something you can't control. You can only control the intention of the execution …"
>
> (Apatow)

Murphy was not intending ironic homophobia in the 1980s, Chappelle was seeking to interrogate racism, and Silverman argues she was looking to unearth latent dimensions of white ignorance, but ultimately, none of them can control the joke. There is always the risk of the audience member thinking "ya, that's our fucking job!" Comedians can refine, experiment, learn, adjust, and sometimes stop what is not working, but the audience plays a significant role. Chris Rock speaks candidly about this process when he announced he would no longer be performing the piece "Ni@#ers and Black People" for he believed an unintended result of this work was endorsing white audience members use of the N-word (*Talking Funny*). In the case of Murphy, you have a reflection of homophobic and uneducated HIV logics, and in the case of Rock, there is the effort to enlist an ingroup critique. However, neither one can control the context, how they are read, if they are read "correctly," and the role of irony in their work. The intended or assumed audience in this new climate may be who the comedian believes they are speaking to, but that doesn't mean they are receiving it as intended. This is a difficult pill to swallow, and it sits at the heart of what we know about communication. The joke is not in the words, nor in the mind of the comedian, but rather it is assembled and produced in the mind of the audience, within and through their own capacities, investments, and processes.

The line (your line) she (actually, you) crossed

The final section of analysis argues that audience social positions, identifications, and investments inevitably co-author the interpretive processing and "understanding" of ironic performativities—centralizing the importance of critical self-reflexivity in the audiencing of this work. Whether an audience reads offense, subversion, or hope into a joke, it has as much to do with the specific audience member and the context, as the content of the joke itself. Amidst all the sexist, homophobic, ageist, and racist doings in Sheen's roast (see Chapter 1), the joke that garnered the most attention for "going too far" ("Amy Schumer Stands") was one that was not, explicitly, about social identity. Addressing Steve-O, whose friend and *Jackass* co-star Ryan Dunn died three months prior, Schumer stated, "Steve-O, I truly am – no joke – sorry for the loss of your friend Ryan Dunn. I know you must have been thinking, 'It could have been me,' and I know we're all thinking, 'Why wasn't it?'" Schumer started sincerely, yet the "why wasn't it?" punchline was delivered with an animated hopeful impatience of someone scratching a lotto ticket. She opened her arms on the punchline, hands upwards, punctuating the line with subtle but committed performative action. The joke was debated for several days after the event in the blogosphere, questioning whether it went "too far," or was uttered "too soon," and has since been listed alongside Carlin's "dirty words" and Lenny Bruce's work as a stand up moment that challenged norms of social decency ("Crossing the Line").

Revisiting the joke, the meanings constructed from this communicative event are complicated by several issues. After Schumer delivers her Steve-O joke, the camera lingers on Schumer for a moment, and we see her calm non-responsive (lack of) reaction. She sits with a lingering frozen satisfaction. After a beat, the camera cuts to a tight shot of a wide-eyed, glazed, and clearly uncomfortable Steve-O. It is this cut and Steve-O's reaction that generated the "controversial joke." Steve-O's reaction was the reason the joke "went too far"—rather than the joke, itself. As a counter example, consider Anthony Jeselnik's joke to Sheen (about his role on *Spin City*) stating, "the only reason you got on TV is that God hates Michael J Fox." Jeselnik's follow through for the joke was his trademark "shit-eating" grin of authority, as if to double down on the joke with, "yep, I said THAT." Michael J. Fox left his show *Spin City* due to complications with his Parkinson's, and Sheen was his replacement. Had Michael J. Fox or his wife been in the audience and laughed, the moment would be lauded. Had Fox or his wife been in the audience and looked upset, uneasy, or sad, it would have "gone too far." That is the standard argument about the context of the joke, but herein the "context" is specifically referring to the audience (both primary and mediated), their reception, embodied reactions, timing, and a wealth of factors that exist *outside* the joke itself. It was how Steve-O *performed* audience, and the aesthetics of that reaction that designated "the offense," more so than the words of the joke that took it "too far" or "over the line."

Comedic meaning making is an interactional process impacted by audience position and identification (Scarpetta and Spagnolli, 211). Even in Booth's project, where he worked to try and locate stable irony and lead an audience to a preferred reading of a text, he found the process of understanding irony to be messy, slippery, and perpetually an infinite endeavor.[3] He argues that, in the end, it is up to the audience to decide what the author intends, what beliefs they espouse, and what beliefs we believe they hold (73). Considering the ever present gendered and raced tensions at work on the stage the night of the Sheen roast, it is significant that the joke from the outspoken female comic is the one that went "too far" (and it is Steve-O that needs public protection). Yet, the audience did not protest or take offense to Steve-O willfully running full speed, face first, into Tyson's fist, just for kicks (or the numerous jokes about rape, drug abuse, female objectification, domestic violence, diabetes, illness, and race).

If the Steve-O joke determines the line of decency for the mainstream audience, what does that tell us about this audience? As mentioned earlier, the space, as with most stand up contexts, was hyper-masculine. When Schumer stepped on stage, she was chided as the "girl" who had to perform fellatio to get her spot. Once she tore into Tyson, her violation of expectation launched a constant push and pull for her entire act, where she was heckled ("If Amy had as many dicks …") yet refused to surrender control in the face of masculine threat. The performativity of her set launched an energetic, affective power struggle where her confidence and her refusal to perform a proper femininity (but rather, enlisted an ironic performativity) created a stir.

At least some of the men on the panel seem to struggle greatly with "taking the jokes" when they came from the body of Amy Schumer. There is a recuperative disciplining in the performativity of the Steve-O camera cut, and the audience's (both local and larger viewing audience) marking of "the line of decency." Discursive systems of patriarchy and gendered expectation worked to construct Schumer as cruel and going too far, eliciting audience protection for poor Steve-O (the man who staples things to his testicles and finds innovative ways to torture himself for mass entertainment). It is not as if Schumer was the only "up and coming comedian" on the panel. Anthony Jeselnik was of similar status when he said to Steve-O, "I saw you perform comedy (beat). Don't give up your suicide." In addition, O'Neil critiques Steve-O for getting sober, telling him he was uninteresting now, and no one wants to see him like this.

Given Steve-O's dangerous history with substance abuse and depression, both jokes have the potential of "going too far." However, the discourses surrounding these jokes, particularly coming from the bodies of men, worked to solidify the joke's meaning and intent as "just a joke" rather than a performative disciplining of "who does she think she is?" In fact, Schumer's joke was not even about Dunn. It merely invoked Dunn, but was a jab at Steve-O that was surely no less harsh (linguistically, verbally) than, "don't give up your suicide." If we look at this larger comedic controversy as a cultural barometer (Gilbert 176), our lines of decency are not nearly as sensitive to doings of racism and sexism as we are to the work of protecting and reaffirming masculine authority and command.

Some could argue that it was Schumer, however, who named Dunn, and by invoking his name, she inflicted hurt—in many ways naming an elephant in the room being left alone (unlike Tyson's domestic abuse, O'Neil's diabetes, Sheen's domestic abuse, drugs, prostitutes, a general acceptance of sexism, or Shatner's doing of racism). She brought up his name, and this set off an alarm that ought be suspect. Performatively, there is a "too soon" commitment around the topic of Dunn that was probed through the combination of naming Dunn and the camera cut to Steve-O. Yet, when Shatner makes his jokes about O'Neil and O'Neil explicitly calls him out for his racisms, this is not "too far," remarkable, nor "over the line." One way to make sense of this is to say that neither the performative resistances of O'Neil's nor Schumer's work were capable of penetrating the discursive field that worked to normalize the hegemonic systems they were directly challenging. A more colloquial way to say this is that we are okay with overt racism, jokes about dying Black men, reducing women to sluts, guys being punched in the face, lamps being thrown at women, and a whole range of racist and sexist doings, but a sobered look of sadness for a joke that hurt the feelings of a white straight male is performatively too much and too far and too soon for our culture. The offense speaks to the power and insidious operations of hegemonic discourse. The performative field in which these comedians are working is hardly a level playing field, and our own cultural responses are inevitably shaped, guided, and constrained by these same discourses.

Where we find and assign offense, humor, or pleasure requires critical self-reflexivity. Context, timing, audience, and our own investments in hegemonic systems of power and privilege enable and goad our laughs, and—as shown by the Steve-O moment—our offense. Our own values, beliefs, and expectations dictate reception (Kreuz and Roberts). As ironic performativity is never stable enough to eliminate any potential ambiguity, there is reason to believe we can always see what we want to see, what we choose to see, or what our positionality allows us to see (or not see). Ironic performativity requires that we, as audience, accept and examine our role, our commitments, and our complicities. Depending on who someone is and how one feels about William Shatner, or Patrice O'Neil, or Amy Schumer, their doings of racism and sexism will come to mean very different things.

Conclusion: What you see is what you get

Whether writing a weblog, developing a tweet, or performing a comedic set, we engage this communicative act with an assumed and intended audience. Early Chris Rock stand up was directed to African American audiences. Amy

Schumer argues her intended audience is women, yet is "appreciative of the guys that can come along for the ride" (Apatow 112). But this assumed and intended audience is a fiction and a projection. The audience is never singular, we engage and make sense of events through the screens of discourse, the framing of the camera, the narrative accounts of others, our critical patterns of reception, and our own investments and identifications with power. We will see what we allow and want to see, attend to what we choose to attend to, and assign intention, trust, shared commitment, or suspicion based upon who we are. The "irony of satire" (LaMarre, Landreville, and Beam) is that the audience's investments, their own beliefs and ways of understanding the world, will work to explain why people laugh in a way that supports their existing belief systems. This is the performative exchange and the processual becoming that occurs in the communicative act. Faced with a joke, the audience, as active and reflective meaning-makers, must, in turn, negotiate their laughing, their politics, their identities and their investments within this humorous exchange.

How is it that amongst an array of comedians doing multiple forms of racism, sexism, homophobia, and ageism, Schumer becomes the comic who goes "too far," Steve-O is the one in need of protection, and Shatner's uncomplicated doings of racism are not a discussion? The Ryan Dunn joke (that was not really about Ryan Dunn) is a point of controversy, but the mocking of O'Neil, who soon passes away from diabetes, is not given critical attention. Such results implicate and indict our cultural racisms and sexisms in ways that, perhaps, ought cross a line that extends beyond our comfort zones. These are the same comfort zones that enable many to laugh easily with Longoria and Ferrera, indict Rebel Wilson and Gervais with paranoid critical-norms, and refuse the reparative opportunity provided when a mirror is placed before us. We, as audiences and producers of critical stories, require just as much, if not more scrutiny than the comedians we attempt to theorize. You have not found a racist joke, but you have co-authored a joke as racist. You were able to locate transphobia in that joke, but its mere presence is not the end of the discussion, but only the beginning. There is no reason why Eddie Murphy's 1980s stand up is more offensive, more dangerous, more troubling, than "Sitting on a cock cause I'm gay." But it is—to me. It is not to my students. Is it because I "trust" Louis C.K.? Is it because I was willing to laugh and so I need to defend that laugh now? Rationalize it? If this broad landscape of audience contestation and negotiation throughout this chapter has accomplished its goal, there are no easy answers to tie up this discussion. It's messy. It's better left messy, as our treatment of audience has been tidy for too long. But, amidst this mess, I offer one very direct assertion to move this project forward. Within the blindness, that paranoia, the shifting contexts, and the competing narratives that assemble the comic controversy, we, as audience members make choices. Interpretation is a choice and it can, in moments, be a radical, inventive, and resistant practice. I choose to laugh with C.K., and I'm compelled to consider what it might mean to laugh with my students in the face of Murphy's ignorance. What can or might that choice, that laugh, *do*?

Notes

1 BAFTA stands for the British Academy of Film and Television Arts.

2 According to Bitzer, the rhetorical situation invites an utterance (62) and a response to a situation (63). The speech, is thus, given significance by the situation. The rhetorical situation is much like a question, presenting the necessary condition for an answer. However, the speech is about altering reality – not merely spinning the wheels of the contemporary. An exigence that cannot be modified is not an exigence, and it can be either a strong or a weak exigence (64). It is a crisis situation where one speaks to respond. After all, according to Bitzer, rhetoric is "the creation of discourse which changes reality through the mediation of thought and action. The rhetor alters reality by bringing into existence a discourse of such a character that the audience, in thought and action, is so engaged that it becomes mediator of change" (61–2).

3 Booth argues the complex demands irony places upon the reader leads us to a place where, "modern critics have tended to stress the value of diversity in interpretation, and they have had no difficulty finding innumerable examples of conflicting interpretations by responsible and sensible readers, and of conflicts between such readers and the stated intentions of authors" (48).

4 "We Saw Your Boobs"

"Bro camp" and subversive coaching

> In other words: He's not racist, he [Daniel Tosh] just plays one on TV. And he doesn't even really do that, does he?
>
> (Hibberd)

> In a world ordered by sexual imbalance, pleasure in looking has been split between active/male and passive/female. The determining male gaze projects its phantasy onto the projected female figure which is studied accordingly. In their traditional exhibitionist role women are simultaneously looked at and displayed, with their appearance coded for strong visual and erotic impact so that they can be said to connote *to-be-looked-at-ness.*
>
> (Mulvey 62)

Daniel Tosh is one of several contemporary comics who have found themselves at the center of public controversy because of their comedic style and approach to humor. Most notably, Tosh received a lot of criticism for a comment he made in response to a female heckler at the Laugh Factory in 2012. The story initially reported via Tumblr (by an anonymous audience member) explains that Tosh, earlier in the set, told a joke that referenced rape. The story reports that a female member of the audience heckled him, yelling out "Rape jokes are never funny!" In response, Tosh was reported to reply, "Wouldn't it be funny if that girl got raped by, like five guys right now?" The accounting of these events, the context, and Tosh's reply have been contested (Masada), yet taking the spoken account as it was reported suggests it was not a sophisticated or responsible comment. Arguments that his comment was a "celebration of a violent crime" (Bassist) or a clear act of "assault" (Bassist) enlist a tragic and uncomplicated narrative of the event, yet simultaneously speak to the treacherous and fraught discourses Tosh is swimming in—seemingly at times rather "off the cuff." Tosh's "rape joke" became a cultural moment, rather than a discussion, wherein there was a lack of engagement or examination of what happened. Instead, there was a resistance to dialogue, and firm ideas were staked out. For example, Louis C.K. famously garnered a lot of criticism for his response on *The Daily Show*. C.K. argued that the "rape joke" events were not entirely surprising, suggesting (what some inferred to be) the claim that feminists and comedy were natural enemies. More specifically, C.K. claimed, stereotypically speaking, "feminists can't take a joke" and "comedians can't take criticism" (Pozner). Many rallied against this claim, citing a long and important history of feminist comics, as well as political comics doing important cultural work. While I fully agree and support the responses critical of C.K., there remains something in C.K.'s statement that warrants serious consideration. Perhaps the argument I see in C.K.'s claim was more effectively articulated by RuPaul in a 2016 *Vulture* interview. When asked about drag's relationship to the trans community, RuPaul replied that the question was boring and opened a line of inquiry they'd rather not talk about. Speaking in reference to drag performers, RuPaul clarified, "We mock identity. They take identity very seriously." Separating, or at least differentiating the work of camp and drag from LGBTQ activism and the ever-increasing seriousness of essential identity politics, RuPaul frames drag as a necessary escape. More specifically, RuPaul references the escape from over-sensitivity, accepting (and investing in) the role of victim, and being locked into these patterns—what RuPaul calls being "part of the Matrix." RuPaul takes a camp approach to drag, embracing gender as a false idol to mock, a site of play, and an illusion that should never be taken seriously. Herein, C.K.'s comment about feminists and comedians can be reframed and contextualized around the tensions between politicized identity and the work of humor and parody, and more specifically camp. In this light, C.K. marks a tension that is foundational in these differing commitments.

It is very likely that your (the reader's) first response to this chapter introduction is discomfort due to the questionable paralleling of international drag superstar RuPaul and Daniel Tosh under a banner of camp. Beginning with an admittedly general definition of camp as a mode of gender play and investigation, which specifically enlists strategies of excess and denaturalization, the chapter will reflect a range of camp aesthetic strategies and how these work to coach a specific mode of critical audiencing.

To provide an introductory frame to this work, this chapter will begin with a close treatment of Tosh's 2015 viral reenactment of Selena Gomez's music video "Good for You." Gomez, a childhood star from shows such as *Barney and Friends* and Disney's *The Wizards of Waverly Place*, has built a pop music career—as well as a career in film—steadily over the last five years. "Good for You," the first single off her 2015 album *Revival*, aims to offer up a more "mature," and also far more sexualized, image for the 23-year-old pop star. The song is a breathy, sexy slow jam, which is accentuated by the steamy video. The music video opens with Gomez lying on the floor, wearing only a large white t-shirt, hair wet, as if she came right out of the shower. The 5′5″ actress/singer still carries a youthful face that reads teenage, innocent, and "made up" with glistening skin, and dark eye mascara. In a moment, the image cuts to Gomez in a sleek and short negligee, slowly tossing and turning on her back, sprawled out restlessly on a large green sofa. She stares longingly into the camera, with a textbook awareness in her eyes that she is being watched, a knowingness of being watched, and smiles directly back at the gaze. The sensual beat of "Good for You" along with the vocals are erotic and masturbatory. She sings in deep, breathy moans:

> Cause I just wanna look good for you, good for you, uh-huh
> I just wanna look good for you, good for you, uh-huh
> Let me show you how proud I am to be yours
> Leave this dress a mess on the floor
> And still look good for you, good for you, uh-huh

Scenes cut to her on a stool brushing her wet hair in only a white t-shirt, to her showering, to her slowly tossing and turning on the sofa and teasing the exposure of her body under the robe. It's an overly sexualized and unapologetically objectified rebranding of Gomez.

In November of 2015, Daniel Tosh released a shot-by-shot reenactment of Gomez's "Good For You" where he attempted to mirror and embody each action, glance, and tease with the technical accuracy of Gomez's original. Daniel Tosh stands 6′3″ tall, with a lean body that lacks defined muscle, but carries a gawky softness. His face carries some of the elasticity in expression of Jim Carrey. He presented the video on YouTube in split screen, playing his reenactment alongside Gomez's in real time to highlight the precision of the remake, and the video quickly was viewed over a million times. Watching the Tosh "parody" on its own, it would be easy to think that he played it up, took the eroticism and camera flirtations to a heightened extreme; however, in the side-by-side version, it is on par with Gomez, and even, at times, the overt sexuality is underplayed. What emerges here is a mainstream and didactic demonstration of what scholars of female representation and gender performativity have theorized for decades. Tosh's efforts to look "Good For You" in the same manner of Gomez looks inauthentic, extreme, artificial, and comical even though there is no explicit wink or joke. He is consciously committing to his task, in the moment, with no necessary or explicit effort at irony (even if ever-present). It directly bombards the audience with a negotiation of how we assign meaning and forge relationships with different bodies, the meanings they carry, and their performative effects.

On Episode 26 of Season 7 of Comedy Central's *Tosh.0*, Tosh discusses a range of responses to his Selena Gomez video, wherein some audience members thought he looked like actress Jamie Lee Curtis and others suggested he resembled the character "Buffalo Bill" from *The Silence of the Lambs*—a cross dressing psychopathic killer that has been strongly criticized as transphobic. Based on these responses, it is safe to assume that there were audience members who engaged the humor in the video rather simply and hegemonically (i.e. "it's funny because he's a man"). Yes, there is absolutely the risk that a more transphobic audience member – who is invested in hegemonic masculinity – can find humor in Tosh's video that works to support, or at least not challenge, their systems of belief. However, the video provides a compelling site and opportunity to examine the rigidity and the ridiculousness of the technologies of gender. Tosh, discussing the video's responses, comments (always with a hint of sarcasm), "Thankfully, some of you were able to look past my sexiness and recognize my true artistic intent." He then reads a comment by viewer Andrea Bobo, "I thought the original vid is propaganda for oversexualization of girls/women, so I feel remaking it with Tosh makes it seem that much more ridiculous. He's not sexy to me in women's clothing rubbing himself all over the place, so why is she? Maybe it's a mute [*sic*] point, but whatev's" (Comedy Central. *Daniel's* ...). As he is reading this comment for the audience, he makes a "whoops/eek" face when reading "mute point." Then, Tosh replies, "Or maybe I just like the song? Whatev's." He chooses to read the critical gender response and put it out there, but refuses to fully align with it. As trademark for Tosh's persona, he refuses to surrender his ambiguous position, as it is central to the work he does as a comic. He allows and maintains incongruity, refusing to shore up or solidify meaning or intent. Just as his love of Selena Gomez may or may not be genuine, his constant teasing of codes of sexuality and gender is both the source of his comedy and the fuel for why many don't know how to read him. His work is destabilizing, resisting fixed meanings. He is a trickster, and in that is pleasure but also risk and uncertainty. "Something about that big grin and his 'I'm just playing' demeanor manages to dial back the edge – at least, in the court of public opinion" (Hibberd). He, like RuPaul, places himself in opposition to the seriousness of identity politics and firm boundaries, and rather plays within and through the malleable "rules" of gender and sexuality. He is somewhat explicit about this in the Gomez video, but he is also fairly consistent with this work through his ongoing comedic persona, navigating a more mainstreamed form of camp aesthetic that both operates within and departs from a long lineage of queer camp work.

A trademark of the show *Tosh.0* is their constant pushing of just "how gay" the show can get. In his 2010 video montage of Season Two's "gayest moments," Tosh opens the video seated in a leather chair, wearing a smoking jacket with a glass of Brandy and a small dog perched on his lap. He asks, in self-righteous and "snooty" performance of confusion, "How could anyone interpret my comedy, *my art*, as homosexual?" The video then cuts to a montage of clips of the season's most sexually ambiguous content and gender play. The video ends with Tosh professing in a slightly exaggerated testimony, "I'm straight. I cannot emphasize that enough." However, this declaration shares the screen with Tosh and three other men in aerobic spandex onesies dancing and clapping in spirited cheer formation. As an exemplar of his style, his professed positions on gender and sexuality are deliberately undercut with incongruity. In future seasons, Tosh continues to play and push with the lines of gender roles and sexuality, perhaps most famously when he brought on pleasure coach Bob Patrick from the website sensitivenips.com. In this episode, Bob a very muscular and tanned gay male who is over 60 (who is fully nude) gives Tosh (also fully nude) a "cranial-anal massage"—a massage where Bob plows his head firmly against and into Tosh's bare anus. This happens on the writing table, with Tosh's writing staff positioned around them. In addition, Bob slides his naked body up and down, while Tosh lays chest down on the table. It could be easy to write off Tosh as just a straight male comedian laughing *at* gayness, a form of "gay chicken" or homoerotic play like on MTV's *Jackass*, but this read chooses to dismiss a broad range of information. He is willfully placing his body, often his naked body, into positions and contexts that completely violate norms of masculinity. He relishes in this ambiguity and, much like the Selena Gomez video, insists on walking this line between joke, transgression, exhibitionism, and pleasure. Furthermore, his pronouncements of his straightness are always contested, excessive and ironic, routinely paired with information or visuals that work to undercut the rigidity of the claim.

This work refuses the ironic dismissal (Miller) where heterosexual masculinity is briefly violated for expression of same sex heterosexual affection but then quickly reified to mitigate threat or ambiguity. Exemplified in 1990s shows, such as *Friends*, straight male bodies briefly flirt with male intimacy, but quickly and explicitly reject that there is anything gay going on. As a common occurrence, best friends Joey and Chandler would hug, but then quickly break apart and "re-butch" themselves to clarify and cast out the possibility of gayness (for themselves and the audience). Miller links this to the emergence of explicitly gay characters and the mainstreaming of gay representation in the 1990s. Prior to this level of gay visibility, characters could flirt, hint at, and offer coded suggestion of gayness without being filed into the either/or boxes of the hetero/homo binary. Post 1990s, the existence and illusionary integrity of the absolutely 100 percent heterosexual male is preserved by the clear and explicit observance of identity boundaries and behaviors. Tosh, in this capacity, works against this form of rigid categorization, engaging in a range of activities that would normally threaten heteronormative masculinity without apology, clarification or explicit dismissal of the presence of homosexual pleasure.

Because Tosh's humor is admittedly lowbrow, relishing in bad taste, and celebrates a degree of adolescence, he actively and insistently resists being taken seriously, or at least literally. His response would be, much like with the Gomez video, "Maybe I just like a good anal-cranial massage, whatevs!" He, like Silverman in the Aoki scandal, strongly avoids and resents having to theorize or explain his work. He loathes that posture of RuPaul's "matrix" and openly mocks it when discussing "his comedy, his *art*." To ask him to drop the mask, give up the game, and settle the ambiguity once and for all robs him of his most effective tool—the ability to never fully pin him down. Thus, rather than try to read him through discussions of identity and identity politics (and the seriousness that these often conjure) this chapter takes a cue from RuPaul and seeks to consider its opposite—the playful and powerful experimentation and celebration of illusion and excess that ushers us into camp.

Having examined in previous chapters the aesthetic complexities of comedy and self-reflexive audiencing in the performative examination of controversial communication events, this chapter digs deeper into the range of audiencing possibilities and potentials that exist through a consideration of camp. Framed as a critical and resistant audiencing practice, which is tied to specific aesthetic cues and reflexive modes of production, variations of camp emerge as an important and productive site for interrogating discourses of gender and sexuality. The chapter will briefly rehearse the lineage of camp literature as a concept and audiencing practice from a trajectory of theorists including Sontag, Doty and Meyer. Next, the chapter will look to the controversial and largely panned 2013 Academy Awards performance of "We Saw Your Boobs" by host Seth MacFarlane. The analysis will examine how explicit and recurring cues for a camp read were resisted or flat out ignored by audiences and critics—generally declaring the number as an offensive and sexist failure. In order to detail and unpack an alternative range of subversive potentials within (and critical responses to) this number, the chapter reasserts camp audiencing practices as powerful and generative spaces of defiance/production. Such practices, even when overtly cued by the aesthetic dimensions of the MacFarlane number, were deemed wholly and undeniably "sexist" through the text-flattening practice of paranoia, the critical norm, and the subsequent Internet outrage. MacFarlane is read through the lens of "bro camp," a mainstream form of masculine camp parody, which can be considered an extension of "Het camp" (Kleinhans 188). The conception of "bro camp," like "het camp," extends beyond traditional modes of queer camp yet maintains key aesthetic and relational elements that carry the potential to disrupt and challenge dominant culture (188, 195). Herein, discussions of audience agency, aesthetic complexity, and comic artistry are co-negotiated within the comic controversy. The examination of a case study of MacFarlane and the analysis of "bro camp" will be considered alongside and through the conception of hegemonic masculinity—specifically examining where and how bro camp works to disrupt or trouble the rigidity of this system of meanings. By looking at how masculinity is performed in their comedic sets, alongside Tosh and MacFarlane, the chapter ends by demonstrating how not all performances of comedic masculinity are productively coached or read through a camp lens. This conclusion is grounded in the example of comedian Jim Jefferies, whose humor offers a counter example of comedy where sexisms are being reified without an explicit camp coding practice at work.

Camp, queer camp, audience training

> In this way, camp provides gay men with a cultural resource for dealing with personal and collective devastation.
>
> (Halperin 200)

> You are not making fun *of* it; you're making fun *out* of it.
>
> (Isherwood cited in Bergman 4)

There are certain definitional debates that, if engaged, can lead into departures so sharp and extensive, the focus of any project might never be able to recalibrate on course. One, as seen in the first chapter, is the contested debate over defining irony. Akin to this tension is the exhausting and, perhaps, futile effort to define the parameters of what is (and is not) "camp." Medhurst suggests the project of defining camp is like trying to seat oneself in the corner of a circular room (cited in Cleto 4). A definitional attempt at camp is often framed as a "slippery" project, for defining a concept that exemplifies artifice, failure, and excess, will always resist clarity, precision, and exclusion. Cleto traces how camp has been cautiously approached "as *sensibility, taste,* or *style,* reconceptualised as *aesthetic* or *cultural economy,* and later asserted/reclaimed as *(queer) discourse*" (2), tracing its "relentless power to frustrate all efforts to pinpoint it down to stability" (2). Shugart and Waggoner suggest that a camp aesthetic is "understood at the most basic level as over-the-top, playful, and parodic" (4). There is an element of intuition to the project of reading camp, for "you know it when you see it" (21). In addition, the term is always on the move, as "Our understanding of Camp changes with the evolving history of gay subculture" (Kleinhans 182).

Perhaps most dangerous is the effort to argue that something "is not" camp, for it is much less daunting a task to argue the presence of camp, or the potential of a camp read, than its absence. This next section will briefly rehearse key themes that have emerged in the scholarly discussions surrounding the concept of "camp," its territory, its processes, and its potential effects. While core definitional discussions will be examined, the central focus of this section is to establish camp as a form of audiencing process, a strategic negotiation of meanings in the resistant act of self-defense and survival (Halperin 200; see also Dyer).

To help us establish a starting place, Babuscio sets forth useful parameters to begin our discussion, suggesting "Camp is never a thing or person, per se, but, rather, a *relationship* between activities, individuals, situations, and gayness" (20, *my emphasis*). Camp theorists have attempted to organize the seemingly spiralling concept through a range of distinctions including Dyer and Babuscio's straight/queer camp, Isherwood's high/low camp, Sontag's naïve and pure/deliberate camp, Booth's Camp/Camp fads, Anderson's true/light camp (cited in Cleto 23).[1] For the purposes of this project, Bergman marks four general themes of camp that share some level of critical agreement; camp is tied to style; camp works in opposition or tension with commercial culture; camp is read through or performed by persons on the outside of mainstream culture; camp has ties to homosexuality and the queer work of questioning desires and ways of being as natural or authentic (Bergman 4–5).

Where scholars such as Ross tend to isolate discussions of camp to the twentieth century, others trace its presence through an extensive literary tradition. Beginning in the twentieth century, in Pre-Stonewall gay culture, camp was an in-group form of communication that allowed coded means of talking to one another in heterosexual spaces that might be hostile or unsafe

(Bergman 13). Both as a social and a viewing practice, camp allowed a double conversation to take place—"a conversation carried on in silence beneath the movie's glossy surface" (Bergman 13). More succinctly, camp offered a coding practice, a wink, a kick from under the table.

Sontag's much-cited essay "Notes on Camp" (1964) famously marks camp as a sensibility "that, amongst other things, converts the serious into the frivolous" (276). She works to detail this "logic of taste" (276) as a "mode of aestheticism" (277) that resists seeing beauty, but rather sees the artificial, the excessive, and the stylized. Using a range of camp canon examples from Tiffany lamps, headlines and stories from *The Enquirer, Swan Lake*, and *Flash Gordon* comics, she sets forth camp as "love of the exaggerated, the 'off,' of things-being-what-they-are-not" (279). Thus, Sontag asserts camp as an apoliticized sensibility and aesthetic that embraces appropriation of kitsch and low culture—an articulation that has continued to anger many gay writers and community members by "detaching the signifying codes [of camp] from their queer signified" (Meyer 5). While Sontag suggests that, "there is no doubt a peculiar affinity and overlap" between camp and Homosexuals, who "constitute the vanguard – the most articulate audience – of Camp" (529), Sontag's conception worked to pry camp from, what many argue is, its necessary context of gay male culture. In other words, Sontag's much-cited discussion of camp introduces an ongoing debate surrounding the contested/necessary/essential foundational connections between camp and queer cultural practice. Furthermore, her articulation of camp resisted definition, yet opened up the field of camp possibility to a broad range of texts—a range and articulation that obscured and downplayed, if not erased the connection between camp and gay culture, gay politics, and gay performance. Thus, Sontag has been strongly and consistently criticized for her "emptying camp of content" (Bergman 8). She worked to "expropriate camp for her own cultural purposes" (Bergman 8), simplifying "strategies and tactics of queer parody" (Meyer 9) "into a degayified taste, a simple matter of ironically relishing an indulgence in what is 'so-bad-it's-good'" (Cleto 10). Thus, Sontag's influential "Notes" minimalized the linkages of camp to gay culture (Kleinhans 186) and stripped away the politic in camp, the resistance, and put forth a more consumable and mainstreamed conceptualization that was more flippant, more fun, but less queer.[2] For theorists such as Dyer, this minimizing of the ties between camp and gayness are significant, arguing "Camp is the one thing that expresses and confirms being a gay man" (cited in Kleinhans 187).

Outside of the constant glossing over gay culture in her detailing of camp (although it is always creeping in through numerous references, such as Greta Garbo, *All About Eve*, Wilde, Isherwood), there is a key moment in her "Notes" that seems to step away from, if not completely miss, what Halperin, Meyer, Dyer and many others would mark as *the* central politics of camp. In Note 12[3] she writes, "The question isn't, 'Why travesty, impersonation, theatricality?' The question is, rather, 'When does travesty, impersonation, theatricality acquire the special flavor of camp'" (280)? Where Sontag wishes to question why one thing acquires camp flavor, and one does not, her resistance to the question of "*why* travesty ..." is an important and telling maneuver. While her carving out camp as "seriousness that fails" (283) brings important insight, the "why" question of camp is a richer and more important mode of inquiry than the classification of what is or is not camp (or pure camp).

The "Why" is key to the queer politic that Sontag obscures, and that Meyer forcefully reclaims in his introduction to *The Politics and Poetics of Camp*. Camp is not merely a thing to be discovered through "objectivist methodologies" (Meyer 8) which assumes a fixed reality that exists outside consciousness. Meyer argues such an approach fails to account for the experiences of individuals, specifically gay and lesbian individuals, and works to set forth a theory of "agency and performance" (9) that "envisions a power – albeit decentered – that is able to resist, oppose, and subvert" (9). Where Sontag "brushed the queer from the discourse" (10) of camp, Meyer works to reclaim camp as a mode of explicitly queer critique, where the dominant original is parodied, exposed, and then resignified from the margins (10–11). The normative, the tragic, the seemingly authentic and natural is resignified—exposed as a failure, as excessive, as trivial, as less-than-serious. This is the very political "why" that Sontag pivots away from, that centralizes the very political workings of camp as a form of queer critique. In this configuration, camp is not a thing, but a critical *process*, an exposure, a pleasure in the exposing, and political dance in the artifice. "Even when Camp is applied as a description to the actions of persons, that person is described as *a* camp. This objectivist bias that reduces people to thinglike status is used to label Camp as extreme aestheticization and therefore apolitical" (Meyer 10). Meyer goes further to assert that this move strips away agency, the critical agency of camp, which denies its political workings. Even as Sontag notes, "the Camp eye has the power to transform experience" (cited in Meyer 13). "Camp is not a property of a text, but exists in the nature of the activations; however, not just any text can be camped" (Feuer cited in Kleinhans 185). The important move here is that camp, rather than a thing to be studied or located as essential to a text, is a process and mode of reception, how a text is taken up, negotiated, interpreted, handled, and how meanings are produced. It presents a political mode of audiencing, a social practice that is "productive, a creative impulse in its own right, a strategy for dealing with social domination" (Halperin 203).

It is this understanding of camp that I wish to take up most directly in this project. Much like the rougher or edgier comedy that has been the focus of these past chapters, I am not interested in lighter, softer, easier to swallow traces of camp that trickle into mainstream scenery. I am interested in camp that willfully embraces foulness, wrongness, deviation, and joyful perversion as a tool—the tradition where camp operates as "queer deconstruction of the opposition between 'original' and 'copy,' 'true' and 'false,' 'primary' and 'secondary'" (Cleto 8). This is a camp that coaches an audience to read in new, challenging and subversive modes, while paying attention to the ways in which the comic controversy undercuts these possibilities. It is not essentialist in that camp is somehow fundamentally tied to a gay essence, but emerges as a gay cultural practice and as a mode of heteronormative resistance, deviance, and pleasure in its perversion. This camp is the cousin, or perhaps the regular trick, of queerness and performance—each attending to brash and unapologetic dismantling of the authentic, the natural, the correct, and the normative. After all, camp is always in quotes (Sontag) and is always a performance (Cleto; Meyer). Through surplus and excess, camp exposes the artifice, the theatre of life, and the critical awareness that we are always playing a role. Dyer links camp to the act of passing in a heterosexist society, wherein gay males "have staked out a claim on society at large by mastery of style and artifice" (cited in Shugart and Waggoner 24). Ester Newton's work is central to this double vision in the theorizing of camp, wherein camp is, "putting on a good show while simultaneously revealing it is, indeed, a show" (35). In this exposure there is "marked pleasure" (25), a "delight in artifice" (35) that is tied to a training to read queer codes and coded actions that work to denaturalize sedimented truths about gender, sexuality, and heterosexist culture. As Dyer states, "So we have developed an eye and an ear for surfaces, appearances, forms – style" (Dyer qtd. in Shugart and Waggoner 2008: 24).

Butler famously theorizes this stylized repetition and replication "brings into relief the utterly constructed status of the so-called heterosexual original. Thus gay is to straight not as a copy is to original, but, rather, as copy is to copy" (1999: 31). It is subversion of the naturalization of straightness through excess (Bergman 11). Straightness and Camp is always a performance that exposes the performance—queers and destabilizes its illusionary truth. They thrive and demand discomfort, disease, and fall short when they are easy enough to digest.

Camp moves mainstream

Looking at contemporary culture, there are ranges of texts that seek to explore, embrace, and perhaps exploit and appropriate camp significations for the mainstream. Shugart and Waggoner argue, "One cannot consume pop culture today without consuming camp" (1), for it has "been absorbed into contemporary sensibilities and practices" (42). Fully tracing this transition is beyond the scope of this project, yet the 1980s primetime soap opera *Dynasty* emerges as a significant text in introducing gay sensibilities to the mainstream (Feuer cited in Kleinhans 185). Alongside *Dallas* and *Knots Landing* and several other primetime soap operas, *Dynasty* was a tale of excessiveness that was too much glitz, and so dramatically over the top, that it was fun. Depicting the extreme rich, with heightened melodrama, big hair, big shoulder pads, big fights, and trashy camped up gender play, audiences found a way into the text that permitted campy removal—a sense of ironic distance—alongside moments of emotional connection. The text straddled the lines of "theatricality and authenticity … intensity and irony" (Feuer qtd. in Kleinhans 185). This trajectory of camp moving mainstream was followed by shows like *Married with*

Children, Rosanne, The Simpsons, and finally a slew of reality television programs that relied upon the audience having access to more sophisticated codes of camp pleasure. From television shows such as *Empire* and *Nashville*, to the *Real Housewives* and *RuPaul's Drag Race*, aesthetic codes of failure, excess, and so-bad-its-good are no longer subcultural, but rather are Must Binge TV for the masses. Applying Bergman's critical themes of camp (specifically its tension with commercial culture and commitment to queer denaturalization of desire), many of these examples seem to step outside of those initial conceptual boundaries set forth by Bergman (out of the mainstream, tied to gay culture, etc.). Yet, the stylistic and aesthetic cues of camp, since the publication of Sontag's essay, have worked their way into mainstream culture (Kleinhans). "Since that time, the media world (television, radio, music, advertising, journalism, etc.) has tended to use and even co-opt Camp, perhaps neutralizing (by naturalizing) its subversive potential" (Kleinhans 187). Thus, it can be argued the mainstream mode of "campiness" of *Ugly Betty* and *Raising Hope* seems to follow in the tradition of Sontag, softening its political edge. This allows the work to be easily consumable, pop, reflective of a consumerist and patriarchal/heterosexist culture, and thus may not work to disrupt audience commitments. It carries the removal of early camp practices, wherein everything is seen in quotation marks (Cleto 25), but the ironic distance does not deliberately call attention to its form, its hegemonic or essentialist production, and its performance as a performance in a way that coaches a critical engagement.

Bypassing the black hole of arguing whether or not these campy texts "are camp"—or rather, do they coach or invite a read that does the work of camp—I want briefly to pivot away from mainstreamed exemplars of pop or straight camp to camp work that operates beyond dominant culture. As these once subcultural codes have moved further into the dominant discourses (Meyer 19), this has created the space and necessity for new articulations and modes of camp to be experimented with by queer artists and audiences. In the last few decades, as camp and gay and lesbian representation moved into the mainstream, new forms of camp have emerged that mirror the critical thrust of earlier camp, but operate on differing registers and with differing intensities. Their pleasure, linked to the pleasure of early camp work, is less decipherable from the vantage point of the dominant and normative. It's a different style of a wink or kick under the table. For example, in the early 1990s, New Queer Cinema introduced a range of bold and experimental queer voices that sought to challenge, disrupt, and reconstruct the softened and apologetic lesbian and gay characters in the mainstream. This historical moment was fueled with the angers and trauma of the AIDS pandemic (and the U.S. government's criminal silence), alongside increased mainstream acceptance (and queer resistances) of the early 1990s. New Queer Cinema emerged in a time of fury, and explored aesthetics that were bold, unaccommodating, and resistently playful (Pearl). Here, camp audiencing practices are cultivated once again as a critical, and somewhat radical, response to the silences and violences of mainstream heteronormative culture. For example, filmmaker Gregg Araki, with his teen apocalyptic trilogy (*Totally Fucked Up (1996), Doom Generation (1996), Nowhere (1997)*) situated a cast of queer teens into a wasteland of popular culture, punishing narrative plotlines, and fatalist angst turned up to a deafening level of absurdity. Araki used intentionally horrible acting, cumbersome dialogue, congested and harsh cinematography, and a blood bath of perverted off-ness to refuse audiences a moment of comfort or identification (Goltz 2012). Araki pleads with his audience to resist (hetero) narrative seductions. He never lets the film draw you in, for when he does, he knocks the audience over the head with violent tragedy coupled with absurdity. For Araki, heteronormative narratives are violent and punishing for queers (Goltz 2012), and his films offer queer audiences a vision of the violence and absurdity from a safer critical distance, coaching us to stand back and to not take the bait. His camp is a cinematic slap in the face (like Cher in *Moonstruck* "Snap out of it!"). His drag teens expose the performance of teen that works to punish and alienate queer youth. Araki's films play off every form of queer punishment cinema has thought to inflict (suicide, hate crime, alienation, rape), but does so in a lineage that speaks to previous camp legacies.[4] "The fact that gay men could so sharply and brightly make fun of themselves meant that the real awfulness of their situation could be kept at bay – they need not take things too seriously, need not let it get them down" (Dyer cited in Halperin 490). Yet, as Halperin points out, "Camp undoes the solemnity with which heterosexual society regards tragedy, but camp does not evade the reality of the suffering that gives rise to tragedy. If anything, camp is a tribute to its intensity" (Halperin 200).

I reference Araki because he exemplifies an evolving style of camp that works to redefine itself and reclaim its edge to disrupt hegemonic systems of meaning. His films can be (and should be, for the right audience) hilarious. However, more often than not when I screen them in class, students are disgusted, appalled, or just furious. Even when framed explicitly as camp, there is this tacit idea about camp with audiences that it should be easy, digestible, light, silly, frivolous, and uncomplicated in its fun. Camp, in the vernacular, seems to connote playful, colorful, and cheerful. I am not arguing that it can't be these things, but I wish to assert that perhaps, some of the most disruptive, complicating, and resistance potentials for this work do not begin with texts that slide down so comfortably.

Extending the lens of camp: Broader conceptions of gender parody

Often, when asked to think of what is camp, or who is camp, we are quick to turn to the mincing, feminine performance of sissiness or the deliciously deviant drag queen—such as the great Divine. While these are often the base images that pop into our heads when we picture what "camp" looks like, its reach and potential offers a much broader landscape of investigation and engagement. Being that "gender and sexuality are key axes on which camp has turned historically" (Shugart and Waggoner 2008: 4–5), there exists a broad range of performances of gender and sexuality—both in the mainstream and in alternative sites—that embrace and work to enlist camp sensibilities. As both a strategy of representation and reception, a coding practice that cues an audience to alternative modes of engagement, there is a broad range of potential explorations of camp that have worked their way into popular culture.

Shugart and Waggoner's *Making Camp* works to explore female camp, where the very conventions of femininity are "'camped' by women" (5). Shugart and Waggoner suggest that scholarly approaches to camp are "frequently – if not always – anchored in conventional notions or 'discourses' of gender and sexuality, and … how camp may function as a key strategy by which those discourses might be renegotiated" (2). Thus, Shugart and Waggoner's project argues that camp should not be confined to strictly a gay male context (26), broadening the terrain to explore how all performances of gender offer the potential for camp examination and engagement. Extending on mainstream artists whose work has been previously read through a lens of camp, such as Madonna, their project zeros in on a handful of significant female cultural figures for their ironic, resistant and playful engagements with discourses of femininity. Shugart and Waggoner look to a collection of "Camp Girls," including *Xena: Warrior Princess* (played by Lucy Lawless), *Charlie's Angels*, Gwen Stefani, Macy Gray, Missy Elliot, and *Will & Grace*'s Karen Walker (played by Megan Mullally). Each of these representations explore a different manifestation of excess and self-referential performances of femininity. Here, Shugart and Waggoner argue how female camp—through the female body—can work to expose, play with, and potentially coach a critical resistance to conventions of feminine performance, rendering naturalized notions of femininity as artificial, cartoon-like, and heightened performative sites of exaggeration and parody.

Shugart and Waggoner's "camp girls" extend a lineage of literature that positions femininity and femaleness as the home of camp. Thus, their project provides a logical extension of camp investigation, for even as it steps beyond gay culture into the mainstream, it carries an investigation of gender performance that is undeniably queer in its investigations. The camp that Shugart and Waggoner examine looks at practices that are critiquing up the gendered hierarchy (female bodies examining femininity) and thus, in execution and reception, are navigating less choppy waters. After all, the lingering sense that camp is, or at least can be, misogynist has contributed to the limited examination of camp outside the context of gay culture (18). This work opens up the question of examining camp from a broader framework of gender parody, considering an extended range of positions and bodies and identities and their ability to enact queer critical interventions through camp-informed gender performance. While camp has been taken up across different forms within mainstream culture, it is not yet clear how camp operates in this popular realm, what its character may be, and what forms of criticism it may accomplish (2).

In considering the frame and possibility of a form of masculine camp, as performed through the male body, there are a few elements that need to be expected and considered. First, camp has a long history in igniting masculine/feminine incongruity (Kleinhans 187), and thus masculine camp would expect to explore this tension in a manner that disrupts the naturalized technologies of gender. However, occupying a historically privileged body, wherein "masculine camp" would be executed through the normative cis-male body, the risks, pitfalls, and discomforts for the male body to do this type of work will be greatly elevated. Hegemonic masculinity marks a dominating and oppressive system, where the straight masculine cis "bro" posture works to reify its logics through the denigration of femininity. As Doyle argues, the first directive of masculinity is "don't be female," coupled with themes of being independent, sexual, and aggressive (cited in Wood 171). Where Shugart and Waggoner's project of feminine camp works to bypass much of this "bad taste" and ideologically fraught terrain, by focusing on women dissecting conventions of femininity in mainstream and consumerable ways, "bro camp" will often plunge directly into the areas fraught with risk and bad taste. Additionally, to expose, engage, and irreverently disrupt the convention and discourses of gender is, by many standards, the opposite of the mainstream. "Bro camp" can be uncomfortable work. The moment by moment investigation of masculine technology, the excess and queering of these patterns, and the use of crude, base, and slightly off performativities is likely to upset a range of sensibilities. It is the embracing and excessive commitment to irreverence and bad taste in the discursive struggle for meaning—especially when this form of critique is emerging from male bodies investigating the conventions and technologies of patriarchal dominance and female oppression—that makes camp a productive and dangerous mode to examine hegemonic masculinity.

Working in the tradition of Shugart and Waggoner, who argue that mainstream and popular performances of gender—whether femininity or masculinity—can provide "a fruitful location for analysis" (5), the next section will consider how the mechanisms of hegemonic masculinity can be engaged and potentially troubled through a mainstreamed articulation of cis male camp that I will refer to as "Bro Camp."

"Masculinity," as a performative accomplishment and a system of cultural meanings, is often seen as "authentic, essential, unadorned, and uncontrived" (Halberstam 1998 cited in Shugart and Waggoner 2008: 5). Masculinity is seen as fixed, standard, precise, and "resilient to imitation" (Halberstam 28). Hegemonic masculinity marks "the culturally idealized form of masculine character" (Connell cited in Trujillo) that is embraced and accepted within the broader culture. It conceptualizes the particular and preferred mode and articulation of what masculinity is, should be, and what it means to achieve the rewarded and embraced status of "manliness." Trujillo sets forth five distinguishing features in the rhetorical production of hegemonic masculinity that will be instructive in examining the workings of "bro camp." Cultural manliness, the system of hegemonic masculinity, is defined through: physical force and control; occupational achievement; familial patriarchy; frontiermanship; heterosexuality (Trujillo). The first feature, physical force and control, draws immediate attention to the male body as a site of "strength, force, speed, control, toughness, and domination" (291). Demonstrated through his analysis of the media production of famed baseball pitcher Nolan Ryan, hegemonic masculinity is theorized through the muscular and athletic body. This body is strong, capable, commanding, and forceful. The second definitional feature of occupational achievement speaks to the reification of what constitutes "manly work" or "men's work," in opposition to "women's work" within a capitalist economy. Masculinity is asserted through occupation and activities that reify power, command, and control (police, firefighter, business, construction), often beyond the domestic space (cooking, cleaning, childcare) and traditionally feminized activities/positions (nurse, teacher). "Familial Patriarchy" marks a range of relational definitions that position the male at the head of the household and in the position of authority within the family structure. This relates to economic power (the male as "breadwinner"), physical power (the male as "protector" and role model of strength), and sexual power (male always sexual and female as sexual object). Furthermore, this definitional theme works to produce and position other members of the family within the patriarchal structure in specific ways (the housewife, the respectful child, etc.). The notion of frontiermanship carries a range of meanings, spanning from connection to the outdoorsman and the mythic American cowboy, to connected themes of rugged individualism and independence often championed in the genre of the Western. Finally, the last defining theme suggests how hegemonic masculinity is "heterosexually defined," marking affinities to heteronormative gender roles and relational structures, where male relationships are distinctly non-sexual and female relationships are primarily sexual. Furthermore, it works to uphold forms of masculine performance that reject effeminacy, "sissiness," and any mannerism or presentation of self that undercuts or blurs a rigid commitment to gender binaries and heterosexual identity.

What is important to consider in the examination of hegemonic masculinity is that these discourses of meaning are written upon, cited by, and performed through the male-coded cis hetero-assumed body. Thus, in order for this linkage and cultural inscription to be examined, the physical body engaging these meanings is central to the type of work that can be performed. Just as drag kings and queens can potentially do certain forms of transgressive work around technologies of gender—and Shugart and Waggoner's "Camp girls" can provide a different site of intervention into the workings of femininity through the female body—this analysis will now turn to the possible work of "bro camp." "Bro camp," as conceptualized here, opens a space to examine the resistant possibilities of cis-male and hetero-assumed comedians to interrogate and denaturalize the performativity of hegemonic masculinity. Central to the "bro" posture are the technologies of hegemonic masculinity, where the "bro" performance is exceeded, denaturalized, and performed in a way that is slightly off. Hegemonic masculinity is presented as a charade, an artifice, a fiction hiding beneath the great and powerful Wizard of OZ (Katz). In the fissures and cracks of the illusion, the performativity of masculinity, the system is opened up. The flow and glide that seeks to render masculinity right, correct and true is stalled, set off balance, and as such opens up the potential for intervention, reflection, and the possibility of humor. Enacted through the cis-male body, the work carries potentials for resistance, yet often emerges in moments of controversy and contest.

Seth MacFarlane's performance of failure

> The "boob" song, as it will be known in perpetuity, may go down as the highest-rated Oscar number in history, but at what cost? … I'm sure public executions would get big ratings too, but is that what the Oscars are truly about? Ratings? When did they turn into a "roast"?
>
> (Jamie Lee Curtis)

> Camp is an ironic and parodic appreciation of an extravagant form that is out of proportion to its content, especially when its content is banal or trivial.
>
> (Kleinhans 186)

By popular account, the 2013 Academy Awards opened up on an "ugly, hostile note" (Donnelly). Host Seth MacFarlane of *Family Guy* and *Ted* (the foul mouthed talking Teddy bear) fame, began his "banal and sexist" (Kornhaber) awards show hosting gig with an opening which sought to spotlight and celebrate that year's theme: music in film. When the evening was over, MacFarlane had critics all talking about musical numbers, but mostly one in particular. In his show opening monologue and musical set, MacFarlane sang and danced to the song "We Saw Your Boobs"—a peppy big band musical number, reminiscent of classic Hollywood show tunes, with the exception of the overly crude and adolescent lyrics. In the song, MacFarlane lists by name and film appearance a number of Hollywood actresses who had shown their bare breasts on camera.

> Meryl Streep, we saw your boobs in *Silkwood*
> Naomi Watts' in *Mulholland Drive*
> Angelina Jolie, we saw your boobs in *Gia*
> They made us feel excited and alive
> Anne Hathaway, we saw your boobs in *Brokeback Mountain*
> Halle Berry, we saw them in *Monster's Ball*
> Nicole Kidman in *Eyes Wide Shut*
> Marisa Tomei in *The Wrestler*, but
> We haven't seen Jennifer Lawrence's boobs at all

Halfway through the number, MacFarlane is joined by the Gay Men's Chorus, and the number builds in a performance that is familiar to convention, perky smiles, and slick Hollywood sheen, yet is totally crass and uncomfortable. Immediately, upon reception, the performance was declared sexist, misogynist, and some claimed homophobic (Davidson; Paskin; Rich and Puchko). From actress Jamie Lee Curtis and Hollywood women's organizations to film and cultural critics, there was a consensus that the number was a cheap, crude, and detestable failure. "'We Saw Your Boobs' was a song-and-dance routine in which MacFarlane and some grinning guys named actresses in the audience and the movies in which their breasts were visible. That's about it" (Davidson). In an article titled "American Dud," in *Time* (a play on MacFarlane's popular animated series *American Dad*), the author argues "MacFarlane was uncomfortable, smarmy, unfunny – and not even bad in any memorably creative way" (Poniewozik). *The Atlantic* questioned, "The host's feeble wisecracking may have been meant to provoke, but provoke what?" (Kornhaber). The inquiry poses a productive question that this next section will work to unpack. I pick the MacFarlane number for a range of reasons, one of which being that after reading dozens of reviews and analyses of the musical number, there seem to be only two primary modes of reception. The dominant (in terms of the most visible online) is the critical assessment that the opening was "crudely sexist" (Donnelly), unoriginal (Rich and Puchko), and did nothing other than perpetuate female objectification. The other responses, which were primarily reactions to criticisms via web comments and reaction threads, fell back on the "just a joke" defense, the argument that "everyone needs to calm down," "people are so sensitive," and "it was funny."

Seth MacFarlane, himself, has come forth and argued that he is fed up with being labeled a "misogynist" and argues that the number was satire (Donnelly). In an interview with *Glamour*, he suggests, "the media ignored the context [of the number] entirely. Comedy and satire being treated with more outrage than *actual* sexism, racism, or homophobia makes no sense at all" (Radloff). While I agree with some of his argument, what is missing in MacFarlane's satire-as-defense position is some discussion of what, exactly, he was attempting to satirize. What moral failing was he bringing to the fore, attempting to expose or resist? What is he doing? I remember watching the ninety-second number at home during the Oscars' telecast and being in a state of suspended confusion, but also, at points, was finding uneasy humor and pleasure in what was happening on stage. It was complicated, layered, and incongruous.

As with several instances in this book project, I am not working to argue that MacFarlane's number was necessarily funny, or objectively resistant in its performative workings. Rather I am working to unpack a densely coded moment in popular culture. Critics of MacFarlane were quick to argue the number took moments of nudity out of context from dramatic and even sexually violent (including rape) narratives, objectified the women, and belittled their artistry. There was no doubt that there was an element and trace of kitsch at work. Kitsch has been defined as "The world of bad taste" (Dorfles in Kleinhans 182), but also "the art of happiness" (Moles in Kleinhans 182). Kitsch, as a trace and a cue can be described as "when the text gives evidence that the makers themselves were aware of their 'bad taste'" (Kleinhans 183), a coaching that MacFarlane was very explicit about (which will be explained in this next section). Yet, the criticisms opted to engage MacFarlane's musical number at face value, wherein his act was a literal and uncomplicated endorsement for female belittlement. The irony and the kitsch that so didactically called for a camp engagement were actively resisted. Thus, in critical engagement, we have the text ("We Saw Your Boobs") forefronted with no consideration in the critical response to the aesthetics of the number.

Before examining the musical number, it is important to establish the context for these controversial ninety-seconds. MacFarlane stands 6′3″ tall, with a soft round matte face, and thin waxed brows. He wears a classic fitted tux and a blindingly white game show host smile. MacFarlane's opening monologue began with a series of jokes that worked with and through all the conventions one would expect when MacFarlane meets the Oscar podium. MacFarlane, as a comedian and personality, enlists certain performative trademarks of ironic communication that set the stage for his humor. Most notably, after the delivery of each "joke" he smiles somewhat arrogantly/expectantly at the audience, cueing extended and complicated meanings that mix pride, cluelessness, and trickster playfulness. His shtick is to probe offense and tease discomfort. As the audience processes his joke, he smiles in a feigned ignorance/arrogance where the meanings of the joke are navigated and suspended between audience and performer. His first boundary was pushed about four minutes in, when he jokes about *Django Unchained*, saying it was "the story of a man fighting to get back his woman, who has been subjected to unthinkable violence. Or as Chris Brown and Rihanna call it, a date movie." The joke parallels a violent legacy of savage racist violence and revenge with a recent domestic violence headline where Brown attacked Rihanna. The punchline, "a date movie," is dropped with all the cues of a canned punchline (ba-dum-bum), indicating that offense is being courted. The audience performs a muffled "ooooo" of discomfort/rejection, and MacFarlane playfully vocalizes the "oooo" along with them, mocking their "outrage." "*That's* what we were afraid he'd do," he vocalizes, performing the voice of the offended audience. The audience laughs in recognition and the meta humor of nervousness around MacFarlane with this platform. MacFarlane reassures them, "That's as bad as it gets, if it makes you feel better." He pauses and shifts, "It's really not as bad as it gets …" In this momentary exchange, the co-presence of an uncomfortable audience groan or a boo, alongside his oblivious and pleased-with-himself grin and self-aware commentary, demonstrates the directed play of ironic performance. Slowly, the opening monologue continues testing boundaries and reflexively working with audience reactions. After a joke about Mel Gibson's voicemails, where the audience groans in some discomfort, MacFarlane quips with a false understanding and discovery, "*Oh*, you're on *his* side?" This back and forth is important as a frame, not only to mark that MacFarlane is cueing a meta-commentary, but he is also establishing a specific form of reflexive humor, where the audience is called to account for when/why they are laughing and when/why they are groaning in resistance. The mere mention of Mel Gibson elicited an audience response that, when called out, actually made little sense.

It was patterned and predictable and anticipated by convention, and MacFarlane worked to call attention to this. Next, he mentions that the show is to be viewed by nearly a billion people worldwide, "Which is why Jodie Foster will be up here in a bit to ask for her privacy." Here, MacFarlane is playing off Foster's infamous coming out [not really] speech at the Golden Globes earlier that year. He plays off the incongruity of Foster's announcement, as well as the public/private tensions and performative nature of a televised awards event. In this speech, Foster, also, was playing with audience expectations in the conventions of the coming out speech (Goltz 2014), which sought to both speak to and work against the Internet and tabloid machine of contemporary media.

It is through this established mode of self-reflexive comedy, and then what comes next, that I argue MacFarlane's opening number is productively read through a lens of camp—a mainstreamed and masculine form of camp. Read as "Bro camp," this work borrows several devices from traditional modes of queer camp in order to deliver one of the most interesting, sloppy, intentionally poor taste, and yet potentially complicating moments at the Oscars.

A low-tech screen drops from the ceiling, amidst some static and buzzes reflective of low budget sci-fi "tuning in" from far away. On the screen is actor William Shatner performing a version of his infamous film and television *Star Trek* character, Captain James T. Kirk. Shatner speaks with a firm authority and a dry, undermining sarcasm of a disappointed father. He calls out, "Enterprise to Dolby Theatre, come in!" Shatner, speaking from "the future" warns MacFarlane to halt whatever he is about to do on the show, declaring "the show's a disaster!" MacFarlane plays it straight and confused, arguing the show is going just fine. Shatner replies, resolutely in contest, "No, (a bit labored) it's not." He declares he has come from the future to stop him from "destroying the Academy Awards." Shatner reads the headline from the next day's paper, which declares MacFarlane as "The Worst Oscar Host Ever." Shatner confirms, he is *that* bad, stating, "your jokes are tasteless and inappropriate and everyone ends up hating you." Seemingly just as appalled by MacFarlane, he, almost in defeat, asks, "Why couldn't they just get Tina and Amy to host the show? Why can't Tina and Amy host everything …?" The audience howls and applauds, as the "sad loser" MacFarlane interjects, "I know, I'm sorry, they will be hosting next year." Playing the defeated innocent, MacFarlane begs to know what it is that he does wrong. Shatner, perplexed, states, "To begin with, you sing an incredibly offensive song that upsets a lot of actresses in the audience." Still performing the humble innocent, MacFarlane asks what this song is, and Shatner agrees to show him a recording of the telecast "from the future." The camera zooms into Shatner's screen (and thus, into this possible, still-to-be-avoided, future) and Shatner cuts away. Three lively beats of orchestration accompany MacFarlane, "in the screen," in his tuxedo on stage, stepping side to side excitedly, before singing the first line: "We saw your boobs."

This is the context in which the infamous and contentious number emerges. Thus, this set-up places a meta frame on the performance wherein MacFarlane is both knowingly, while also "innocently," performing/witnessing his wrongness and failure, yet this did little to affect the interpretive frames of many critics. Poniewozik argues, "A metajoke about telling an unfunny joke is still an unfunny joke." Other critics of the joke reiterated the "meta" frame of the number did not "excuse" the joke (Davidson), and MacFarlane simply "wanted to have its cake and eat it too" (Donnelly). Thus, many suggest that the context of the failed performance, and the meta-discussion around it, was (in their read) a weak effort at an excuse or an attempted "get out of jail" card for what was about to come. It was a qualifier, in their read, that sought to undercut the backlash of the assault because he showed he knew he was being offensive. Yet, the critics argue this set-up and context does not *change* the assault or insult. The underlying logic is, if someone says, "I know this is wrong" before hitting another person, the preemptive inoculation does not change or alter the assault (as someone is still being hit). While this is true with regard to physical violence this logic does not so easily translate when it comes to the workings of comedy, irony, and communication. As a comedian, he quite literally (and almost exhaustively) worked to establish his pretense of ignorance and failure. MacFarlane, even in the moments before the song, lets us know he is the fool here, and contextualizes the performance as a gross and utter failure. We are literally watching him, as he watches his ignorance play out. While I do see where the meta frame of failure doesn't necessarily make the joke, itself, funnier, it does fundamentally change the joke and opens up a range of ways it can or ought be audienced. This context and pretense, I would argue, should (or at least productively could) work to cue an alternative form of engagement prior to the number even beginning. It both coaches an ironic read and works to cue a broad range of audience positions through several traditional and modified invitations to a camp read. Everything that comes next is in quotes, artificial, and framed as fundamentally wrong. It does alter the communicative action.

Camping masculinity, aesthetic tensions, and playing the gaze

> What kind of gender performance will enact and reveal performativity of gender itself in a way that destabilizes the naturalized categories of identity and desire?
>
> (Butler 1999: 139)

> Camp – whether its source is gay subculture or nongay appropriation – relies for its effect on casual excess, deviant decorum, and libidinal obviousness. (Kleinhans 189)

As the camera zooms into the lowered screen on stage, into a glimpse of the future, we are dropped right into a musical number, an exemplar of camp aesthetics where everything is heightened, overly dramatic, excessive, overstylized, and extended. MacFarlane plays the ludicrous and objectionable song very straight, with a stone-faced, showstopper, and big band presentation. The musical style, his appearance, and his affect are all reminiscent of cool classic Hollywood elegance. You'd think he'd be singing a song from *The Music Man*, a Rodgers and Hammerstein musical, or one of the celebratory and playful opening numbers from past Academy Awards by recurring host Billy Crystal. Everything about it is Hollywood glamour and sophistication, with a rollicking upbeat tempo, citing this year's theme: music in movies. Well, everything except for the crass and juvenile lyrics, which MacFarlane delivers matter of factly. This irreverent incongruity is reflected in much of his previous work, where the basic premise of the film *Ted* is a cuddly child's toy that talks like a sailor and smokes a lot of marijuana. *Ted*, like the "boobs" number, is about extreme juxtaposition, the corruption and perversion of the seemingly pure, wholesome, sterile, and nostalgic. The strategy here is to take something pure and normative and disrupt its ease, corrupt its innocence, and trouble its correctness—offering a slightly less violent and slightly more mainstreamed version of Araki's slap in the face.

As MacFarlane performs, he sings the word "boobs" with little inflection or emphasis, offering only a subtle and understated wink that there is anything off here. His delivery feels almost clinical, if not hollowed, rather than the crassness one would expect with the content of the lyrics. But, the pacing, the repetition, and the story of the song is so incongruous, it completely jars. This is not about subtlety, yet his cooled Disney-charmed affect in the delivery creates a discordant awareness of trying way too hard. Something is just not working. The distance is reminiscent of the famous *Ellen* coming out episode, "The Puppy Episode," when Ellen Morgan was trying to convince herself of her straightness. Running unconvincingly to her male romantic interest Richard, Ellen says, rather flatly "men, men, men, why do I love men sooooo much" before jumping on top of him awkwardly. She follows up this awkward seduction by saying "show me the money, baby" while ripping open his shirt. Following sex, with a stereotypical post-coital cigarette (all a bit heightened, contrived, and never convincing), Richard asks Ellen her secret for why she's such a good lover, and she replies, as if smooth (but not), "I guess I'm just a sucker for man/woman sex." It's a moment that cues an audience in its excess, its wrongness, and all the ways this is simply (but intentionally) not working. Shugart (2001), in an earlier analysis of *Ellen*, examined how the show, and specifically DeGeneres, presented a conspicuous performance of femininity, that was labored, excessive, and incongruous. The incongruity continually works to tip off the audience that femininity was being performed here in a manner that provides a deconstruction of gender and sexuality (102).

Similarly, MacFarlane's performance exposes the "contrived, artificial nature" (Shugart 2001: 108) of some elements of masculinity, cueing a conscious reiteration and performative intervention in a way that feels both juvenile and completely artificial. There is a lack of desire, and a performance of multiple forms of masculinity (the old Hollywood, the slightly queer musical theatre, the playground preadolescent use of "boobs") that rub in tension, yet never fit or work through MacFarlane's body. In the *Ellen* coming out episode, the show uses a device where her awkward sexual encounter is continually intercut with Ellen relaying the events to her friends. With each awkward line ("men men men," "Show me the money," "man/woman sex") her friends are appalled and confused, asking in disbelief, "you said *that*?" It is this distance, this parodied excess, that MacFarlane is cueing, using Shatner as a similar sounding board. Shatner exposes both the inappropriateness of it, but also MacFarlane's failure. Where James T. Kirk is a mythical beacon of masculinity,[5] MacFarlane is failing at every turn. His body is softer, he is in a musical number, he is more primped, his eyebrows waxed, sexually suspect, and under a pretense of lacking any authority, control, or power.

After singing about Meryl Streep, whom we do not see (MacFarlane is gesturing from the stage as if speaking directly to her in the future), there are three pre-taped "reaction shots" from actresses explicitly named in the song. In reaction shot one, Naomi Watts hears her name and faux-instinctively lights up, until he sings "Naomi Watts in *Mulholland Drive*" and her smile turns to a shameful pout. At that moment, in the cut away, a gentleman sitting next to Watts in the shot glances down at her chest. Next, the song references Angelina Jolie in *Gia*, where seeing her "boobs" is said to have "Made us feel excited and alive." His song and dance here is stagey; with a bouncy back and forth side step. His delivery of "excited and alive," again, hits an extended note, and lacks any cue or hint of sexual arousal. He could, based on his oddly flat but perky delivery be singing about cotton candy, a nice spring day, or G-rated Disney-fied romance. As he sings about Anne Hathaway, he trots his arms to the four deliberate beats to "Broke-Back-Moun-Tain" as if riding a horse, seemingly referencing Hollywood singing cowboys like Gene Autry. He lists several more actress/films, and the camera stays on him, where he is deliberately focusing on the stone-faced work of performing, with, again, an absence of erotic pleasure. He concludes the stanza with, "We haven't seen Jennifer Lawrence's boobs *at all*." The words "at all" are held for several notes. In this moment, the camera "cuts" (again, pre-recorded) to Lawrence, who raises her fist to eye-height, offering a little fist pump/cheer—a faux-celebratory triumph—as if to say, "I nailed it." When we cut back to MacFarlane, who we are to assume is singing to Lawrence because of the camera angles, it's the first time we see him smiling, and near amused within the number. Herein, a relation and shared understanding is established in this connection and reaction. In the next verse, there is also a reference to Charlize Theron, which offers the third pre-recorded reaction, on Theron, a mimicry of shame, as she covers her face with her hand and slowly sinks into her chair.

Many critics, again, argued the pre-recorded segments with Theron, Lawrence, and Watts were merely cheap justifications to "get away" with the misogyny of the number. Where some suggested that just because the actresses were in "cahoots" with MacFarlane, it didn't change the offense. Davidson argued, "It just seemed like a way for MacFarlane to make fun of viewers for being prudish and not 'getting it.' (See, the cool girls think that it's funny!) We got it." Others went so far to suggest the women were probably forced or required to "play along," less they be accused of being "humorless bitches" (Rich and Puchko). When considering the pre-recorded segments of the actresses, I would argue it is important to not erase or downplay the agency each of these actresses has in their involvement. While surely there can be a range of ways their pre-recorded shame (or in the case of Lawrence, her triumph) can be interpreted, they chose to be a part of this number. Surely, as three of the most powerful and successful actresses in Hollywood, and ones known for taking strong leading roles (and for fighting for gender equality in compensation and representation), it's dangerous and troubling to infantilize and downplay their involvement or choices. A key question, which emerges with many of the choices that are present in this controversial number, is why? Why would they do this? In fact, the vast majority of the critics all dance around similar questions surrounding the number, asking what is he trying to accomplish, what were they thinking? Why would these three successful actresses film these small cutaways, designed to evoke laughter (and an uneasy laughter), through a seemingly crass and simplistic song and dance, if it overtly and merely works to undermine their craft and integrity as artists? There is an unsettling itch in the camp cue, the offness and slightly wrongness of the number, yet the critics opted to indict MacFarlane and not engage the hints and whispers any further.

Reading MacFarlane's performance of masculinity through a "bro camp" lens, there is little or no insight or revelation by the dozens of articles and responses arguing "sexism." There is no question, MacFarlane was invoking sexism, but the articles failed to step past that dangerous trap where the invocation of sexism, the doing of sexism, is purely and wholly only "sexist." Each of the cutaways of the three actresses was an explicit play on how they were being framed, positioned by the camera, in an ironic performance of shame/triumph. It was an ironic performance of victimhood that made its performance visible. Its distanced and playful self-awareness offered the opportunity for audiences to rethink the male gaze and the positioning of the female, as well as the relationship between the actresses and MacFarlane, the role of the camera, and the positioning of the assumed viewer.

Jamie Lee Curtis and Jane Fonda, along with many others, expressed negative reactions, believing the number was sexist because you would never see that type of attention and objectification paid to the male body. I agree that the way the number was constructed was about women, and it was intentionally so, but I think this criticism deserves some close attention. When thinking about nude male bodies in film, there is surely (and sadly) a lack of penises. This is a valid critique, yet the fascination with the penis is not something the media or even the Academy Awards has shied away from. In the film that won him a 2012 Oscar nomination, Michael Fassbender "played an emotionally distant sex addict and went full frontal nude for Steve McQueen's drama *Shame*, which earned the film an NC-17 rating and, ironically, far more press than it would have gotten otherwise … his immense talent has almost been overshadowed by incessant talk about his member" (*Michael Fassbender's …*). At the Golden Globes Awards, a year before MacFarlane's number, George Clooney famously joked "Really Michael, honestly, you can play golf like this [shaking his waist side to side] with your hands behind your back." While not arguing that the male body is equal or parallel in how it is culturally represented via media, I am marking how the male actor's anatomy is also a site of much discussion and intrigue by audiences, media, and the Internet.

Jane Fonda, after the 2013 Oscars said, "I agree with someone who said, 'If they want to stoop to that, why not list all the penises we've seen?'" (West). Answering her call, it did not take long for a video to be created and uploaded by "CheersKevin" titled "We Saw your Junk" that lists notable male penis visibility in film. The video, while in many ways paralleling MacFarlane's number, has certain key differences that help to identity key tensions in the original. Most notably, MacFarlane's number avoids any sense of evaluation or assessment of the bodies exposed. He does not say more than mark the presence of "boobs," never using descriptive or evaluative language (actually the sterilized opposite), yet "CheersKevin" most clearly puts on a "that's gross" face when he mentions seeing Harvey Keitel's "junk." Next, while the "junk" number is stylistically the same in terms of music, pacing, and genre, the absence of the cutaways to the actresses (or in this case, male actors) removes an important interruption. The faux-shame and discomfort commenting on MacFarlane is central to how a camp read and a complex ironic tension is called for. Additionally, the use of the word "junk" in the song simply operates differently than "boobs." It sounds like the word a straight man would choose to comfortably describe his own genitals, or those of another man "I don't want to see your junk" or "Get your junk away from me." "Boobs" has an adolescent quality to it, that is a little silly, and when spoken by a man performs/cites a specific form of "bro" masculinity. Perhaps a more appropriate equivalent would be "We Saw Your Peen" or "Dong" or even "Wiener." What does come across in both videos, that is incredibly important, is the sexual ambiguity of the singers. Just as "CheersKevin" may or may not be gay or sexually excited by male penis, as it is unclear how he feels other than displeasure with Harvey Keitel being naked, MacFarlane walks a similar line. There is matter-of-factness, along with a show tunes flare, in both performances that resists a fully straight read. And, it is a musical number.

On MacFarlane's third verse, about a dozen tuxedo-clad male dancers trot onto stage, performing behind him in a choreographed sequence of step touches, jumps, turns, and jazz hands. Their faces are bright, smiling, and doubling down on the reference to old Hollywood pizazz. MacFarlane then breaks from the song, announcing "Ladies and Gentleman. The Gay Men's Chorus of Los Angeles!" The curtain behind him rises, and a swelling "Ahhhhh" of dozens of male voices is heard. MacFarlane turns to perform the role of choir director to a booming multipart choral repetition of the line "we saw your boobs" over and over in a swelling finale. MacFarlane turns and sings the dramatic final note. Like much in the number, it posed more questions than definitive answers. Davidson argues, "And who knows what the Los Angeles Gay Men's Chorus thought that it was doing by serving as MacFarlane's backup singers; one does wonder what the rhetorical point was meant to be."

Perhaps, not surprisingly, a homophobic critique of MacFarlane emerged in this segment. Following the song, MacFarlane, who toys with and was once rumored (though he denied this) to be gay, himself, cuts into the applause and clarifies for the audience, "Just so you know, I'm not *actually* a member of that chorus, I was just joining in the end there." He holds a smile, performing a self-aware ironic refusal that undercuts his claim. Shatner, in playful condescension of a hard truth, replies "Ohhhhhhh, trust me. In July 2015 *you join* the chorus." As a punchline, MacFarlane's cluelessness is, once again, unmasked through Shatner, the symbolic pillar of hegemonic masculinity. The audience laughs for several seconds, and MacFarlane lets the joke sit for a minute (a joke he set up for himself) before "nervously" (performed) changing the subject. Here, Shatner, as some towering figure of hyper masculinity, once again works to undercut and discipline MacFarlane's masculine performance. The ironic read of MacFarlane's future outing or the presence of the Gay Male Chorus is not to argue that gay men cannot take part in sexism or female objectification, but it cues the intentional presence of queerness, parody, and camp play with gender and sexuality. MacFarlane's gaze, and how he is positioned as audience to these texts, as well as the actresses, is troubled and disrupted from traditional norms of hegemonic masculinity. As a reading strategy, irony was cued in his playful and exaggerated resistance of his gender and sexuality, much as irony was cued at the top of the number when Shatner warns him his hosting is "offensive." That pretense, that awareness as a frame constructed prior to the "boobs number," opens up the space for an ironic read and a camp consideration of the juvenile "bro" masculinity that MacFarlane's work often plays with and against. "The result is a kind of humor often dismissed as adolescent. And it is" (Kleinhans 192).

We saw your "ism" and the struggle for artistry

There is also a dimension to the performance that I believe was, perhaps the most productively resistant, and it is likely what strongly contributed to the most angered responses. The Academy Awards, as a telecast and a process, tends to take itself very seriously. It's self-congratulatory back patting of its own integrity and artistry is something that has soured many mainstream viewers from the show for years—a trend that bringing MacFarlane in to host was designed to address. This was his rhetorical weight as the host, much as Chris Rock's was centered around engaging the #OscarsSoWhite controversy. MacFarlane makes films and television shows that audiences go to see, appealing to a base juvenile crowd, and has a reputation (like Gervais) of always thumbing his nose at Hollywood elites. There is something so deeply irreverent in him naming the presence of nudity in artistic films, juxtaposed with the sophisticated and refined viewer who is not supposed to speak of it. It is "tasteful nudity" (Rush *et al.*). It serves the narrative. It tells a story. It's about integrity and vision and artistry. This is the pretense around Oscar films. However, only in that room does that story hold up. Prior to the film being made there are long and extensive contract negotiations of exactly what parts of the body, at what angle, in what lighting will be shown for how long. It is a business and long before MacFarlane uttered a lyric on Oscar night, Theron, Watts, and every other actress in that song has had to sit through meetings and negotiations regarding the choice to expose parts of their body. It might be artistic, but it's an artistic business. Halle Berry famously received a $500,000 bonus for going topless in *Swordfish*. There seems to be something normative in the tacit expectation that we pretend it's not there. In terms of the news media, whenever there is nudity in a film, reporters harp on the question, promoters want it discussed (and advertised) in the press interviews as a selling point to market the film. It's not the crude and direct, "Do we see your boobs," but more "tasteful" inquiries like, "You have a series of love scenes where you are nude in the film. Was that challenging?" As for audiences, since the advent of the Internet, there is no limit to the amount of websites, Tumblrs, and databases that screen cap, stream, and discuss at extensive length nudity in film. Thus, there is a larger culture here that seems to be ignored in the critical responses to MacFarlane, and the satiric possibilities of MacFarlane's discussion of female nudity in Hollywood. He is not inventing a discussion but reflecting it. Davidson strongly indicts MacFarlane, saying "The women were not showing their bodies to amuse Seth MacFarlane but, rather, to do their jobs. Or did they just *think* they were doing serious work? You girls think you're making art, the Academy, through MacFarlane, seemed to say, but all we – and the "we" was resolutely male—really see is that we got you to undress." While resisting a range of aesthetic cues to trouble this linear read, it also plays into the narrative of the Academy Awards as sacred art, where the mention of the bodies that are negotiated, marketed, and exploited (but then not to be talked about) is profane.

Considering bodily citation, there simply were limits and obstacles to what MacFarlane was able to accomplish in this number, even though he worked to produce a camp-laden aesthetic with a range of productive tensions. MacFarlane, who is most known for writing and producing animated series (or the animated bear *Ted*), has found greater freedom through the art of animation. He is capable of speaking voice through the drawn body of cartoons that do not carry the weight of meanings his physical body conjures and cites. As a body on stage, rather than an animated rendering of a person, his humor is constrained. There is an invulverability tied to the white male body on stage (Peterson 124) that always, in some ways, will comfortably be positioned within discourse (128)—even if he works to expose its arrogances and foulness. There are limits to what MacFarlane, through his body, can accomplish, and there are additional obstacles he may have not fully accounted for. Consider, hypothetically, how delightfully uncomfortable the past Oscar host Ellen

DeGeneres would have been singing "We Saw Your Boobs," perhaps playing on tropes of the aggressive older lesbian. Or, consider past host Whoopi Goldberg, whose sexuality is always a bit playful and queer, tackling the number. Her body and persona would likely reshape meanings to be more about comradery, if not surprise ("Molly, we saw your boobs, Girl"). If Tina and Amy had stepped into the routine, their bodies and personas would have immediately taken an audience to a more willing and generous feminist read, where the "we" in "We Saw Your Boobs" would not so easily slip into a male gaze that so simply and only objectifies. Yet, MacFarlane, in his white cis male body, carries certain citational elements—alongside his celebrity persona—that redirected how it was received (even if he offered multiple cues to read otherwise). Through the cutaways, the camp musical aesthetic, the gay chorus, the gender play, the sexual ambiguity, and the broad frame of failure—the critics still chose to locate the sexism at play and concretize it as a defining *sexist act*.

Herein marks a core irony. Remember, what was argued as the most offensive was how the female actresses, their work and their artistic contributions were merely reduced to a body part, a breast shot, without any regard for the larger context in which these topless actresses were operating within. "Ha, ha, ha, ha, breasts – it's not like women in film do other things, right?" (Lyons). Feminist lawyer Gloria Allred told *The Daily Beast*, "It's one thing to be topless and to have that in the context of the film, for a purpose in a particular scene for a particular reason. It's another to take it out of context and just focus on women's breasts" (Grove).

However, just as the female breasts were stripped of context and seized upon in ways that offended, this is not unlike how critics have responded to MacFarlane. There was a whole production of aesthetic complexities to factor in and wrestle with, as this section has detailed, and yet, critics performed their own reductive song and dance of "we saw your sexism." To simplify the number to mere endorsement of female objectification, ignoring the presence of ironic cues, fails to factor the aesthetic layering at work—fails to consider the complexity or artistry of his humor. This is not to claim the sketch was either good or bad, effective or not, so much as to argue the terms by which the humor is being categorized are overly simplified and reductive. Beyond self-mockery as a potential read (where MacFarlane plays off the worst fears of what he might do to the Oscars), he also draws attention to a masculinist culture that does obsess on nudity in film, female objectification, the reduction of complex artistic works to "boob shots" and this collision of "high brow" cinema with "low brow" audiencing—the very tension and Academy disconnect with younger mainstream viewers he was brought on to help address. Perhaps this was no more visible than the following day, where dozens of articles on *Huffington Post* were lambasting MacFarlane's sexism, yet were placed directly next to a main page article reporting, "Anne Hathaway's 'nipples' on The Oscars Red Carpet Are Super Distracting (PHOTOS)." Not exactly "Congratulations Anne Hathaway for your 2013 Academy Award and artistic achievement in *Les Miserables*." When asked what MacFarlane was attempting to satirize, one need only look a few inches down on the screen.

Hegemonic masculinity and the boundaries of a camp reading

> Jefferies then joked about fat women, lying women, beautiful but boring women, dumb women, and made plenty of references to different types of women he had sex with. He also admitted that he'd like to have sex with a 16-year-old.
>
> (Scaunich)

Given my treatment of MacFarlane, as well as Tosh at the opening of this chapter, one might assume that this project is moving towards the argument that many, if not all, performances of hegemonic masculinity warrant a "bro camp" engagement. While Tosh and MacFarlane are presenting comedic work that overtly and consistently cues an audience to an alternative form of reception, it is not my argument that all work is worthy or benefits from this framework. While Chapter 3 worked to explicitly trouble any notion of a correct or uniform read of a comedic text, camp is not solely and completely in the eye of the beholder. Rather it exists in tension between the camp audience and a form of coaching enacted through the comedian. Some masculinist work, if not most work, falls short of justifying/calling for a camp engagement. To explore this position, we will turn to the stand up comedy of up and coming Australian comedian Jim Jefferies, and most specifically his stand up comedy special *Bare* from 2014.

Jefferies, 38 at the time of the special, stands 5′10″ tall, with an average build, short dark hair, a brown leather button up shirt and blue jeans. His overall presentation of self is quintessential "everyman"—a mix between the working class vibe of Kevin James and the more frat/dude bad boy image of Dane Cook. His body would exemplify the "dad bod," yet the advertising for the comedy show presents a slightly more toned and muscular Jefferies on the cover, naked, covering his genitals with a teddy bear. His thumbs are covering the stuffed animal's eyes, with each index finger pointing down, framing his "package." The copy on the promotion, just left of his crotch reads "You can't unsee this."

In Jefferies's comedy special, he spends the first twenty-five minutes of his set discussing opinions and experiences specific to gender, heterosexual relationships, and his family (specifically his girlfriend and son). He introduced his girlfriend by saying, "I got my girlfriend pregnant after knowing her for two months," to which the audience applauds with a loud masculine hooting—the audience equivalent of a "high five, bro" rather than a "congratulations, dad." He nods his head and takes a half committed bow. He follows up with, "She's a nice girl and I love her in a way, sure," dryly indifferent, as he paces back and forth in a conversational stream of consciousness style. There is not the effort to hold the audiences' attention after each line, enlisting smiles or pauses to shape the meanings. Rather, there is a sense that the joke ends with the utterance and he allows laughter without an effort to shape its direction. By introduction, his girlfriend is nameless and passive, but continues to be the focus of a few quick jokes. For example, he comments that his girlfriend is "shit at telling stories, and I'm awesome at telling stories, so it really bothers me when she talks." Again, the meaning is left untroubled, wherein his degradation of this woman is untouched as the punchline—an offering that the boisterous audience seems to eagerly consume. He soon references that his girlfriend used to be a model, but then quickly qualifies to the audience, without a beat, "I'm not bragging. I didn't get the model years." He says the line with a subtle squint that hints at confession and regret/loss. Jefferies then talks about back when his girlfriend was a model, she once dated a center for the Miami Heat. Upon finding out this information, he describes the mental process a man goes through upon hearing that the "mother of your child" dated a basketball player. He narrates, "the first thing is, that's why your c*nt's so fucked up!" The audience screams in aggressive, hooting, audibly male, support. Again, the comment marks the close of the joke, and he leaves the audience to take the utterance untroubled. Jefferies is excessive in his use of the "c-word" to both describe women, as well as refer to specific parts of their bodies—a result and assumed excuse based upon his being Australian.[6] Still, there is a constant objectification and dehumanization of his girlfriend throughout the set. For example, when she is discussing her "model days," back when she was having sex with Madonna and Dennis Rodman, he screams, "Shut the fuck up! Just shut the fuck up! You are the mother of my child!" Relationally, his unnamed girlfriend is enlisted throughout his humor to position him in a range of positions that work to reify his commitments to hegemonic masculinity, while simultaneously denying her voice or agency.

Beyond the language, his positioning of women within his set does not appear to be doing anything with sexism, but merely relying on it for his identity production and audience constitution. As a frustrated female audience member from one of his Melbourne performances wrote, "His jokes against women were delivered with passion and conviction, and sections of the crowd consumed them like hungry wolves" (Scaunich). For example, he opens a joke by marking how women only make "70 percent of men in the workplace, and of course that's disgusting." The joke turns on the punchline, however, as he continues "how dare women earn so much!" The execution is straight, non-ironic, and delivered as a statement expecting endorsement. The line is awarded with loud and thunderous applause from the audience in support, with noticeable male voices in the room hooting above the rest. He follows up this joke, marking that he will be saying a lot of jokes tonight he "doesn't actually mean, but this is something I am really passionate about. Women DO NOT deserve to make as much money as men in the workplace, I'm sorry!" There is no cue or suggestion that this is an ironic position, but rather a smug sense of satisfaction in a manner that "takes a stand"—a masculinist manifesto reifying an untroubled claim to authority and power. He argues he is not a misogynist, and is not claiming women do not work as hard, but insists they do not deserve to earn as much money. He follows out the joke, suggesting women do not deserve to make that much money because (get ready for it ...) men are supposed to pay for everything all the time. He uses the example where, if a guy "parties hard," he wakes up having spent $5,000—implying he either paid for a prostitute or a stripper. When a woman wakes up and says, "Oh my God, I partied so hard," he jokes that she will have made $5,000—the implication being she either stripped or sold herself for sex. His set up marks how women are paid less and appears to be troubled by this point. However, his unexpected turn to arguing that women still make too much is never upset, reflected upon, or troubled, but supported in a linear directed set that went on for several frustrating minutes. Jefferies elaborates that he knows that there *are* women in the room who pay for themselves, to which he tosses out the punchline, "Don't think we don't appreciate the uglies. We do." Furthermore, as the men in the audiences hooted in support, Jefferies offered no corrective, pause, or effort to shift the meaning in that moment. He merely cites and reaffirms textbook hegemonic masculine meanings without trouble or contest.

Jefferies continues to dig into the financial disparities of being an (assumed cis heterosexual) male in a relationship with a woman, arguing that Valentine's Day and Mother's Day are all about men buying women presents. In reference to Valentine's Day, he suggests the holiday is really a question of, "How much money do I need to spend today so that you don't act like a c*nt?" When thinking about what he wants for Father's Day, he replies, "How about for 24 hours you don't touch my fucking money?" When reflecting on what kind of holiday men would want, he posits an "anal sex day." He then further considers this, admitting that anal sex, for him, is not like it appears in porn. "The thing is, is you can't smell porn," he says, now seated in a leather chair, his legs crossed tight, as if a bit fearful. He makes a face that hints at disgust and discomfort, with a performed artifice of trying to be tactful. Unlike porn, where he narrates that women seem so happy, "the experience I have had in my own life has been vastly different." It seems like, for a moment, Jefferies might be building to a critique of the unrealistic, offensive norms of straight porn when a woman is positioned purely for the pleasure of the male. He continues "my experience [with anal sex] has been a lot of crying (he pauses for a laugh) and while that can help you cum at times, it's not what you want for every day." Rather than disrupt, he doubles down on a punchline that suggests his occasional pleasure and arousal by inflicting pain, and it is here where he allows the joke to land and to concretize. After several more minutes of discussing anal sex in porn, he concludes that even though he does not like anal sex that much, men like anal sex because "we know you fucking hate it!." His face is stilled, unreflexive and resolute on the delivery of this line, lacking emotion, and carrying the certainty and down speak that indicates the "final word" on this topic.

The manner in which systems of sexism are engaged in Jefferies stand up marks a strong example of where hegemonic masculinity is being reproduced and cited in ways that fail to invite a camp or layered audience engagement. His treatment of women is not only degrading, but he positions women as merely sexual objects, mothers of children, and gold diggers. He asserts a highly sexual, dominating, individualistic, breadwinner construction of his masculine self (and the constituted male audience) that is assumed to be heterosexual and connected as a "we" in this misogynist positioning of women.

So, why linger on Jefferies? I came to Jefferies because he, along with Tosh, MacFarlane, and a handful of additional comedians like C.K. and Maher, regularly pop up under web searches for the most sexist and misogynist comedians. Yet, when studying the work of these comedians, there were those whose work was couched in a complex negotiation of meanings, and those that lacked critical reflexivity. When I started watching *Bare*, I was taken aback. I had wrongly assumed this level of crude and uncomplicated enlisting of sexism was simply no longer acceptable in the mainstream. It reminded me of the foul and obnoxious stand up of Andrew "Dice" Clay and Sam Kinison in the 1980s—work that if my students were to view now might view as ironic because its reliance of sexism is so extreme. One might even look at a few moments from this set and consider, for a moment, the utility of "bro camp" as a frame of analysis. However, I would argue the text does not warrant such consideration. This is due to an absence of codes and cues that would coach a camp engagement. I chose Jefferies because, while these codes were mostly absent with regards to gender, they were present and activated elsewhere in his work. Jefferies is quite able to push, extend, flip and trouble meanings when he opted to (and when it came to sexism, he simply opted not to). For example, in a relatively benign set about when a household pet dies, you go out and replace the pet so the pet's owner won't notice. He then extends this strategy to the scenario of a child dying and contemplating going out and getting "a replacement child." He clarifies, that it is "Easier if you're Black or Asian." The audience responds with booming applause and laughter, clearly assigning some troubling meanings and demonstrating approval through their response. Jefferies interjects, "Boston no. no. No! Shut up! I will not put up with racism at my shows, okay? I'm not saying, 'cause they look the same!' I'm saying 'cause they are easier to purchase.'" The joke is followed by loud and supportive applause, now redirected. Again, the joke is uneasy and uncomfortable, and he plays with this tension with the audience. Here, he's working with racisms in the set, which feels significantly more complex and negotiated than the sexisms he's been dropping left and right over the first twenty-five minutes of his show. He does not merely allow the reification of racism, but his attention to hegemonic meanings is not extended to gender which is a cornerstone of his set.

Perhaps most frustrating about Jefferies' stand up is the moments where he chooses to offer a meta frame, trouble meanings, and challenge his audience's understandings (and when he does not). Later in the set, he explicitly warns the audience that some are going to get offended, as he is venturing into the controversial part of the show (as if everything prior was peachy keen). Yet, following this warning he launched into a very smart, mostly funny, and satirical set challenging American policies and cultural narratives on gun control. The humor in the section is quite hilarious, insightful, and for the first time, it's clear to me why Jefferies (in spite of the way he enlists untroubled sexism) has achieved his level of popularity. He calls out the 10 percent in the room who are seething and just "fucking furious" for his comments. He stops to list a few reasons why this 10 percent in the audience are mad. One, "I am making good points," and two, "I'm foreign and that's pissing you off." He adopts his best "Murica" accent and parodies the line, "If you don't like it go home!" a few times before interjecting smugly in his own voice, "Your first amendment means I can say your second amendment sucks dicks." Next, he mocks people yelling, "You can't change the second amendment," pointing out, "yes … you can. It's an AMENDMENT." In this set, his authoritative "bro" masculinity is being mobilized to challenge a set of logics in an effective way, rather than simply reproduce its performative dominance. He further breaks down the arguments of safe gun owners, and the limited logics of "responsible ownership." Referencing the "if only they had a gun logic," with regard to recent school shootings, he asks the audience to think back to that substitute teacher that everyone would incessantly mock and tease—the sad single woman driving the Volkswagen. He leapt into a quick line of cruel mockery, implying "we all" had that teacher who we told would never get married, would die alone, and who burst into tears as she ran out of class. Then he followed this up with, "Ya, give that c*nt a gun." Again, with all the care and qualification he builds into his set for the gun detractors, there is no hint, wink, or encoded pause that suggests his use of sexism is anything other than functional in his logic.

After moving systematically through a range of limited arguments put out there by pro-gun Americans, challenging their logic and reasoning every step of the way, he returns to a meta frame. He acknowledges those marginalized or implicated in his critique, and attends to them, even as he mocks them. What becomes clear with the racial joke, and then the gun control set, is Jefferies is capable of pulling at meanings, using irony to complicate through humor, and enlisting satire to push and trouble social norms and values. He just opts not to do this with regard to his treatment of hegemonic masculinity. In terms of his oft-referenced girlfriend, he continues to refer to her as "the mother of my child," and even makes jokes about how one day his son will watch this routine, to hear his father discuss wiping cum off his mother's face. The positioning of women in his set are merely objects and prostitutes (he mocks Madonna's "muscular vagina" and talks at length about strippers). He positions himself and his audience as a "we." He assumes a shared heterosexuality, a sexual power over women, a financial burden incurred by "gold digging" women, an assumed authoritative position, and an untroubled command. When discussing his son, he says he does not care if his son is gay or straight, but just hopes he gets laid a lot. His body and his text, as well as the constitution of the audience, present an untroubled model of "bro" humor—a masculinist and misogynist mode that relies on and reifies the citation of male dominance without complication or contestation. Much like Shatner at the Sheen Roast (as discussed in previous chapters), he is enlisting sexism, standing on its shoulders, but not offering a critical intervention or disruption. Its foundation remains untroubled and naturalized. His doing of sexism is hegemonic and uncomplicated.

Seriously, take a hint: Active audience coaching

> Subversive parodic performances may be a particularly effective way to denaturalize these hallmarks [of gender], especially in cases of women and men performing femininity and masculinity, respectively.
>
> (Shugart 2001: 108)

> Low camp deliberately celebrates bad taste and often intentionally offends aesthetic and social sensibilities in order to make a statement.
>
> (Kleinhans 189)

This chapter explores the performative complexity of three contemporary and controversial privileged-bodied comedians, Daniel Tosh, Seth MacFarlane, and Jim Jefferies. Engaging their humor, specifically Tosh's "Good for You" parody and MacFarlane's Oscar musical number, this chapter set forth to explore and articulate a mainstream form of gender parody conceptualized as "bro camp." The concept becomes instructive in helping to trace how both of these comedians are coaching and coding discourses of sexism in ways that are performatively distinct from merely reifying sexist logics. By placing their work alongside comic Jim Jefferies, whose satire and investigation of meanings works to productively trouble other systems of meaning, but lazily relies on sexist logics without complication, the chapter sought to draw a stark contrast. Where Tosh and MacFarlane are troubling the discourses of hegemonic masculinity through a series of aesthetic and performative interruptions and interventions, Jefferies wrongness and bad taste fails to denaturalize gender or cue an alternative or resistant read.

Returning to comedian Eddie Murphy, and the question posed at the close of the previous chapter, can I read Murphy's homophobic stand up as ironic, Murphy as the fool, and his work as an interrogation of heterosexist ignorance? Sure. It is possible. It could also be possible to put on a camp interpretive frame and seek out hints, slips, and moments of failure and excess that might, maybe, assist in this process. Thus, I am not going to argue that his work, or the work of Jefferies *can't* be camp, but rather I would suggest it fails to justify a camp read. The meanings seem concretized rather than troubled. The audience laughs comfortably *with* oppressive meanings, and without the pause, dis-ease, or tension from Murphy to coach the laughing *at* oppressive meanings. It falls short of cueing or coaching the camp eye, both in terms of camp aesthetics, but also in terms of the ever-important wink. Camp is always a matter of specific coding practices (Bergman 94), and while camp is often attracted to the most questionable texts (Halperin 232), "wherein bad taste is celebrated as good taste" (Kleinhans 189), this must be accompanied by a wink of the excessive, the falseness, and the failure that emerges in the exposure of gender's artifice.

So, Murphy's stand up is not something I would read ironically. Yet, I will continue to explore alternative modes and positions to engage/navigate his humor, for laughter in the face of his extreme homophobia is a mode of survival and an act of resistance. After all, from its inception, "Camp does not do away with the dominant society, but rather finds a way to live within it" (Bergman 108). I look at Murphy's ignorance from a distance, willfully play with sexualized and queer meanings that I map onto his tight leather pants and his almost-too-good dips into feminine mockery. I joke with friends on city street corners when hailing cabs, to "Puuuuo Ovvveh," re-appropriating his gay mockery as our own joke, our own property, and I take pleasure in the hypocrisy of his very famous arrest for soliciting a trans female prostitute—placing his "authentic masculinity" into question and quotes. In camp, we take and make apparent the core understanding of "life as theatre" (Kleinhans 187), and Tosh and MacFarlane are extending and citing this performative mode. Their engagements with sexism are significantly different than Jefferies, and there is a value, importance, and potential in mining and engaging those differences. Sure, placing all of these comedians under the banner of sexist is one way to order this content, but there are different ways of assigning meaning to this work. As Shugart and Waggoner argue, surely there can be normative functions, but mainstream camp can be critical and playful, "infused with critical promise" (3). To paraphrase RuPaul, there is value in mining the subversive play of camp, rather than only investing in the seriousness of identity. When looking holistically at the ways they use the body, the pause, and the destabilization of masculine codes, (rather than merely what is spoken), a more complex analysis is called forth. However, when the audience goes right for the offense and insists on pausing upon this singular element, then the joke, the comedian, and the complexity of this communicative moment will always be reduced to the "boobs."

Notes

1 Cleto extends this discussion, arguing, "on the other hand, we find a series of oppositions whose finality is the description of camp in its operative modes, and of its representational effects within culture; camp as sensibility vs. camp style and taste; camp as fully cultural and inauthentic vs. camp as their opposite nature, and expressive authenticity; camp as fully modern vs. camp as metahistorical; camp as a sign of homosexuality vs. camp as an aesthetical dimension; camp as a secret, closeted code vs. camp as flaunting, flamboyant, histrionic; camp vs. private, seclusive vs. camp as community experience; camp as index of visibility and homosexual expression vs. camp as invisibility strategy (the acting required in order to pass for straight) and homosexual (self)-reticence; camp as strategy of homosexual integration into

heterosexist culture vs. camp as subversive of that culture's very assumptions; camp as aristocratic vs. camp as democratic; camp as ironic mode vs. camp as parody; camp as apolitical and conservative vs. camp as political, and progressive" (23).

2 Marcie Frank marks how post-Stonewall, about a decade after Sontag published "Notes," there is a shift in how Sontag negotiates the relationship between camp sensibility of politicism (178–9).

3 The numbering of the listed "Notes" by Sontag was designed to spoof more definitive texts that are antithetical to camp (Bergman 92).

4 The teen apocalyptic trilogy provides a brash, biting, and violent assault of conventions of heteronormative narrative. For more about Araki's form of camp, as a queer critique of heteronormativity and temporality, see Goltz 2012.

5 Kate Bornstein, in "My Gender Workbook" jokes that if you answer every question with the most rigid, cis, and normative possibility, her quiz tells you that you are "James T. Kirk"—mocking the extremity of his masculine performance.

6 While there is still a strong resistance and offense assigned to the word "cunt," it has a range of uses in the Australian context that some argue is more acceptable than in the U.S. While it can be thought of as synonymous to endearing terms such as "mate", and circulates more regularly in Australian speech (Esposito), it still carries degrading meanings for women (Scaunich).

5 Conclusion

Racial humor and performing white innocence

> Chelsea Handler: I'm a comedian. What am I allowed to say, what am I not allowed to say?
>
> Rev Al Sharpton: I think you have to be able to laugh at yourself without making your culture the joke. There's a fine line there and I think that people ought to be sensitive to where that line is.
>
> (Chelsea Does … Racism)

"Racial humor" is one of the, if not the, most complicated and delicate forms of comedy. It is often smack dab in the center of the most notorious comic controversies. The practice often traces, defines, and questions the cultural limits of what words can or cannot be said, by whom, in what context, for which audience, and for what purpose. One need look no further than the quintessential example of how violence and historical weight can be encapsulated into a single word, the "N-word," and the ongoing cultural discussion of whether the word should ever be uttered, and if so by who, and when, and where? Talking about race is dangerous, and differently dangerous depending on whose body and in what context. Telling jokes about race is even more fraught. Navigating the line between a joke being "about race" and a joke being "racist"—these are treacherous waters that our mainstream cultural discourse is simply incapable of navigating with much complexity. When thinking about the risks of racial humor, the easier (or at least culturally safer) answer would be to adopt a framework that helps to mitigate or bypass clear areas of risk: leave the race jokes to persons of color. Period. Although boxy and essentialized, such an approach works to privilege marginalized positions in racial discourse and err on the side of audiences feeling more at ease. However, that might also be the very reason the approach to racial humor needs to be expanded.

Dick Gregory was one of the first mainstreamed African American comedians in the U.S. to perform for both white and Black audiences. It's been said, Gregory, "Could turn racial turmoil into a fun evening. He was so sweetly and serenely reasonable, so nonthreatening, so downright amiable, that you didn't realize until you were walking out of a club that he had heightened your sense of civil rights" (Nachman 481). Although seemingly tame in this historical context his work was groundbreaking and bold. "There is no problem so serious that it cannot be leavened with humor. This is Dick Gregory's credo" (484). However, Gregory walked a tricky line between exposing racism without calling out his audience—a necessity for the time, for his success, and for his comedy to land. It was the difficult balance of not making "fun of himself, or whites, but tried to get both sides to laugh at themselves" (485). Although marked as a master of this impossible dance, the constraints of what he could accomplish led him to leave comedy. He decided "It was too easy … The world, he decided, needed to hear more candor, a harsher, more urgent message" (482). Comedy in the mid 1960s was limited in terms of what it could do, the meanings it could carry, the political work it could accomplish, so Gregory moved to activism. Yet changes in racial comedy emerged, from mainstream assimilationist voices like Cosby to raw and political work from Pryor. These voices were in community with white comics who took on the racial turmoil facing the country, such as Lenny Bruce and George Carlin. Since that time, the topic of race has been front and center for many comedians of color and some white comedians. The burden of speaking about race, of always being raced, still weighs on the non-white body in contemporary U.S. culture.

Historically, the world of mainstream comedy has been dominated by white comedians, and thus white voices had greater access to shaping racial comedy. Common wisdom began to shift to an understanding that, perhaps, racial comedy was best handled by non-white comedians, and helped usher in a call for more diverse voices in mainstream comedy—a call that remains not fully answered. Yet, to argue that comedians of color are the only ones accountable to cultural racisms (and should primarily be tasked with dealing with race), while white comedians are free to talk about anything but race, seems dangerously simple and limited. This chapter forges into the messy limitations and potentials of racial critique in comedy as enacted through the white body—a central site of the comic controversy—tracing a range of postures, pitfalls, and possibilities through a handful of contemporary white comedians. To begin, I turn to the controversial opening monologue of Louis C.K. on the 40th season's final episode of Saturday Night Live in 2015.

C.K. steps out to uproarious applause, wearing a simple black t-shirt and jeans. Facing the applause he awkwardly raises his arms half way, accepting the applause with performed awkwardness and humility. "Thank you, uh stop, um Hi." He quickly introduces the final episode of the season and launches right into the set up for his monologue. "I was born in 1967, so I grew up in the '70s, so I'm not racist." His tone is uneasy, rising higher at points, but lands with a punctuation of declarative certainty. The comment sits for a beat, and a trickle of laughter emerges from the audience. C.K. keeps his smile steady, hinting awareness as the hesitant laugh emerges. He then raises his finger, qualifying, "However …" and a brief but more confident laugh comes from the audience, as they begin to pair up meanings and rhythms with C.K. He takes his time in these few moments, working to establish a set of foundational meanings. "However, I do have mild racism, (building a playfully defensive argument). It's the best I could do coming out of the seventies, because it was a very racist decade. People said racist things all the time, and nobody got offended …" Here his voice moves upwards, as he starts to make his case, explain his position, and contextualize his self-labeling in a posture of white nervousness. He works at a rate that is quick, not looking for a laugh, nor allowing his pause, but building. "The *only* time someone got offended when you said something racist is when they would say, 'Hey! You interrupted me! *I* was saying something racist!" Here he allows space for the laugh, both in pause, but through a vocal and physical shift in the "Hey, you interrupted …" persona he switched into. The laugh is a bit hesitant, uneasy, not fully allowing comfort or full audience release. He interrupts the medium laugh and pushes through, "So I have mild racism. It's benign, it's not aggressive, it's not even negative racism, it's mild racism." The audience is quiet, but he is also allowing little space for them to enter. He quickly pivots, "Let me give you an example. Like if I go to a pizza place I've never been to before, and it's run by four Black women, I'll go like, uh … hmmm." His performance is of a thoughtful and contemplative gesture, not fully shock or surprise, but a less extreme "who would have thought?" In the "hmmm" the audience finds their laugh and he leaps on top in defense excitedly, "See, it's *very* mild! It's *extremely* mild racism!" The audience release happens here, and the laugh is loud, large and seemingly unhesitant. Now that he and the audience are negotiating some understanding, he pushes on, marking how this would be weird, unless "it's called Four Black Girls' Pizza" and that was "the whole point of the place." He extends his explication of "mild racism" to when he finds out his doctor is from China or India, "I'll think, well *good*" as he puts his hands on his hips and nods his head with comfort. "Good, *more* of that, why not?" His final example is in a mini mart, late at night, where he imagines a young man walking up behind him, wearing a hoodie. If the man is white, C.K., narrates, "I'll think, Oh, he's an athlete. If he's Black, unless he has a big smile on his face, then I become mildly racist." He then performs his "mild racism" with a nervous, over compensating smile, nervously spewing, "That's fine. Everything's FINE. Nothings gonna happen, of course, I'm fine." He adopts a "shame on me" tone with his hands on his hips, "why did I even think that for a moment." As he performs this, he holds an aware smile on his face, and the audience giggles with him, but with some disease. In this bit, C.K. is calling out the audience to reflect on their own positioning to "mild racism." He is not inventing it, and he's not endorsing it in any clear way, so much as calling upon the audience to deal with themselves in relation to it. Where to laugh, how to laugh, and what that laugh means.

The set was quite controversial, both for his examination of "mild racism"—that some saw as "racist"—as well as for some later jokes that involved Israeli/Palestinian relations to the U.S. and child molestation. But, for the purposes of the introduction to this chapter, what is unique about this brief set is the way C.K. positioned himself within systems of race and performances of racism. Rather than planting himself rhetorically outside of racist culture and pointing fingers, he locates himself as a part of and within a racist culture—a move that many white comedians actively resist or evade. In addition, he locates racisms in the mundane, the everyday, and the pedestrian, and thus he is implicating everyone in the audience to think through the racisms they all carry and perpetuate, even if "mild." His body, his voice, and the relationship he forges with the audience affords a very distinct and pointed mode of inquiry.

When engaging systems of race in comedy, there are a fairly limited number of ways this has been approached. With specific regard to racial humor performed from the position of a white subjectivity and through a white body, these postures became even more constrained. This chapter will set forth and examine these postures, discussing their possibilities, as well as their limitations in engaging our understandings and complacency in systems of whiteness, white privilege, and white racisms. Grounded in some key concepts from critical race and whiteness studies, the chapter will begin with a discussion of *white invisibility* as a posture, wherein discussions of race are comfortably located as the purview and property of comedians of color. Next, the chapter will examine what comedian Margaret Cho refers to as *white fragility* and discuss avoidance and finger pointing engagements with racial humor that seek to absolve the audience from racist systems. Finally, the notion of *white innocence* will be explored as an additional posture returning to comedian Sarah Silverman as a case study in this work. In conclusion, the chapter will reflect on the limitations of what humor can and cannot do, continuing to hold onto the subversive possibilities of humor, while marking how there are some discussions where humor simply may not be effective for many audiences.

Safe identifications and white invisibilities

> The sense of whites as non-raced is most evident in the absence of reference to whiteness in the habitual speech and writing of white people in the West … An old-style white comedian will often start a joke: 'There's this bloke walking down the street and he meets this black geezer,' never thinking to race the bloke as well as the geezer.
>
> (Dyer 10)

As discussed in Chapter 3, when Eva Longoria and America Ferrera presented at the 2016 Golden Globes, their comedic bit about racial misrecognition was widely positively received and considered a success. As the two Latina actresses stood on stage and teased the audience in a quick back and forth about who they are not (not Salma Hayek, not Eva Mendes, not Charo, etc.), the audience responded with loud laughter and support. The joke references the racist conflation and confusion of all Latina actresses through the bodies of two Latina women. Thus, audience identification was solicited for the audience to relate to Longoria and Ferrera and laugh at the abstracted racist. The joke was funny and poignant, allowing an understanding and a shared laugh to emerge between Latina women. It also allowed those outside this identity to laugh at the racist practice and find delight in these women who playfully indict the practice. The bit was, however, able to cite and speak against the practice of erasure, yet the practice remained abstracted and general, removing the interrogation from white bodies, white performativities, and a referent of whiteness.

A similarly themed joke was explored on *The Daily Show* in 2016, when correspondents Roy Wood Jr., an African American male, and Jordan Klepper, a white male, co-presented the report, "How to Navigate Race-Based Humor." The report begins with the two men framing the discussion, as Wood admits racial jokes "can be tricky." Klepper follows up, somewhat sing-songy, "But if you work together, listen, and keep an open mind, it can really pay off." The bit proceeds where the two explain the importance of their friendship off camera, which helps them navigate racial humor on camera, yet Klepper keeps dropping offensive racial stereotypes. For example, Wood begins to tell a story about a stand-up gig the two were performing recently at a college, and Klepper drops in, "Yeah, the first time this guy has ever been to college." Klepper keeps a large smiley shit-eating grin, where Wood appears frazzled for a moment, starts to refute the claim, and then corrects himself. Calming himself, Wood Jr. explains, "Jordan is playing with the idea of the undereducated Black man, and it's okay because we are friends. He is using stereotypes to create satire. It's a powerful weapon." Klepper cuts in again, "Almost as powerful as Roy's unregistered handgun." The joke is that because the two are friends, Klepper sees his racist jokes to be acceptable. Klepper tells the jokes and then Wood unpacks Klepper's joke as a performance of white ignorance, marking how Klepper is only pretending to be so ignorant. The two return to a moment of shared positioning, discussing how context and audience is central to racial humor, and it is their great friendship that allows them to joke as they do. But, slowly, the frame of white ignorance as ironic satire is pulled back (although not entirely, as we know Klepper is still in on this joke) and taken to a gross extreme. Klepper keeps referencing shared experiences with Wood, who stone-faced, continues to point out it was not him, and that Klepper is "thinking of another Black guy." Klepper spirals off, discussing shared high school memories with Wood, who replies, deadpan, "We met six months ago." Klepper continues, talking about how in high school Wood played every position on the basketball team. Host of *The Daily Show*, Trevor Noah, interrupts, "Jordan, Do you think all Black people are the same?" Klepper shifts to performed defensive nervousness and retreat, quickly backtracking and shifting tone. He gasps and points in an accusatory deflection, "No, no no, I see what you are doing right there. I see what you are doing. You are trying to flip this to make me look like a racist, alright?" Klepper faces the audience and doubles down on his support of his "friend." He declares, "Roy was *the man* in high school. I mean, you were the science teacher, the hall monitor, the bus driver, you were a couple of the kids, you and my dad would have cigars and talk about Vietnam together …" Wood, deadpan, states, "We are not friends anymore." Jordan replies, "That's a little heartbreaking. I cannot believe I'm losing my best friend *and* my favorite Uber driver. By the way, you are doing a great job hosting this show" (now pretending to mix up Noah and Wood as they are right in front of him). Noah intervenes, "Jordan, I don't think you are racist. I think you have a brain tumor." As the final joke, Klepper replies dismissively to Noah, "Uh, why don't you chill out Jessica, I'm talking to Roy" (as if he thought Trevor Noah was Jessica Williams, another correspondent on the show who is an African American women).

Much of the racial content of this sketch is similar to the Longoria and Ferrera bit, working to call out and indict the erasure and conflation of all persons of color, denying their unique individuality and personal integrity. However, there are a range of differences that enable and constrain its potential effects. The extreme degree that Klepper enacts his misrecognition and conflation is so far-fetched that the audience is quickly relieved of negotiating ambiguity or engaging in murkier self-reflexive processes. White privilege is both marked and identified, but also distanced and contained to the extremes of Klepper's idiocy. Because they work off one another, Wood and Noah's presence helps contextualize and legitimize the satiric value and presence of irony in Klepper's performance of blind racism and privilege. Yet, the presence of Klepper's white male body performing white ignorance forces a white audience to negotiate identifications between both Klepper and Wood, rather than so simply removing oneself from an abstracted and disembodied racist tendency (as with Longoria and Ferrera). This next section will review some foundational literature in critical race and whiteness studies to begin examining the question, within the context of racial humor, what can the presence of the racially privileged body potentially offer in the project of anti-racist work.

Whiteness and the white body

> They know that they are white, but they cannot know that such a thing has social meaning; they know that they are white, but they must not know that their whiteness accrues power. They must not call it whiteness for to do so would be to acknowledge its force. They must instead feel themselves to be individuals upon whom nothing has acted. That's the injury, that their whiteness has veiled from them their own power to wound, has cut down their sympathy to a smaller size, has persuaded them that their imagination is uninflected, uninfiltrated. It has made them unknowing. Which is one reason why white people take recourse in innocence: I did not mean to do any harm.
>
> (Loffreda and Rankine 20)

The easier, or at least safer, answer has been to rely upon the grammars of essentialization, where comedy about race and racial systems (especially in the form of irony) is best delivered by a comedian of color. We need to continue to demand more comedians of color gain visibility and platforms to do this work. There is, quite simply, important work around racism and privilege that the white body cannot do. However, this does not mean to suggest the white body is incapable, or without significant potential and responsibility, to intervene and engage racist logics through humor. There is different work to be done. As Schneider points out in relation to performance artists, the artists who are non-white can work to make sedimented and dehumanizing meanings of primitivism most visible, yet "it is incumbent on white feminist performers to strive to make whiteness explicitly visible in their work, or better, to make its structural invisibility visible" (Schnieder 9). In other terms, white artists, or specifically for our purposes—white comedians—have unique access for examining and intervening into the cultural workings of normativity—in this case, whiteness and the performance of white privilege. The problematic alternative is to "leave whiteness in the realm of the implicit" (9), and continue to place the burden and responsibility of engaging racial systems and white privilege only upon those who are marginalized by its operations.

Naming whiteness and marking the performative workings of whiteness has been found to be a slippery and contested project. The study of whiteness begins with understanding "the social construction of both racial and ethnic categories" (Martin, Krizek Nakayama and Bradford 127), wherein race is a biological fiction, a discursive set of meanings, and a performative accomplishment. What does whiteness mean? When asked to define this identity, students responded that "white means white" in a tautological spiral, and this "absence of a reference demonstrates the ideological masks that hide the powerful functionings of 'white'" (139). Whiteness is the "phantom center" (141) of racial systems of power and meaning—which makes it particularly difficult to study (141), as well as understand or interrupt. As Shannon Jackson notes, "The act of remembering a condition such as white privilege is akin to the paradox of retroactive waking, like trying to recall an experience that you slept through" (52). Whiteness is elusive, violently resistant to looking at itself head on, and works to make itself invisible from those who most benefit from its logics. This slippery and elusive cluster is not so easily seized, marked or pinned down, and thus "future research will necessitate in depth interviewing and other qualitative and perhaps more confrontational strategies, as part of our larger program of research to uncover the meaning of white" (Martin, Krizek Nakayama and Bradford 141).

As one confrontational strategy, one of the most famous and culturally relevant moments in performance art in the last few decades is the much-cited collaboration between Coco Fusco and Guillermo Gómez-Peña. Positioned within a series of museums, the artists placed themselves in a cage and performed the fictitious and outlandishly exoticized characters of the Amerindians, a "primitive" and "discovered" tribe placed on display for Western observation. As bell hooks argues, "The 'primitive' is entrenched in the psyches of everyday people, shaping contemporary racist stereotypes, perpetuating racism" (353). Working off these entrenched meanings, Fusco and Gómez-Peña's "reverse ethnography" of the colonizing gaze placed the audience under critical examination, challenging the "limits of 'happy multiculturalism'" (131), while dramatizing and interrogating what Fusco calls the "colonial unconscious" (132). Although, remarkably, some audience members took the performance of the "newly discovered" Amerindians as real, granting extreme authority to the museum spaces in which the performance was held, many understood this was a comment on Western colonialism and primitivism. Yet, as Fusco points out, even those laughing off at a distance were still complicit, implicated, and quick to step into colonizing and dehumanizing roles with uncomfortable ease. It was a prank where audience members were "caught off guard" and in that setting where "their beliefs are more likely to rise to the surface" (132). Fusco marks these beliefs as the "psychic investment" in racial stereotypes, arguing the "desire to look upon predictable forms of Otherness from a safe distance persists" (134). In this reversal of gaze, Fusco marked how the performers of colonization seemed to, even when understanding it was not real, derive pleasure in these roles, locating an investment in colonial mindsets that "does not simply wither away through rationalization" (133). Rather, these audience engagements reflected bell hook's indictment of white consumption of otherness, "as new dishes to enhance the white palate – that the other will be eaten, consumed, and forgotten" (359). When placed into an embodied context and asked to engage other (othered) bodies, the invisibilities of whiteness and white colonial entitlements—so often hidden from sight (or at least to one's self)—become alarmingly present.

The Fusco and Gómez-Peña collaboration is significant because it speaks to the power of the performance as a site of interrogation, self-reflexivity, and accountability for white bodies—the mundane and pervasive way racism is *done* through the body in daily acts and behaviors. Even though many might generally agree there are some privileges that accompany being white, "they do not overtly acknowledge their white privilege because they think of themselves as average, morally neutral non-racists" (Crenshaw 255). Privilege, and particularly white privilege, operates through its own invisibility. Yet what was so impactful in this performance piece was not Fusco and Gómez-Peña's performance, but the audience performances they brought forth. "In academic and political discourse, it is also rare for white people to explicitly reference their whiteness" (Crenshaw 253) and yet there is a cultural necessity to "make whiteness visible and overturn its silences for the purposes of resisting racism" (254).

Deflective postures: Whiteface-saving

Making whiteness visible is further complicated by a broad range of performative strategies that work to deflect, resist or deny one's personal accountability to systems of racial privilege. When faced with the accusation or implication of white racism, privilege often works to adamantly preserve its innocence, point fingers elsewhere, and yet still manage to re-center itself at the fore of the discussion. This next section will explore a broad range of postures that help to trace and categorize a series of strategies in which whiteness functions within the comic controversy, specifically with attention to race and racisms.

Gresson sets forth the concept of *white pain* to mark the experiences of guilt, shame, anxiety, fear, and discomfort when one's racial privilege is interrogated or denied. This sense of loss and attack, while a mechanism to deny privilege and protect hegemonic systems, marks a deeply felt experience that is too often more real, tangible, and embodied for white persons than the material violences inflicted through whiteness (Zingsheim and Goltz). While counter-intuitive, white pain provides a conceptual frame for understanding how the most significant racial experience often felt and understood through white subjectivity is not the violent effects of racism, but the discomfort of interrogating and questioning of one's own privilege. Because whiteness operates through silence and invisibility, as a steady and unremarkable experience of 72 degrees, it is only when the temperature is discussed or potentially altered, that discomfort emerges. While those who exist beyond the comforts of normative whiteness surely experience the temperature outside that room in far more extreme and severe ways, it is only when the door is opened and the discussion of temperature is introduced that whiteness is faced with this at all. White pain, while minimal and fleeting in the grand scheme of systemic racism, helps to mark the seemingly extreme and yet very real discomfort white persons experience within explicit racialized contexts and discussions.

Beyond the recentering of self that emerges through white pain—a form of self-victimhood that reframes the discussion—the interrogation of whiteness also produces a form of *white liberal deflection.* Weigman marks a "racial 'hyper-consciousness,' which simultaneously exhibit[s] anxiety about racial identity *and* reproduces white power" (Owen and Ehrenhaus 136, their emphasis), but also "privileges an inchoate white agenda, precluding the legitimacy of other readings by devaluing other interpretive communities' own claims on history and memory" (136). In other words, white racial anxiety can over-privilege its own anti-racist analysis, its way of seeing racism, in a way that shuts out how other communities might come to understand a text or event. In their study of differing interpretive communities' readings of the film *The Green Mile*, Owen and Ehrenhaus identify "Negative reviewers' efforts to control the legitimacy of others readings (i.e. to frame them as racist) as evidence of their own anxiety, particularly in the construction of black masculinity" (136). They detail and question what is at work when minority voices have positive identifications with texts "that mainstream (and mostly) white liberal reviewers denounce as racist" (140). Owen and Ehrenhaus suggest the presence of an "anxiety of representations of blackness" (142) for these white critics, which entangles meaning making processes because of their own relation and position within racist systems. In other words, the leap to a wholly racist indictment is tied to the white liberal critics own anxieties around race and white racism.

The posture of deflection is strongly enmeshed with Madison's conceptual frame of the *anti-racist white hero,* wherein the framing of an event or narrative constructs a tale of the *white savior.* This trope of the Atticus Finch character, or more recently Leigh Anne Touhy from the film *The Blindside*, presents morally pure and narratively heroic tales of white persons who come to the aid of persons of color. "In doing so, these benevolent white men typically 'saved' people of color from the ignorant violence of white, working-class vigilantes" (Pierce 45). Within the realm of comedy, this helps to mark the limitations of the white comic who rhetorically casts themselves as the noble anti-racist comedian, by primarily vilifying and distancing themselves from cultural racism. This posture is tied to the practice of *whiteface-saving*, which Shannon Jackson refers to as "a test of whether I will allow myself to look bad" (Jackson 53). Herein, whiteness works to present and perform itself as innocent of racism, removed from a racist system, and outside a system pointing a finger elsewhere. In presenting this form of story and self-presentation, the comedian still, will often keep the discussion focused upon, "white, elite, and predominantly male experiences and understandings" (Pierce 45), yet removes the gritty material realities of white privilege. This is not to suggest that white comedians should not be taking anti-racist positions or calling out racist practices. As a concept, however, "whiteface-saving" draws our attention to the rhetorical implications of a comedian positioning themselves as the pure, innocent, and noble ally, somehow divorced from practices that reify systemic racism. This would also include the self-flagellating posture of white guilt. Although this can surely be read as a gesture toward anti-racist solidarity, the limitations here are that the mechanisms of whiteness are pushed outside, elsewhere, over yonder at those "other whites." This is the same framing that permits us to more comfortably laugh with Longoria and Ferrera rather than face our complicities with Klepper or Louis C.K.—for these two men are not only willing to "look bad" but solicit an audience to locate their own identifications with racist systems.

An additional posture, while one perhaps least noticed, is *outright avoidance* of racial discussion—relegating the topic of race elsewhere beyond the unraced white comedian's body. When considering the comics who are so often criticized for engaging difficult or dangerous topics, it is important to contextualize their work in an expansive field of comedians who simply avoid the topic altogether and perpetuate white invisibility. Let there be no mistake that silence around issues of race and whiteness is always rhetorical (Crenshaw 272). For the white body, particularly, race is a topic that requires travel or interaction with a non-white body in order to be seen, as race is problematically exoticized as a "sort of wildlife preserve separate from ordinary, everyday experience" (Loffreda and Rankine 15). Thus, avoidance becomes easy and unstated for the white comedian's body. This posture, perhaps the easiest of all, helps to bypass the thorniest of trappings—the false conflation of race and racism. The "trope" in racial discourse that "race is racism" (Loffreda and Rankine 15) marks the uncomplicated triggering of racist interpretation by the mere mention or citation of racial discussion—especially when mentioned by a body coded with privilege. This intuition fosters and strengthens the problematic tie between any racial discussion and scandal, creating a climate where race is feared to be interrogated, discussed or engaged in. Fear that its treatment, no matter the tone or objective, will be turned into the accusation of racism. As Loffreda and Rankine, founders of the Racial Imaginary project, have stated, the intuition that "a lot of us here when asked to talk about race are most comfortable, or least uncomfortable, talking about it in the language of scandal. We're all a little relieved by scandal. It's so satisfying, so clear, so easy. The wronged, the evildoers. The undeserving. The shady. The good intentions and the cynical manipulations. The righteous side taking, the head shaking. Scandal is such a helpful, such a relieving distraction" (13). For a comedian attempting to engage in the complexity of racialized systems, scandal becomes both a vehicle and a severe limitation. While it can surely create a forum for notoriety and discussion, it also leads to a tragic and binaried framework for engagement (see Chapter 2 for multiple examples). Specifically looking to racial discourses, and the project of tracing postures of white deflection and facesaving, I turn to a recent controversy involving comedian Margaret Cho to ground these concepts in a specific site of analysis.

"Why not Amy and Tina?": White postures of white fragility

> There can be no significant context-shift until members of subordinated groups are the ones who are telling the jokes, regardless of their content. Indeed, in such cases the material may be similar to "politically incorrect" comedy.
>
> (Littlewood and Pickering 308)

> What's really annoying is that nobody really cared about race until white people got involved, and now all we do is talk about race … It's like, all the white fragility is so annoying. You've got to walk on eggshells around white people.
>
> (Cho qtd. in Herwees)

While referencing the inevitability of Seth MacFarlane's hosting failure during the 2015 Oscars, William Shatner playfully complained that the show's producers should have just brought in "Amy and Tina." The side comment received a large audience laugh, as calls for more Amy Poehler and Tina Fey hosting the Oscars (rather than MacFarlane) were already well established. The two comedians had been brought in earlier that year as a corrective to Gervais following one of his most controversial Golden Globe hosting years. Yet, in 2015, when Fey and Poehler returned to the Golden Globes as hosts, their show was not without its own controversy. In the aftermath of the Sony hack and the drama surrounding the film *The Interview* (a comedy in which dictator Kim Jong-un is assassinated which strongly angered the North

Korean Government), Fey and Poehler had several sketches through the show with comedian Margaret Cho. Cho played the part of Cho Yun Ja, a fictitious North Korean journalist (and newest member of the Hollywood Foreign Press) who writes for a magazine called “Movies Wow!” The character held a stoic and affectively flat expression, holding up a magazine with the image of Kim Jong-un. When asked if they wished to take a picture with someone, Cho slightly nodded and then pointed directly to Meryl Streep, a few feet away. The bit dragged on for about another minute, as “Cho Yun Ja” and Streep staged an awkward photo for “Movies Wow!” In a second appearance of Cho as “Cho Yun Ja,” she joined Poehler and Fey on stage. They asked if Cho Yun Ja was having a good time, so far. Cho shook her head slowly. When asked by Fey why it was not fun, she said, in a slightly over-the-top accent where inflections and emphasis would shoot out in unexpected points in the sentence, “In North Korea, we know how to put on a show. This is not a show. No! You no have a thousand babies playing guitar at the same time. You no have many people holding many cards to make one big picture. You no have Dennis Rodman, no basketball at all!”

The character is not new territory for Cho, whose stand-up has included various members of her Korean-American family for years. She has also performed a similar characterization as Kim Jung-il on Fey’s *30 Rock*. However, the portrayal on the Golden Globes received a range of negative responses, with audiences on Twitter and critics calling it “racist” (Oldenburg) and “minstrelsy” (Ma). As with most tragic commentaries within controversial comedy, one does not have to look hard to see where the responses are coming from. Cho adopted an affect and an accent that is stereotypically Korean, and heightened these vocal shifts and facial expressions to the level of caricature. She is working in a tradition of political parody, and is playing with and through exaggeration to critique a dictator. What was most interesting about the recurrent bit was all the ways it was awkward. It failed from the first moment, yet it kept getting brought back, only to once again sit in the uncomfortable dryness of Cho’s performance. Watching Meryl Streep fumble and try to hold an uneasy smile, for a suspended period, next to Cho’s frozen scowl felt eternal. As a “member” of the Foreign Press, Cho’s slow and exaggerated critique of the show’s failings, by holding it up to the perceived norms of North Korean television, fell out of time with the banter of the program. It was, temporally, a cultural collision, though one orchestrated through excess, failure, and something so tangibly “off.” The campy style and workings of Cho’s bit were directly winked at, when Cho Yun Ja spoke out about the placement of *Orange is the New Black* in the comedy category. Cho self-referentially critiqued the show as “funny, but not haha funny.”

When discussing or evaluating the quality of humor, a common metric to determine success or effect is ‘the laugh test.’ For certain types of comics, the laugh is the win, even if navigating dangerous content. By this metric, at the Globes, Cho’s comedic bit failed. However, the laugh is a limited criterion of evaluation in this case. As a constant disruption and violation, Cho’s performance of "Cho Yun Ja" complicated everything it came in contact with. From the polished Hollywood celebrities who did not know how to respond, to the stereotypes being enlisted that were large and present and uncomfortable (and not wholly consumable), Cho brought about a dis-ease. She turned the show inside out for a few moments, where the very white and Western show of the Hollywood Foreign Press, was gazed back on with disapproval. In turn, the disapproving stare of North Korea was then parodied. For a few uneasy moments, there was a standstill. It failed, but in a very interesting way. When the show was ending, Cho Yun Ja announced "show over; I host next year," already offering a threat and a jab to the negative responses simultaneously occurring on Twitter.

When faced with critiques of racism, Cho was quick to completely dismiss them. She responded on Twitter, "I'm of mixed North/South Korean decent – you imprison, starve and brainwash my people you get made fun of by me." She additionally responded, "I'm the only person in the world, probably, that can make these jokes and not be placed in a labor camp" (quoted in Feeney). She has since gone further to criticize a trend she calls "white fragility," which she rather directly critiques as "so annoying" (quoted in Geddes). In dialogue with Stephen Colbert, she marks a sensitivity and lack of sophistication occurring in the culture that is quick to pounce and correct, without even considering the workings of the joke.

Cho's "white fragility" response invokes and calls out a range of postures that her critics are performing. One, in the calling out of "white fragility," she is primarily addressing a white audience of critics—critics who can just as easily be criticized for their performance of anti-racist white heroism. Beyond the white savior model being enacted through a form of white liberal deflection, there is surely a space to discuss how this critical posture was a form of whiteface-saving, a paranoid response of anxious white pain to deflect the critic's own discomfort in dealing with race (equating the presence of race with racism). Thus, by calling out Cho and producing a scandal around her performative choices, there is a social drama that obscures any real form of racial discussion. Just as one can label Cho "racist" for performing a North Korean stereotype as a Korean woman, it's just as easy to apply a broad range of conceptual labels to her critics. Sure, we can apply these labels, but more importantly we should be examining what the labels *do* (beyond feed tragic scandal). What is lost in this pseudo and momentary scandal—which only serves to fill headlines and op-eds until the next day's scandal—is any discussion of the other racial performances in the event. Streep's nervousness, Fey and Poehler's "straight" rationality, and all of the awkwardness surrounding Cho's persona marks the co-presence of white racial performances that were ever-present in Cho's segments. Not unlike long standing critiques of television series where the show is never "about race" until a person of color appears (and usually, just as quickly in 1970s and 1980s, exits), only Cho's performance is raced. Meryl Streep might just be the greatest living embodiment of whiteness on the planet yet our critical racial gaze remains locked on Cho, and how she performs race.

Given the discursive terrain conflating race and racism and the gravitation toward scandal, alongside a broad range of postures for whiteness to preserve its privileged invisible and noble status, the prospect of engaging racial systems through a white body is daunting. There is a safety and an investment in keeping the white body unraced, unremarkable, and always 72 degrees. Yet, combatting white silence is imperative. "If we silence talk about race, we perpetuate whiteness' silent privileges" (Crenshaw 272). Yet, there is a double-bind at work. "The logic of this argument follows this pattern: if our talk about race causes racism, then reason dictates that we should quit talking about race. It equates race consciousness with racism" (272). Crenshaw points out that there are many dangers to this line of thinking, and calls for us to think about privileging alternative mobilizations and performances through bodies of privilege. She asks (274):

> What if we conducted our teaching and scholarship as an ideological enactment of the *rejection of privilege*? … First, it would require a consistent commitment to revealing how ideologies that determine meaning 'work' to conceal silences about our own privileges, privileges that exist in what we take for granted or think is 'natural' not only in writing but also in our offices, hallways, and classrooms, the places where we live, work, and communicate with each other.

Extending this work to our two areas of analysis—the comedian's body and the critic's identity—it calls for greater examination of how racial privilege operates in both of these performances. It calls for us to be steadfast and complicated in the work, and not "to stand apart from our ideological criticisms" (Crenshaw 274), but rather centralize and infuse the comedians and the critic's work with an awareness of their privileged affiliations and performative operations.

Upon being told to check her privilege at the door, Jackson reflects on this request. "I remember being unclear how to examine baggage that had been checked at the door, but I am sure I nodded my head anyway" (54). Herein, Jackson feared her whiteness being seen, recognized, and what it meant for her to be explicitly associated with these meanings, systems, and histories. Rather than checking one's privilege outside the room, which is more of an expression than a possible act, we return our attention to the white body and what it, as a discursive and critical tool can uniquely accomplish *in* critical comedic work. Rather than checking it, as in leaving it aside, what happens when that privilege is front and center, rendered visible and open to scrutiny and intervention? There is no question that so much of the important critical cultural work to be done around racialized experiences can and needs to be performed through the bodies and subjectivities of persons of color, but what happens when white bodies commit to the anti-racist and deconstructionist project of critically performing whiteness? Warren and Kilgard argue that "performing whiteness puts flesh on theory" (262). The practice works to engage theory in and through the body "and make present what is often left absent in conversations about racial identity and whiteness" (262). Because "whiteness is a discursive/material (re)production – an accomplished identity, (re)created through the word and the body in continual, mundane processes" (263)—the critical performance of whiteness helps to expose, denaturalize and potentially disrupt these moment-by-moment reiterations of whiteness. This encourages critical visibility of this often silenced and unmarked norm, this luke-warm yet seemingly temperature-less system of meanings that fights to disguise its constant and ongoing reproduction.

The face wars of Sarah Silverman

> Joking as a form of human interaction plays disrespectfully on our sense of what is socially respectable or ethically correct. Some would go even further and say that all instances of the comic are founded on the transgression of decorum, propriety and the gravity in human affairs, that this transgression is its very raison d'entre.
>
> (Littlewood and Pickering 292)

> We are having a hard time talking about race separate from racism.
>
> (Loffreda and Rankine 21)

Given what we know about whiteness, its invisibility and its resistance to interrogation, it should come as no surprise that the comedians (and specifically the white comedians) who are often at the center of the racial comic controversy are the one's who dare discuss and engage racial discourses. Afterall, the most "common languages for race" are evasion, and unlike the production of scandal, which works to simplify and polarize the discussion, evasion "smudges" and obscures (Loffreda and Rankine). The smudge of evasive tip toeing around race resists complex, complicated and messy interrogations, yet those who attempt to wade into this fraught and self-defending discourse of whiteness and white privilege (beyond proud heroics) too often become the easy scapegoat for all our cultural racial anxieties. Pointing fingers elsewhere and/or positioning self as the noble or self-reflexive hero evades the risk and messiness of interrogating and unpacking white privilege. It is messy work. It requires, not just owning, but actively investigating one's complicity (and calling for the audience to investigate their own complicity). It resists whiteface-saving and seeks ways to identify, map, and render visible what whiteness *does.* Few comedians, who occupy a white body and seek to trouble the meanings of that body, have made more concerted efforts in recent years than the continually controversial Sarah Silverman. Too often Silverman is lazily framed as an "edge" comic or one of those comics who simply aims to shock and offend. The implication of this assessment is that the end goal, objective, and operations of her humor are simply to rattle the audience. In this next section, I want to examine Silverman's work as an intervention that is far more pointed than mere "shock" and much denser than simply seeking to offend.

In the absolutely hilarious and deeply uncomfortable third episode of the second season of *The Sarah Silverman Program* (2007–2010) titled "Face Wars," Silverman unflinchingly jumps right into the deep end of issues of race, privilege and representation. The larger premise of the show is centered around Sarah, who plays an ironic, bubbly, mishap-prone, and cluelessly privileged buffoon (much like her stand-up persona). Her real life sister, Laura, plays her older sister and is often stuck taking care of, and cleaning up after, her foolish Magoo of a sibling. The set up for "Face Wars" is simple, and is introduced in the opening moments of the episode. Sarah joyously and cluelessly walks into a country club, in her tennis outfit, and requests a tennis court. An employee, with a friendly smile, says, "Sure, what's your name?" "Silverman," she confidently answers. The perky employee looks through the register and then looks up, confused. "I'm sorry, I don't see your name in our member book. Are you a member?" "No," Sarah says, in a confused whine, as if she is not entirely sure what bearing membership has on this issue. "You need to be a member to use our facilities" she politely informs her, while waving in recognition at two (we assume to be members) as they pass by to the tennis courts. Sarah seems flustered, if not offended, by the membership inquiry and the women simply walking past. The employee states, "I'm sure you understand." Silverman, clearly cobbling together a conspiracy in her mind, replies, rather accusatorily, "Yeah, I understand. I read you loud and clear." Sarah turns and walks away. There is a performed humiliation and accusation in Silverman's tone, that is clearly confusing to the woman working the counter. The scene cuts to Sarah running into the diner to meet her sister and friends, interrupting their discussion and dramatically declaring, "I'm the victim of a hate crime!" Sarah quickly recounts the story, greatly embellished, where the woman said "What's your name, Silverman? Get out Jew!" Laura, suspicious of her often exaggerating sister, asks, "she said that?" Sarah, replies, "Yeah, basically, *with her eyes.*" Sarah them dips into a deep victim narrative, insisting "It's like everywhere I go I'm a second-class citizen. There is nothing harder than being Jewish in the entire world." Their waiter, Eugene, an African American male standing right next to her, walks up rather soberly and says, "excuse me?" Silverman, clueless as ever, corrects herself, saying, "I'm so thoughtless, I'm sorry. I didn't realize we were ordering." Sarah scans the menu, obliviously, and then order some pancakes. The waiter, calmly says, "Miss, I believe there are harder things than being Jewish – like being Black" The argument of whose life is harder escalates into a competition between the two and Sarah asks, "Um, did Black people have the holocaust?" "No," he replies, "but we did have 400 years of slavery." Silverman, in mocking and flustered disbelief, "Oohhhhh, I'm so sorry you guys had to, like, uh, have great singing voices and really catchy songs while we got, oh, yeah, murder showers!" Sarah looks to the table of friends for support or recognition, and the four white friends all stare down in silent discomfort. In calmed disbelief by Silverman's idiocy, the waiter walks away, in shock, to which Silverman replies under her breathe, slightly annoyed, "I don't think he got my order." The waiter returns, insisting she could not last one day as a Black person. A competition is established where they attempt to switch places for a day. Silverman says condescendingly and playfully, "And then we'll settle the score once and for all," while touching Eugene on his nose. She says, "I'll be black (correction), I'll be *back*. I'll be *white black*." She laughs at her less than clever word play and exits.

Prior to the introduction of the competition storyline, there are central foundations presented that frame the larger racial discussion of the episode in important ways. First, Sarah's white ignorance and victimhood is, from the outset, a joke. Her "hate crime" is really tied to her ignorance and blinded white entitlement that she should be able to go wherever and do whatever she wants at all times. This white entitlement to space is depicted, not only at the country club, but even in her physical engagement with the diner. Her blindness is compounded by her literal erasure of the waiter's body and racialized experience as a Black male in America. This is coupled with her clear over reliance on sanitized mediated representations of Black oppression, where slavery is reduced to "great singing voices and really catchy songs." There is no question, from the outset, that we are in the hands of an ironic fool, whose cluelessness about the reality of hate crimes or racial injustice is taking us into a deeper reflection on white ignorance and the blindness of privilege. She is the idiot who is engaging in the short-sighted and self-serving practice of oppression Olympics. The episode is structured around her foolish and selfish effort to demand the centralization of white experience and white pain.

In order to engage this competition, Silverman turns to her makeup artist friend Eddie, who will be able to transform her into someone who looks Black. The scene alludes to the Harvey Fierstein transformation segment from *Mrs. Doubtfire*, where we watch the artist's face and their careful labor as the physical transformation occurs. The audience view is delayed as we only see Sarah from the back. Soft, sentimental piano music plays, as the camera pans across a work station filled with makeup, spirit gum, latex masks, and tools. On the mirror, behind Silverman hangs a collection of head shots of actors, whom we assume have worked with this artist. The expectation of what will appear after the transformation is also informed by a recent FX reality show that garnered a lot of attention (around the time of the original airing of "Face Wars") titled *Black. White*. In this program, professional makeup artists alter the racial significations of two families (one white and one Black) so they can swap places with each other to learn about racialized experiences. Yet, when the artist is finished and hands her the mirror (accompanied by soft music that creates the expectation of self-discovery and understanding) we see this is not the sophisticated makeup transformation the scene anticipates. Rather, she is painted in the most stereotypical, not remotely convincing, blackface makeup. Her pale white skin has a dark brown oval of makeup that starts about halfway down her forehead and goes to her chin. Her lips are widened with white make up. It is the most hideously awful and offensive thing, yet Sarah, in her ironic innocence, is amazed by the "realistic" transformation. Accompanied by the piano, she gently looks in the mirror and says, slowly and in amazement, "I look like the beautiful Queen Latifah." "You're a genius, Eddie" she declares, and then comes to a hardened and sobered realization of what is now ahead of her. "I guess it's time to start my adventure." Sarah sprints to the door, sentimental music beginning to swell, when Eddie stops her. "Hey, take this! It could get windy out there." He tosses her a red checked scarf, which she ties around her head, sentimentally, unaware that the offensive blackface is now coupled with an equally repulsive "mammy" head scarf. "Thanks!" she says, "I love it, it's so Rhoda" she declares before offering an impression of Rhoda and running out the door.

Silverman's comedy, in this episode (and in much of her stand-up) takes on the persona of the blinded white fool. Through this perspective, she creates a space for a persona to become the bull in the china shop of racial rules and guidelines. She embodies an extreme wrongness that works to unearth and expose all the tacit logics and silences so often protected from muffled racial speech. These rules, as they are adopted and perpetuated by mainstream culture, work to disguise racist beliefs, attitudes, and behaviors from public scrutiny. As Cole tweeted after the Paula Deen controversy, "The real reason Paula Deen's in the news is not because she's racist, but because she broke the unwritten rules about how to be racist" (cited in Roxana Gay). Silverman's show is also breaking many of the rules of race, but it would be too easy to argue she is merely working to reinforce and strengthen their logics (promoting racism) or simply using them to elicit a reaction (shock or edge). Rather, her work is investigating and talking about racism, specifically white racism and the distortions it perpetuates. There is no question, it is gross and offensive, as racism is all these things. But the citing and interrogating of the gross and the offensive as a means of examining its operations is quite different. The humor, from the episode, is purely coached from a perspective of ignorance, working to actively prevent an audience from fully identifying with Silverman. The jokes, the laugh, is continually coached at the awareness of the racial rules and her idiotic lack of awareness. There is discomfort in these violations, but also a self-reflexive identification coached with her persona, for even in the extreme, she carries and enacts more subtle white performativities. She brings forth the tacit and the buried beneath the surface and forces us to deal with them in uncomfortable ways. She embellishes and calls attention to white distortions and assumptions, and calls to the audience to take part in this work.

As Sarah ventures out into the world in blackface, everyone she encounters is instantly appalled. They call her "disgusting" and shun her on the street. An older Jewish man says, "I spent my life trying to rid the world of people like you! Seeing you burn in hell will be my personal heaven." Silverman, the fool, is baffled and horrified by this treatment. She says, to herself, "I had no idea. I had no idea how cruel white people could be to us." Sarah is so clueless to the implications of her makeup and the meanings they carry that she completely confuses anti-racist criticism of her blackface *with* racism. Overwhelmed with sadness, she says she needs to be with her "own kind" now and runs into a Black Baptist church. She dances in, singing and clapping, completely oblivious to how everyone is floored by her, her makeup, her buffoonery, and her really bad dancing. The religious service screams to a halt, and Sarah announces. "Oh, I'm sorry, I'm Black today," to which she is quickly kicked out the door. Sarah, broken and defeated, returns to the diner, admitting she had no idea how hard it was to be Black. Eugene, the waiter turns around wearing a false Jewish nose, an "I love money" t-shirt, and an Orthodox Jewish hat and wig. He, equally broken, says being Jewish is harder. In a perky and simplified faux resolution, a chipper Sarah says, "Well, I guess we will just have to agree to disagree," with a large smile. The moment ties a fake bow of understanding that references the absolute limits of sanitized "after school special" types of engagements with racial difference. Clearly, neither of these two have any new understanding of the other, and, if anything, their absolute lack of understanding is only further highlighted. The awkward smile lingers, but then shifts. Then Sarah awkwardly backs up from Eugene, suspicious, and seemingly uneasy. This is only halfway through the episode, and the second half takes a radical turn in terms of content, shifting to a complicated examination of the comic controversy and the conflicted roles of whiteness in these moments.

White ignorance and white innocence

> The point of seeing the racing of whites is to dislodge them/us from the position of power, with all the inequities oppression, privileges, and sufferings in its train, dislodging them/us by undercutting the authority with which they/we speak and act in and on the world.
>
> (Dyer 10)

Sarah steps back slowly from Eugene, with an over-staged indication of "suspicion" and heads out the door of the diner. Moping down the street, a white lady pushing a stroller stops Sarah and starts up a conversation with her. Sarah quickly reassures her she is not Black. "I know it's just make-up," the women replies. Sarah, responds, "Well I'm done with it, alright? There is nothing harder in the world than being Black." "Exactly," the women, interjects, "Which is why you can't stop now. I get what you are doing, you are starting a dialogue about race, and I think it's fantastic!" Sarah's defeated expression suddenly shifts to a cartoonish large smile, loving the praise and attention. With no clue as to what the woman is talking about, Sarah beams, "Really? Thank you." Her moment of feeling self-righteous, once again, is bolstered by noticing a parking ticket on her car. Sarah, who is parked illegally, sees the ticket and explodes into a tirade about "liquor stores on every corner and now this," asking if there is any end to "our struggle." The women with the stroller seems to be on board with her outrage. Sarah yanks the ticket from her windshield, marches to the car parked behind her and proudly shoves it in into their windshield wiper. Then, as she is returning to her car, a policeman (it was a police car she moved the ticket to) steps out of his car and calls for her to stop. As the cop approaches, Sarah instinctively performs a whiney, helpless, and cutesy "I'm sorry," using the justification that she did not see him in the car. Sarah seems to expect this helpless flirting to work, but it doesn't. When the officer says he needs to arrest her for breaking the law, she replies, "Well gee, that wouldn't happen to be because I'm *Black*, would it?" The cop, quickly responds in dismissal, "No," and follows it up conversationally with "What the hell are you doing looking like that, anyway?" Sarah, outraged, replies, "Why, do you have a problem with me being Black, officer?" Sarah, now aware a woman is recording this incident, performs dramatically for the camera. "Well ya, it's revolting" the police officer says, "completely over the line" (of course, referring to her wearing blackface). Sarah is now over-performing the role of victim, forcing herself down on the hood of the car, while yelling into the camera, "Show the world! Tell the people what you've seen and heard. The people must know my story!" Sarah is tossing and struggling, against nothing, as the police officer has stepped back several feet and is holding his arms in the air. In the precinct office, in the next scene, Sarah sits next to Jay, a police officer who is dating her sister Laura. Jay asks, quite reasonably, "Sarah, have you given any thought to wiping that crap off your face and paying your unpaid parking tickets?" Self-righteously, Silverman replies, "And abandon everything I believe in?"

In the second section of the episode, Silverman's ironic examination of white ignorance takes a turn and digs deeper into a series of issues beyond mere blindness. Her arrest sparks a local outcry, where about a dozen incensed white protesters, wearing blackface in the name of "racial justice," scream in front of the police department. A man in blackface with a bullhorn yells, "What do we want?" The small crowd of blackface wearing race warriors (all white) yell (the extremely and intentionally cumbersome) "THE FREEDOM TO EXPLORE ISSUES OF RACE IN AMERICAN CULTURE THROUGH THE USE OF POSTMODERN IRONY!" He yells again, "WHEN DO WE WANT IT?" They reply, less enthused, "We think it's fairly obvious." The commentary seeks to satirize self-righteous white activism, questioning its self-serving ambitions, its desire to consistently re-center self, and the very material, personal, and experiential rift that exists between those who experience oppression and those who strive to speak to that oppression (even with seemingly good intention). The white allies in this episode are obsessed with their own image, their own righteousness in ways that have little to do with actual racial injustice. Both fragile and facesaving, these ironic saviors may be the ones grabbing the media headlines, but they are satirized as buffoons. Their whiteface-saving performance is being executed through blackface and the right to use blackface becomes the ridiculous point of debate.

The overt and biting criticism of white racial activism is loaded and messy. It is significant that all the African Americans in the episode (who were focused on in the church scene) kick Sarah out and want nothing to do with her, feel no affinity with her, and share collective eye rolls and dismissals. The anger and outrage she experiences in the street is all from white persons, just as all her supporters are white. The episode is dealing with whiteness, white privilege, white activism, and the culture of white heroism. Engaged through white bodies, this episode mobilizes a legacy of performative discourses around whiteness, blackface, racism, minstrelsy, and dehumanizing buffoonery, and recasts these meanings upon white bodies and white collectives. We are called to laugh at the acts so commonly reproduced in the mainstream for nobility and heroism, and witness their detachment from racial violence. This is an example of the work these bodies can explore and engage. The episode places Sarah, the most self-serving and socially clueless character imaginable, as the idiot hero who starts a dialogue about race, when really all she is trying to do is get attention for herself and gain access to a club she never joined. By doing so, the show launches this meta-critique in order to create satire around whiteness. When she is being interviewed on TV for the local news, Sarah proudly says, "Well Grace, I don't want to compare myself to Abraham Lincoln … but there are some undeniable factors. We are both white people fighting for the rights of African Americans and we are both attracted to men." She goes on to unintentionally flaunt her selfishness, falsely lauded as activism, when she says, "I encourage people to join me in this movement. It's a great way to contribute to society without really taking away any of your 'me' time." She is someone who likes the spotlight, enjoys praise and attention, and quickly falls into a series of racial justice declarations that are immediately exposed as hollow, self-serving, and suspect. Yet, the audience of blackfaced white protesters cheer for her. She responds, "Thank you. Look at these beautiful Black faces. I woke up this morning with a vision. A vision of playing tennis … But how can I exercise when justice is not exercised? And that is why I stand before you today an angry blackfaced woman!" So many clichés of white activism and white heroism are not only cited but worn with prideful arrogance in a way that exposes that the emperor has no clothes. The rousing crowd of do-gooder white liberal protesters cheering her on becomes the largest punchline of the episode, and the show uses Sarah to launch a broader critique about white liberal saviors who claim solidarity with civil rights, yet really are protesting for their own freedoms.

The self-centered critique of the white characters was even extended beyond the always bumbling Sarah. After a mishap where Jay accidentally shoots Sarah, and Sarah lies in the hospital unconscious, her seemingly self-less sister Laura sits at her bedside tending to her. Laura begs her to not die and says she cannot possibly imagine life without her. Yet, even as she says these words, we see a fantasy sequence in Laura's mind. Laura sits at the center of dozens of men who are all focused on her and laughing at her corny jokes. Her vision is set in the 1920s, where she speaks in an old Hollywood dialect and dons a curly bob and a flapper dress. She is the center of attention and is getting the same praise and attention her sister also craves. In other words, amidst this whole ridiculously offensive blackface spectacle of her sister's, the thing Laura is most concerned with is getting her own attention.

The episode ends by taking everything just one step further. Laura wipes off Sarah's blackface, but Sarah swats her away before she is completely finished, leaving a small, Hitler-esque line just above her lip. The woman from the country club, from the opening of the episode, sheepishly enters Sarah's hospital room. Sarah, slowly and deliberately raises her mechanized hospital bed. Sarah's rise is slow, her eyes angry and intense, and, along with her Hitler-stache, creates the effect of the rise of a Vader-like villain. Sarah barks at the woman, "Hate any Jews lately?" The woman, ashamed, after everything that happened, confesses, "I didn't let you into the club today because you were Jewish. But then, when I saw you on TV today as a Black woman, I realized it could have been a lot worse. I just want to say I'm sorry, and that you are welcome to play tennis at our club any time you'd like, that aren't during the peak hours." Here, Silverman takes on representational symbols that are probably only second to blackface as culturally weighted with oppression—Nazi's and Hitler. She is villain and fool. The innocent victim and the violent racist. She claims Jewish victimhood even as she wears the signification of Hitler, himself. Furthermore, the country club worker makes a final and punctuated move to reiterate the hollowness and violence of whiteness in the U.S., stating "when I saw you on TV today as a Black woman, I realized it could have been a lot worse." Here, the subsuming of Jewish identity under the umbrella of whiteness, as a means of further alienating persons of color is stated, explicitly. Like most of Silverman's work around race, she speaks the thing that should not be said, yet is culturally tacit and ever-present. Silverman can get access to the exclusive club she never joined, so long as she stays white and prevents the possibility of "worse"—a Black women entering the club. This, for Silverman, requires no thought or struggle with conscience, because she never was invested in racial justice in the first place. She wanted attention and tennis, and she got both. The irony calls out a range of white obliviousness, but also the concessions of being subsumed into systems of whiteness in the project of racism and segregation.

What's so powerful about Silverman's ironic performance of whiteness is the absolute commitment to *not seeing* the violence and offense she leaves in her wake. She genuinely believes, as she says to her dog Doug in the closing credits, "It's like I'm the only open minded person in this whole world." She justifies hating Jay, not because of his race (he is white), but because "I *took the time* to get to know him." There is no willingness or capacity to see a broader system and no recognition of the pervasive, historical oppression of people of color. She is an innocent and an ignorant. She closes with a smiling sense of self-satisfied pride, realizing that her dog, Doug, is black and she loves him "to pieces." She smiles at her own belief in her innocence and her perceived distance from white racism. But then, she reflects, speaking to Doug, "I never really think of you as Black because your hair is straight." This is a show and persona who is dealing with racism, doing racism in a broad range of ways, but, I would argue is not "racist"—or better yet, is poorly engaged as merely racist. Silverman refuses to take the safer, simplified, heroic white posture of innocent finger pointer. Rather, her work forges into the far more treacherous waters of interrogating white innocence and obliviousness. She seeks to examine the experience, forge critical identifications and make an audience do more laborious work. It's tricky, it's dirty and it's layered, and so it is not easily digestible. Discomfort is expected and needed.

Going too far: Negotiating lines and contexts

> But comedy does not believe all limits can be transcended. Instead, it embraces ambivalence that can't be resolved.
>
> (Stone xvii)

> Man has two ways out of life—laughing and crying. There's more hope in laughing.
>
> (Dick Gregory qtd. in Nachman 494)

The choice to closely read a single episode of Silverman's short-lived series helps to trace the core thematic progression of this text, while also presenting some additional questions for further inquiry. While the episode is now several years old, Silverman has referenced the episode in recent interviews for a few key reasons. In 2016 on *Watch What Happens Live*, hosted by Andy Cohen, a call-in listener asked Silverman which joke she most regrets in her career. For a comedian like Silverman, who has had a lengthy list of controversial jokes (including the infamous Aoki incident and her much-regretted Brittney Spears joke that she discusses in *Bedwetter*), there are several places this could have gone. Surprisingly, to answer the question, she begins by recounting the basic premise for the episode of "Face Wars." With reference to her persona, and the character of Eugene, she states, "It's really aggressively stupid and we're both idiots." She continues, "I'm in like the most racist blackface and he's wearing paius and a yarmulke and a big fake Jewish nose and he's wearing a t-shirt that says 'I Love Money.'" She still stands by the episode, arguing, "It's great, but there's a still (picture) of me on Twitter in blackface and it's totally out of context." She explains, "I tweeted it when Twitter was new and the people who followed me watched that show and it was from that show … Now it's forever there and it looks … it's totally racist out of context and I regret that" (quoted in Maglio).

The complex aesthetic and ironic workings of Silverman's episode are by no means present in this single Twitter image that is forever out in the world. The image is, due to absolutely no contextual framing, a visual depiction of Silverman modeling racism. Interestingly, the short article written about this Silverman interview got it slightly wrong in ways that inform the workings of the comic controversy. For one thing, the writer of the piece claimed that Silverman "Admitted, 'It's really aggressively stupid and we're both idiots,'" but this was not an "admission"—as if there was some form of guilt being owned up to. This word was a verb selected by the writer. But, she was *explaining* the work. The stupidity she marks was not a later realization, but a choice in its composition. The verb choice is subtle but shifts the story in important ways. The article also reports, "Sarah Silverman has made a living pushing the envelope comically for quite a long time – but there's one gag that the actress wishes she could take back." Actually, while a click-worthy headline, Silverman never apologized for the episode or the joke, but rather regrets the decontextualized image being uploaded to Twitter. So, just as the comedic work is so often decontextualized and rewritten, so is the critical self-reflection of her work. Even when she works to carefully explain her work and clarify her answers, the complexity of what she is working with is quickly watered down and forced into a tragic frame of apology. The distinctions between being racist and the comic doings of racism are lost. The shifting contextual extensions of audience are ignored. The choice to enlist the privileged body in its own critique is disciplined and corrected, rather than thoughtfully self-reflected upon. It is true that nuance is not usually click-bait, yet the implications for the perpetuated tragic simplification are significant.

So, it should be clear that as a performing body, carrying a range of meanings around whiteness and white privilege, I find complexity and value in the interventions of Silverman's comedy. I believe her work, like the work of many others, warrants a deeper read, a closer examination, and a more sophisticated critical discourse beyond tragic indictment. Should it have "free reign" under the banner of "comedy?" No, I am not saying this. Should it be commended? Not necessarily. Perhaps, at times, but surely never without close scrutiny. This is less about championing the work than permitting it a range of performative workings and fostering consideration for a breadth of performative effects. What this work does is messy, skilled—and even when critically indicted—merits a sophisticated discussion. That is my primary call—greater scrutiny and complex critical discourse for humor, especially humor that makes a practice of intentionally breaking the rules.

There surely remain limits and shortcomings in the work Silverman does, and the work she seems willing to do (and was capable of doing at that time, as an evolving artist). I have lingering questions and concerns about the rhetorical strategies she relies upon in her investigations. While whiteness is visualized and reflected in "Face Wars" through both ignorance and innocence, the notion of innocence can and should be troubled further. All the while that hegemonic whiteness works to argue, fight, justify and rationalize its innocence—as part of its operations—attention to its postures of removed cluelessness ought not erase that there *is* violence in its daily performances. Silverman taps into this, somewhat, but opts to do so through her infantilized persona. Sarah's persona is not only an idiot, but is also a child. The shortcomings of this approach are that whiteness (white privilege, white oppression and white blindness to that oppression) is then *only* criticized through the optic of childhood, a "back when," and thus a *different* mode of innocence (not only an “I don’t see race” innocence but also a “I can’t be held accountable” innocence of the child). By infantilizing the whiteness under scrutiny, there is a different form of facesaving that is permitted. Just as racism is so often problematically relegated to the past tense, a “back then,” Silverman’s ironic criticism via childish ignorance/innocence allows a rift and a distance for the audience. Whiteness is about ignorance but not always innocence. For the white body to call out and also implicate self, marks a complex rhetorical effort, but this is softened and tidied up by the infantilization of whiteness. As this book has argued many times over, there are certain performative effects and engagements that differing bodies can enact, and this is not always easy or even enjoyable. Whiteness is not always nice, cute, foolish, or misguided. It can be ugly, violent, and dehumanizing—even when it does not see itself engaging in this work.

This discussion is thematically tied to the C.K. monologue on SNL discussed at the top of the chapter, in his articulation of 1970s “mild racism.” It was about a particular time, a “back when” in the process of growth—thus perpetuating some illusionary story of racial progress linked to maturity and adulthood in 2016. But, racism and the violences that continue to occur in the wake of white privilege is not merely kids stuff, is not merely childish and in the past, and so there are still rhetorical fields that work to preserve whiteness from a range of interrogations. The work of Silverman, nor the work of C.K., is without places of criticism, but it is best served by criticism that is willing to invest in a range of meanings, workings and performative effects.

Perhaps, this leads up to a closing point of inquiry: are we butting up to the limits of what comedy can do? Are there some types of work comedy cannot do? Shouldn’t do? Sure, it can work to bring levity to situations, but can comedy always do the penetrative work of critical humor? Is there a line of when and where and which bodies can engage a discourse—especially when that engagement is framed around the laugh?

Shaun King, in response to Chris Rock’s much-discussed 2016 Oscar hosting monologue (as discussed in the Introduction) placed this in terms that help to trace where these limits might reside. Rock dealt with the #OscarsSoWhite protest and backlash around all white nominees in the major categories with a series of jokes that worked to engage, but too often, undercut the critique. First, he laughed off Jada Pinkett-Smith’s boycott by suggesting she was never invited. But, then he compared the protest in 2016 to the state of civil rights in the 1960s, saying no one was protesting the Oscars in the 1960s because “we had real things to protest at the time … They were too busy being raped and lynched.” It has, since, been pointed by Gene Denby from NPR’s *Code Switch* blog that the Oscars actually were protested for lack of diversity in 1962. However, where Rock most clearly stepped over a line, for many, was his doubling down on this joke. He continues, “When your grandmother is swinging from a tree, it’s really hard to care about best documentary foreign short.” Shaun King writes, in his critique of Rock:

> Listen, I know Chris steps on toes for a living, but I don't ever want to hear a live audience laughing about the lynching of our grandmothers. I can't imagine the deepest, darkest pain of any other group of people being used as a prime-time punchline. Not only that, but we indeed live in an era where black bodies, riddled with bullets, choked lifeless, Tasered repeatedly, are strewn all over this country from coast to coast.

Yes. Agreed. It's a fair and important line. There is something deeply and not productively unsettling about a primarily white and extremely privileged audience at a protested event (and protested for its perpetuation of hegemonic whiteness) to be laughing at a joke where the punchline is about Black grandmothers being lynched. The severity of the joke, I understand, was a commentary on the stakes Rock was attempting to argue. The severity was about putting the #OscarsSoWhite protest into perspective. But the brutality of his lynching invocation was not about exposing or dismantling racism. It was about diminishing the violence of contemporary racism, and so the cost and effect of the joke's brutality was simply out of proportion. The jokes were not merely a citation of racist past, but were used as a means to actually undercut and belittle the violence facing Black bodies in the United States in 2016. It *did* racism in a manner that "gave the distinct impression that Black people were either petty for being frustrated with The Academy or that we live in a time without injustice, and, therefore, have too much free time on our hands" (King).

Even more so, from a performative perspective, this performer and audience exchange enacted something else that was quite troubling. Rock, in this space, carried a large burden for sure—a burden that reflects the very burden of liveness Muñoz discusses when he talks about the mandate facing minoritarian performers on stage to "'perform' for the amusement of the dominant power bloc" (1999: 187). He was there to perform, to entertain, address the protest, but only so far as to do so in a way that allows everyone to also enjoy the show. For his body to make light of that joke about grandmothers being lynched, to offer that up to a highly privileged and primarily white audience, reifies a range of racial and racist performativities around power, surveillance, and self-degradation at the pleasure of whiteness. More so, the laughter that followed from this primarily white and very privileged audience at this joke—this belittlement of contemporary racial critique through the invocation of lynched grandmothers—is deeply haunted. Traces and discourses of the past—delight, pleasure, and white community constructed around the murder of Black bodies—echoes strongly in this citation. It is harkened back to and made present in this performer/audience negotiation. I wanted so badly for Rock to redirect that moment. I wanted, at the minute that joke landed—in the moment that audience felt any laughter emerge from their (perhaps our) deeply racist guts—for Rock to stop and say "There! Right *there* is the fucking problem! It's not funny and if you laughed at *that*, then clearly you want me to tell you a story about your race, your history, your privilege, and your innocence that is *a lie.* Do better!" No, this did not happen. One, it's not what Rock does. Two, it's not something Rock is likely able to do, given the confines of his performance while trying to keep his career. Three, it's not funny. That no longer becomes comedy. Sure, a joke might unearth the gross underbelly of these investments, but sometimes it takes more than a joke, perhaps, to bring it into the light of day. It takes a necessarily seething indictment that nobody (or at least not certain bodies) should be laughing at.

What Rock's joke did was reify and embolden a legacy of racist performativity. It was this one joke, one of many in this expansive set, and it does not mean there was not a range of interesting and complicated work being done throughout the broadcast. It was this joke, however that crossed a line, and it was a line that can be described as moving from offense to causing pain. Curtis Luciani, in response to the Tosh controversy in 2012, attempts to parse out a distinction between causing pain and offense.

> All of us who like comedy are generally in agreement with the idea that "taking offense" is lame, and a comedian should be willing to "offend" whenever he or she wants to. But causing pain is quite a different fucking matter. Your job as a comedian is to take us through pain, transcend pain, transform pain.

Returning to Madison's metaphor, Rock was mirroring racist legacies, but he did not provide a clear hammer to that reflection. The pain was not transformed or transcended. Rock can dangle a forceful critique about well-meaning modern day Hollywood racism, and call it out in a way that people can identify but still not fully leave their comfort zones. After all, a white audience likes to be implicated, to a degree, so long as there is enough psychological wiggle room to secretly narrate themselves on the right side of the issue—to psychologically construct their own, personal innocence. Or, an audience can accept being implicated if the tone is calmed, rational, intellectual and not too affectively charged as to upset the temperature in the room. For some topics, the line between offense and wound can be so loaded, so tricky, it's too affectively packaged to parse. The mere citation of a meaning can be so powerful, so startling that the audience shuts down and can only see pain.

When Sarah Silverman, in 2016, walked onto the Conan O'Brien show dressed as Adolph Hitler, it should be no surprise that she garnered some negative responses. She played the role of Hitler in order to address recent comparisons between Hitler and 2016 presidential candidate Donald Trump. Hitler came on the show to defend his reputation against that "unfair" comparison. It was a simple bit with a very clear pretense that required minimal intellectual work: Hitler is the definition of evil, and so Hitler's offense to the Trump comparison is ironic. Silverman, because she is Jewish, is offered some level of cultural leeway (for some, not others) to do this bit. It's fine, easy enough, and digestible—so long as you can deal with the reference to Hitler and are not resistant to Trump being placed into this ironic tension. Earlier this year, I was on a discussion panel around humor and pedagogy, and this Silverman appearance was raised. A gentleman, also a humor scholar, spoke very definitively that this bit was both unfunny and unacceptable. He pronounced, in very absolute terms, "As a Jew, I can tell you that this was offensive." I found the statement fascinating, as if he had been authorized to speak to this joke from some official Jewish council (of which, as a Jew myself, I never received a ballot—was there a vote?). There is no doubt that, in our political rhetoric, Holocaust and Nazi comparisons have been painfully overused. However, they invoke powerful warnings, concerns, and the most grotesque of human cultural patterns that are not without relevance, power, use, importance, and cultural guidance. The bit on Conan made its point. It did the work it sought to do, although I am not sure if it was particularly funny. I am also not entirely sure if that matters.

Some topics simply push an audience to a place of discomfort, and I have attempted to argue throughout these pages that that comfort can come too fast, the offended response can be too rapid, and our engagement can so routinely become highly simplified. Returning to the C.K. monologue from the beginning of the chapter, it was not only his "mild racism" set that caused a wave of offense and controversy. After this discussion he moved to two additional topics, both using metaphor to talk about very dangerous "hot button" issues. First, he tackled U.S. relationships with Israel and Palestine. He examined these through the metaphor of his two fighting children. The metaphor spoke to secret deals and favoritisms under the guise of being fair and neutral in treatment, but also framed these relationships in terms of pouting, whining, teasing, and the assumed mature adult role of the U.S. as "the daddy." Next, he leapt to a discussion of child molesters, marking how they are "very tenacious people. They love molesting childs. It's crazy. It's like their favorite thing!" He continues, "There's no worse life available to a human than being a caught child molester. Yet they still do it! Which from, you could only really surmise that it must be really good!" The audience discomfort was audible. Responding to their apparent disgust, C.K. replied, "How do you think I feel? This is my last show, probably." Unable to understand the degree that child molesters like children, he enlisted the metaphor of a Mounds Candy Bar, which he professes to love. But, "If someone said to me, if you eat another Mounds Bar, you'll go to jail and everyone will hate you, I would stop eating them, because they do taste delicious, but they don't taste as good as a young boy does …" The audience discomfort pinnacles, and C.K., playing with meanings, again clarifies "to a child molester! Not to me! Not to us, cause we're all awesome!"

Even through a metaphor, the topic of child molestation as a site of humor is so fraught. He wasn't condoning the act. It could be argued he was somewhat trivializing the act, through the metaphor, or obscuring the lines between right and wrong. I think his work was doing that, yet the response of offense and anger is an interesting one. As a metaphor (child molestation and candy) he was examining the tension between desire and punishment. Yet, by bringing the audience into the joke, it asked them, for a brief moment, to consider the extreme degree of compulsive desire one must feel to commit this act. He made it about consumption, chocolate, and the act of taking something forbidden into one's mouth. Yes, this is an uneasy hailing of the audience, for sure. It does something, rhetorically and performatively that is simply uncomfortable. To suggest it trivializes the violence, however, works under the assumption that comedy is only for light topics. To bring serious topics into a comedic space somehow cheapens them, makes them fodder for laugh, relegating comedy to fluff and silliness. Rather, to bring these topics into the set worked to tackle hard and messy topics through a piercingly uncomfortable metaphor. Lack of audience comfort was not the failure of C.K.'s set. It was the point. It was the power. Too often, the minute an audience stops feeling comfortable, we leap to it being a failure of comedy rather than a rhetorical strategy of art. The work, the read, and the laugh reside in the audience, and that means the "fragile" or the paranoid audience will routinely slam on the breaks and leap from the car screaming "fire!" Perhaps the mainstream, particularly the increasingly paranoid terrain of the comic controversy simply cannot or will not deal with the ambiguities of more piercing and indicting forms of humor—those that require an audience to dig through their own shit before locating the joke. This is not the slip on the banana laugh, or the goofy mishap laugh. It is a laugh that comes from accountability, a sense of bravery, a willingness to open your eyes when the mirror is placed right in front of you, and engage a part of you that tugs at your very comforts and foundations. It's a laugh of dis-ease, of pain, of sadness, and of recognition. There are forty pit-stops for offense along the way to this laugh, and not everyone, at all times, is up for the journey. It's work. It's a process. It's a difficult laugh that sometimes doesn't follow the rules of the GPS. We get lost, often. I think this is one of the most important things that good art *does.*

Ricky Gervais has said, "You have the right to be offended, and I have the right to offend you, but no one has the right to never be offended." Although I really like this quote, it's important to mark that I found it being used as support inside a gross piece of right wing propaganda called "Indoctrination Prevention: 10 Ways College Professors Indoctrinate America's Youth and How to Prevent It." This pamphlet was handed out at a county fair I stumbled into in Wisconsin a few years back, while on vacation, by a kindly Midwestern woman who warned me about gay professors taking away our freedoms (beginning with our guns!). I believe in what the Gervais quote offers and suggests, but the context in which I found it also speaks to its dangers and risk. It places us all on watch. As a queer man, as a critical academic, as a performance artist, and as someone who has been told their work is "hate speech" and received threatening mail before performances, I know the stakes are high. I know that the minute controversial ideas and thoughts are silenced or shutdown, the precedent of this silencing will come back to us threefold. As critical citizens committed to work in social justice, silencing or tragic vilification of art and critical commentary should not be our strategy, for we historically know how dangerous it can be. We need to mine the distinctions to develop a broad vocabulary and series of frameworks that trace the lines between offense and wound.

For anyone, this is a complex and imperfect distinction, and for those invested in communication, performance, critical comedy, and anti-racist social justice efforts, this line is likely more muddled than for others. Yet, accepting its limits, it articulates both the potential values of pain in comedy and the dangers of offense leading to restricted or simplified dialogue. Comedy is an art form, and the work of opening up new ways of thinking, new approaches to speaking, and new modes of being requires some allowance for offense, pain, and discomfort. There ought to be limits, for sure, as the reckless infliction of pain (rather than offense) should not be uncritically permitted. Humor and comedy, if not held to scrutiny, can too easily become a place to disguise and defend the uncritical regurgitation of oppressive meanings. Yet, the boundaries need to be negotiated, troubled, complicated, and read through performative frames. Their doings need to be scrutinized, investigated, and fiercely debated with both suspicion and hope.

From the field of communication, we have learned the dangers of certain words and the rhetorical violence they can and might bring forth. Surely, the term "offense" is not always enough to hold the weight of the violence that words can carry. Still, our work for opening, complicating, and democratizing public discourse needs to consciously factor the role of performance and communicative aesthetics into these engagements. Bodies must not be written out of the account, audiences drive contextual meanings, and the words, in the end, are but a small piece of a much larger image. This text calls for a complex alternative to the "just a joke" dismissals, the textualized (and decontextualized) condemnations of "ists," and the "you are being too sensitive" refusals to engage the complex doings of humor. Rather, when engaging humor, we need to be sensitive to a broad range of channels that shape meaning. We need to know that even as humor works to call us to the fore, this will be resisted through our complicities, our self-defenses, our mechanisms of self-sustaining blindness and our narratives of innocence. When faced with the mirror, too often these postures work to slam our eyes shut and turn us away from self-reflexive engagements and meanings. This is, no doubt, the easier choice. But, when facing the performativity of comedy, when engaging that text, through that body, in relationship to that audience, across that complex affective field, and through this self-reflexive yet refractive perception, surely it can never be merely "just a joke."

References

"Amy Schumer Stands by Her Controversial 'Charlie Sheen Roast' Ryan Dunn Joke." *Radar Online*. September 20, 2011, www.radaronline.com/exclusives/2011/09/amy-schumer-stands-ryan-dunn-steve-o-charlie-sheen-roast-joke/.

Apatow, Judd. *Sick in the Head: Conversations About Life and Comedy*. Random House, 2015.

Apte, Mahadey. "Humor." *Folklore, Cultural Performances, and Popular Entertainments: A Communications-Centered Handbook*, edited by Richard Bauman, Oxford University Press, 1992, pp. 67–75.

"A Quote by Stephen Colbert." *Goodreads*. Goodreads Inc., www.goodreads.com/quotes/44606-if-our-founding-fathers-wanted-us-to-care-about-the/.

Babascio, Jack. "Camp and the Gay Sensibility." *Camp Grounds: Style and Homosexuality*, edited by David Bergman, University of Massachusetts Press, 1993, pp. 19–38.

"BAFTAs 2016: Rebel Wilson Courts Controversy with Transgender Joke." *News Australia*. News Limited, February 15, 2016, www.news.com.au/entertainment/awards/bafta/baftas-2016-rebel-wilson-courts-controversy-with-transgender-joke/news-story/0f2dd818439f50562c35f2f4da8757cc/.

Bahr, Lindsay. "Sean Penn Has 'No Apologies' for Green Card Joke at Oscars." *Huffington Post*. March 7, 2015, https://www.yahoo.com/movies/sean-penn-has-no-apologies-for-green-card-joke-113012775522.html/.

Bassist, Elissa. "Why Daniel Tosh's 'Rape Joke' at the Laugh Factory Wasn't Funny." *The Dailey Beast*. The Dailey Beast Company, July 11, 2012, www.thedailybeast.com/articles/2016/06/20/the-real-story-of-afghanistan-s-harrowing-battle-of-ganjgal.html/.

Batalion, Judy, editor. "Difference at Work: The Live Comedy Audience." *The Laughing Stalk: Live Comedy and Its Audiences*, Parlor Press, 2012, pp. 3–27.

Bedhead, Agent. "11 Generally Unfunny Comedians Worthy of Contempt." *Pajiba*. Disqus, August 8, 2012, www.pajiba.com/seriously_random_lists/11-generally-unfunny-comedians-worthy-of-contempt.php/.

Bennert, Kate. "Here Are All of Seth MacFarlane's Predictable Sexist Homophobic and Racist Oscar Jokes: Video." *Gawker*. February 25, 2013, www.gawker.com/5986601/here-are-all-of-seth-macfarlanes-predictable-sexist-homophobic-and-racist-oscar-jokes/.

Bergman, David. "Introduction." *Camp Grounds: Style and Homosexuality*. University of Massachusetts Press, 1993, pp. 3–18.

Bergman, David. "Strategic Camp: The Art of Gay Rhetoric." *Camp Grounds: Style and Homosexuality*. University of Massachusetts Press, 1993, pp. 92–112.

Berteaux, Anthony. "An Open Letter to Jerry Seinfeld from a Politically Correct College Student." *The Huffington Post The Blog*. TheHuffingtonPost.com Inc., June 9, 2015, www.huffingtonpost.com/anthony-berteaux/jerry-seinfeld-politcally-correct-college-student_b_7540878.html/.

Bitt, Barry. "The Unbearable Silence of P.C ." *Vanity Fair*. February 2016, pp. 72–74.

Bitzer, Lloyd. "The Rhetorical Situation." *Readings in Rhetorical Criticism*, edited by Carl R. Burgchardt, 2nd ed., Strata Publishing, 1995, pp. 60–68.

Booth, Wayne C. *A Rhetoric of Irony*. University of Chicago Press, 1974.

Bornstein, Kate."My Gender Workbook." *American Queer: Now and Then*, edited by David Shneer and Caryn Aviv, Paradigm Publisher, 2006, pp. 45–51.

Bradley, Bill. "Bill Maher and Jeff Ross Slam PC Culture, Defend Jerry Seinfeld." *The Huffington Post Entertainment Comedy*. TheHuffingtonPost.com Inc., June 13, 2015, www.huffingtonpost.com/2015/06/13/bill-maher-jeff-ross-pc-culture_n_7577192.html/.

Burke, Kenneth. *Permanence & Change: An Anatomy of Purpose*. Revised ed., Hermes, 1954.

Burke, Kenneth. *A Grammar of Motives*. California ed., University of California Press, 1969.

Burke, Kenneth. *Attitudes toward History*. 3rd ed., University of California Press, 1984.

Butler, Judith. *Bodies That Matter: On the Discursive Limits of Sex*. Routledge, 1993.

Butler, Judith. *Gender Trouble: Feminism and the Subversion of Identity*. Routledge, 1999.

Butler, Judith. *Giving an Account of Oneself*. Fordham University Press, 2005.

BytesMaster, "Tuesday Quotes: Ricky Gervais, Salman Rushdie and Cat Stevens." *Bytes*. Blogger, March 12, 2013, www.bytesdaily.blogspot.com/2013/03/tuesday-quotes-ricky-gervais-salman.html/.

Calner, Marty, director. *Whitney Cummings: I'm Your Girlfriend*. HBO. 2016.

Chait, Jonathon. "Not a Very P.C. Thing to Say." *New York Magazine*. January 27, 2015, http://nymag.com/daily/intelligencer/2015/01/not-a-very-pc-thing-to-say.html/.

Chambers, Emily. "#thetriggering just Took Down PC Culture and not in the Way You Think." *Pajiba Web Culture*. Disqus, March 10, 2016, www.pajiba.com/web_culture/thetriggering-just-took-down-pc-culture-and-not-in-the-way-you-think.php/.

CheersKevin. "We Saw Your Boobs – Seth MacFarlane Oscar Parody." YouTube. February 25, 2013, https://www.youtube.com/watch?v=RD5NLYjBiQA/.

Chelsea Does. "Chelsea Does … Racism."Netflix. 2016.

Cho, Alexander. "Queer Reverb: Tumblr, Affect, Time." *Networked Affect*, edited by Ken Hillis, Susanna Paasonen, and Michael Petit, MIT, 2015, pp. 43–57.

Chu, Arthur. "How Seinfeld Became a Bad Joke: The Threat of a Hyper-Vigilant Left-Wing Outrage Machine Has Been Greatly Exaggerated." *Salon*. Salon Media Group, June 11, 2015, www.salon.com/2015/06/11/how_seinfeld_became_a_bad_joke_the_threat_of_a_hyper_vigilant_left_wing_outrage_machine_has_been_greatly_exaggerated/.

Clark, Herbert H., and Thomas B. Carlson. "Context for Comprehension." *Attention and Performance*, edited by J. Long and A. Baddeley, Erbaum, 1981, pp. 313–330.

Clark, Herbert H., and Richard J. Gerrig. "On the Pretense Theory of Irony." *Journal of Experimental Psychology: General*, vol. 113 no. 1, March1984, pp. 121–126.

Cleto, Fabio, editor. *Camp: Queer Aesthetics and the Performing Subject*. University of Michigan Press, 1999.

Colletta, Lisa. "Political Satire and Postmodern Irony in the Age of Stephen Colbert and Jon Stewart." *Journal of Popular Culture*, vol. 42 no. 5, 2009, pp. 856–874.

Comedy Central. "Daniel's Selena Gomez Video." Tosh.0. Season 7, episode 26. Viacom, 2015, www.tosh.cc.com/video-clips/5ofn8f/daniel-s-selena-gomez-video/.

Comedy Central: "How to Navigate Race Based Humor." *The Daily Show*. Performances by Trevor Noah, RoyWoodJr. and Jordan Klepper. Viacom, April 12, 2016, www.cc.com/video-clips/falnyc/the-daily-show-with-trevor-noah-how-to-navigate-race-based-humor.

Comedy Central UK. "Black Bush: Chappelle's Show." YouTube. July 7, 2015, https://www.youtube.com/watch?v=KTDFGQ5OiLo/.

Conquergood, Dwight. "Beyond the Text: Toward a Performative Cultural Politics." *The Future of Performance Studies: Visions and Revisions*, edited by Sheron J. Dailey, National Communication Association, 1998, pp. 25–36.

Conquergood, Dwight. "Performance Studies: Interventions and Radical Research." *The Drama Review*, vol. 46 no. 2, 2002, pp. 145–156.

Cornell, Drucilla. "What Is Ethical Feminism?" *Feminist Contentions: A Philosophical Exchange*, edited by Seyla Benhabib, Nancy Fraser, Judith Butler, and Drucilla Cornell, Routledge, 1995.

Crenshaw, Carrie. "Resisting Whiteness' Rhetorical Silence." *Western Journal ofCommunication*, vol. 61 no. 3, 1997, pp. 253–278, doi:10.1080/10570319709374577.

Curtis, Jamie Lee. "And the Oscars Go to … Hell." *Huffington Post*. March 1, 2013, http://www.huffingtonpost.com/jamie-lee-curtis/and-the-oscar-goes-to-hell_b_2793392.html.

@danieltosh. "All the out of context misquotes aside, I'd like to sincerely apologize." Twitter, July 10, 2012, 1:56 p.m., twitter.com/danieltosh/status/222796532653629441/.

Davidson, Amy. "Seth MacFarlane and the Oscars' Hostile, Ugly, Sexist Night." *The New Yorker*, February 25, 2013, www.newyorker.com/news/amy-davidson/seth-MacFarlane-and-the-oscars-hostile-ugly-sexist-night/.

DeBoer, Fredrik. "Admitting that White Privilege Helps You Is Really just Congratulating Yourself." *Washington Post*. The Washington Post, January 28, 2016, www.washingtonpost.com/posteverything/wp/2016/01/28/when-white-people-admit-white-privilege-theyre-really-just-congratulating-themselves/.

Denby, Gene. "#OscarsSoWhite, #ForSoLong."*NPR's Code Switch*. February 25, 2015, http://www.npr.org/sections/codeswitch/2016/02/25/468002136/-oscarssowhite-forsolong/.

Derschowitz, Jessica. "Amy Schumer Says She Won't Do 'Safe Material' on Race despite Criticisms." *Entertainment Weekly*. Entertainment Weekly Inc., June 28, 2015, www.ew.com/article/2015/06/28/amy-schumer-twitter-jokes-race/.

De Mann, Paul. "The Concept of Irony." *Aesthetic Ideology*, edited by Andrzej Warminski, University of Minnesota Press, 1996, pp. 163–184.

Deggens, Eric. "For Better or Worse, Chris Rock Made the Oscars as Black as He Possibly Could." *NPR's Code Switch*. February 29, 2016, http://www.npr.org/sections/codeswitch/2016/02/29/468566401/for-better-or-worse-chris-rock-made-the-oscars-as-black-as-he-possibly-could/.

Derkson, Céleste. "The 'Attack behind the Invitation': Gender Parody in Karen Hines's Pochsy's Lips." *Performing Gender and Comedy: Theories, Texts and Contexts*, edited by Shannon Hengen, Gordon and Breach Publishers, 1998, pp. 233–246.

Diamond, Elin. "The Shudder of Catharsis." *Performativity and Performance*, edited by Andrew Parker and Eve Kosofsky Sedgwick, Routledge, 1995, pp. 152–172.

Donnelly, Elisabeth. "Seth MacFarlane Sick of Being Called Misogynist Says We Saw Your Boobs Was Satire." *Flavorwire*. Flavorpill Media, November 13, 2014, www.flavorwire.com/488234/seth-MacFarlane-sick-of-being-called-misogynist-says-we-saw-your-boobs-was-satire/.

Dyer, Richard. "The Matter of Whiteness." *White Privilege: Essential Readings on the Other Side of Racism*, edited by Paula Rotherburg, Worth, 2005, 9–14.

Esposito, Brad. "9 Outrageous Words that are Said Every Day in Australia." *BuzzFeed*. BuzzFeed Inc., February 20, 2014, www.buzzfeed.com/bradesposito/outrageous-words-that-are-said-every-day-in-australia?utm_term=.vjONK657X#.mow1PgZn6/.

"Face Wars."*The Sarah Silverman*. Season 2, Episode 3. Comedy Central.

Fairclough, Norman. "Political Correctness: The Politics of Culture and Language." *Discourse & Society*, vol. 14 no. 1, 2003, pp. 17–28, doi:10.1177/0957926503014001927.

Feeney, Nolan. "Margaret Cho isn't Sorry about Mocking North Korea at The Golden Globes." *Time*. January 12, 2015, http://time.com/3664746/golden-globes-2015-margaret-cho/.

Feldman, Josh. "Is Jon Stewart's Epic Takedown of CNN a Good Thing or a Bad Thing?" Mediaite. October 29, 2013, www.mediaite.com/tv/is-jon-stewarts-epic-takedown-of-cnn-a-good-thing-or-a-bad-thing/.

Framke, Caroline. "Tina Fey on the Internet: It's a Real Culture of Demanding Apologies, and I'm Opting Out." *Vox Culture*. Vox Media, December 18, 2015, www.vox.com/2015/12/18/10621924/tina-fey-interview-unbreakable-kimmy-schmidt-racism/.

Frank, Marcie. "The Critic as Performance Artist: Susan Sontag's Writing and Gay Cultures." *Camp Grounds: Style and Homosexuality*, edited by David Bergman, University of Massachusetts Press, 1993, pp. 173–184.

Fusco, Coco. "The Other History of Intercultural Performance." *The Routledge Reader in Politics and Performance*, edited by Lizbeth Goodman and Jane De Gay, Routledge, 2000, pp. 130–135.

Gambino, Lauren. "Daily Show's Trevor Noah under Fire for Twitter Jokes about Jews and Women." *The Guardian Arts*. Guardian News, March 31, 2015, www.theguardian.com/culture/2015/mar/31/trevor-noah-backlash-highlights-jokes-jews-women/.

Garcia, Catherine. "Joan Rivers Won't Apologize for Her Joke about the Cleveland Kidnapping Victims." *The Week*. Dennis Publishing, April 25, 2014, www.theweek.com/speedreads/454463/joan-rivers-wont-apologize-joke-about-cleveland-kidnapping-victims/.

Gardner, Josh. "Margaret Cho Accused of Promoting Racist Stereotype as She Lampoons Sony Hack with North Korean General Sketch at the Golden Globes." *Daily Mail News*. Associated Newspapers, January 11, 2015, www.dailymail.co.uk/news/article-2906146/Margaret-Cho-accused-promoting-racist-stereotype-lampoons-Sony-hack-North-Korean-general-sketch-Golden-Globes.html/.

Geddes, Travis. "Margaret Cho Tells Steven Colbert White People Ruined Racist Jokes: 'White Fragility is So Annoying'." RawStory. November 3, 2015, http://www.rawstory.com/2015/11/margaret-cho-tells-stephen-colbert-white-people-ruined-racist-jokes-white-fragility-is-so-annoying/.

Gibson, Megan. "Trevor Noah Faces Backlash over Twitter History." *Time*. Time Inc., March 31, 2015, www.time.com/3764913/trevor-noah-twitter-backlash/.

Gilbert, Joanne R. *Performing Marginality: Humor, Gender, and Cultural Critique.* Wayne State University Press, 2004.

Goltz, Dustin Bradley. "Frustrating the I: Critical Dialogic Reflexivity with Personal Voice." *Text and Performance Quarterly*, vol. 31 no. 4, 2011, pp. 386–405, doi:10.1080/10462937.2011.602707.

Goltz, Dustin Bradley. "Lovesick Aliens in the Wasteland: Queer Temporal Camp in Araki's Teen Apocalyptic Trilogy." *Critical Studies in Media Communication*, vol. 29 no. 2, 2012, 97–112, doi:10.1080/15295036.2010.514935.

Goltz, Dustin Bradley. "Perspectives by Incongruity: Queer Theory and Kenneth Burke." *Genders*, no. 45, 2007, n. pag, www.genders.org/g45/g45_goltz.html/.

Goltz, Dustin Bradley. "The Critical Norm: The Performativity of Critique and the Potentials of Performance." *Text & Performance Quarterly*, vol. 33 no. 1, 2013, pp. 22–41, doi:10.1080/10462937.2012.733887.

Goltz, Dustin Bradley. "Weighted Expectations upon Jodie Foster's I'm Not Coming Out to You Speech." *QED: A Journal in GLBTQ Worldmaking*, vol. 1 no. 1, 2014, pp. 180–187.

Gottfried, Gilbert. "A Pre Emptive Apology from Gilbert Gottfried." *Playboy.* Playboy Enterprises, June 28, 2014, www.playboy.com/articles/stop-saying-sorry-on-twitter/.

Gournelos, Ted, and Viveca Greene. "Introduction: Popular Culture and Post 9/11 Politics." *A Decade of Dark Humor: How Comedy, Irony, and Satire Shaped Post 9/11 America*, edited by Ted Gournelos and Viveca Greene, University of Mississippi Press, 2011, pp. xi–xxxv.

Grove, Lloyd. "Gloria Allred: Seth McFarlane's a Boob." *The Daily Beast.* Daily Beast Company, February 25, 2013, www.thedailybeast.com/articles/2016/06/20/the-real-story-of-afghanistan-s-harrowing-battle-of-ganjgal.html/.

Halberstam, Judith. *Female Masculinity.* Duke University Press, 1998.

Hall, Edward T., and Mildred Reed Hall. "Key Concepts: Underlying Structures of Culture." *Readings in Intercultural Communication: Experiences and Contexts*, 2nd ed., edited by Judith N. Martin, Thomas K. Nakayama, and Lisa A. Flores, McGraw-Hill Higher Education, 2002, 165–171.

Hall, Stuart. "Encoding Decoding." *Media and Cultural Studies: Keyworks*, edited by Meenakshi G. Durham and Douglas Maria Kellner, Blackwell, 2001, pp. 166–176.

Halperin, David M. *How to Be Gay.* Belknap Press, 2012.

Ham, Mary Katharine, and Guy Benson. *End of Discussion: How the Left's Outrage Industry Shuts Down Debate, Manipulates Voters, and Makes America Less Free and Fun.* Crown Forum, 2015.

Harbidge, Lesley. "Audienceship and Non Laughter in the Stand Up Comedy of Steve Martin." *Journal of Audience and Reception Studies*, vol. 8 no. 2, 2011, pp. 128–144.

Hartsell, Carol. "Chris Rock White People's Day July 4th Tweet Sparks Controversy." *The Huffington Post.* TheHuffingtonPost.com Inc., July 5, 2012, www.huffingtonpost.com/2012/07/05/chris-rock-white-peoples-day-july-4th-tweet_n_1651833.html/.

Herwees, Tasbeeh. "Margaret Cho: 'White Fragility is Annoying'." Good. November 3, 2015, https://www.good.is/articles/margaret-cho-white-fragility-ruined-comedy/.

Hibberd, James. "Daniel Tosh at TCA: I'm Not Sexist or Racist, I Just like the Jokes." *Entertainment Weekly.* Entertainment Weekly Inc., January 5, 2011, www.ew.com/article/2011/01/05/daniel-tosh-defends-jokes/.

Holmes, Linda. "Pop Culture Happy Hour: A Conversation with Trevor Noah." NPR Pop Culture Happy Hour. NPR, November 27, 2015, www.npr.org/sections/monkeysee/2015/11/27/457375043/pop-culture-happy-hour-a-conversation-with-trevor-noah/.

hooks, bell. "Eating the Other: Desire and Resistance." *The Consumer Society Reader*, edited by Juliet Schor and Douglas B. Holt, The New Press, 2000, pp. 343–359.
Hughes, Geoffrey. *Political Correctness: A History of Semantics and Culture*. Wiley-Blackwell, 2010.
Jackson, John L. *Racial Paranoia: The Unintended Consequences of Political Correctness*. Basic Civitas, 2010.
Jackson, Shannon. "White Noises: On Performing White, on Writing Performance." *The Drama Review*, vol. 42 no. 1, 1998, pp. 49–65.
Jones, Ken. "Talking Funny HBO." YouTube. December 30, 2012, www.youtube.com/watch?v=OKY6BGcx37k/.
Jung, Alex. "Why Amy Schumer Reacted to Criticism of Her Race Jokes Like Stand-up." Vulture. June 29, 2015, http://www.vulture.com/2015/06/amy-schumers-not-a-racist-but-she-is-a-comic.html/.
Keller, Tim. "Seth MacFarlane Has this VERY Strong Message to Bernie Supporters." *Bipartisan Report*. April 8, 2016, http://bipartisanreport.com/2016/04/08/seth-macfarlane-has-this-very-strong-message-to-bernie-supporters/.
Kelley, Seth. "Darren Criss Apologizes for Caitlyn Jenner Remark During Hedwig and the Angry Inch." *Variety News*. Penske Business Media, June 26, 2015, www.variety.com/2015/legit/news/darren-criss-caitlyn-jenner-hedwig-and-the-angry-inch-1201529656/.
Kickham, Dylan. "Bono's Senate Proposal to Deal With ISIS: Send in Amy Schumer and Chris Rock." *Entertainment Weekly Music*. Entertainment Weekly Inc., April 13, 2016, www.ew.com/article/2016/04/13/bono-isis-amy-schumer-chris-rock/.
King, Shaun. "King: Chris Rock Oscars Opener Dropped the Ball and Lynching Jokes Went over the Line No Matter How Tough a Spot it Was." *New York Daily News*. February 28, 2016, http://www.nydailynews.com/entertainment/oscars/king-chris-rock-oscar-opener-lynching-jokes-article-1.2547017/.
Kleinhans, Chuck. "Taking Out the Trash: Camp and the Politics of Parody." *The Politics and Poetics of Camp*, edited by Moe Meyer, Routledge, 1994, pp. 182–201.
Kornhaber, Spencer. "The Banality of Seth MacFarlane's Sexism and Racism at the Oscars." *The Atlantic*. The Atlantic Monthly Group, February 25, 2013, www.theatlantic.com/entertainment/archive/2013/02/the-banality-of-seth-macfarlanes-sexism-and-racism-at-the-oscars/273460/.
Kramarae, Cheris. "Classified Information: Race, Class, and (always) Gender." *Gendered Relationships*, edited by Julia T. Wood, Mayfield, 1995, pp. 20–37.
Krefting, Rebecca. "Laughter in the Final Instance: The Cultural Economy of Humor, Or Why Women Aren't Perceived to be as Funny as Men." *The Laughing Stalk: Live Comedy and Its Audiences*, edited by Judith Batalion, Parlor Press, 2012 pp. 140–156.
Kreuz, Roger J., and Richard M. Roberts. "On Satire and Parody: The Importance of Being Ironic." *Metaphor and Symbolic Activity*, vol. 8 no. 2, 1993, pp. 97–109.
Krishna, Raechel. *People Are Unhappy with all the Asian Jokes Made at the Academy Awards. BuzzFeed*. February 29, 2016, https://www.buzzfeed.com/krishrach/people-are-unhappy-with-all-the-asian-jokes-made-at-the-acad?utm_term=.nqJmoAO5aN#.pvxYgZQMKw/.
LaMarre, Heather L., Kristen D. Landreville, and Michael A. Beam. "The Irony of Satire: Political Ideology and the Motivation to See What You Want to See in the Colbert Report." *International Journal of Press/Politics*, vol. 14 no. 2, 2009, pp. 212–231, doi:10.1177/1940161208330904.

Langellier, Kristin M. "Personal Narrative, Performance, Performativity: Two or Three Things I Know for Sure." *Text and Performance Quarterly*, vol. 19 no. 2, 1999, pp. 125–144.

Langellier, Kristin M. *Storytelling in Daily Life: Performing Narrative.* Temple University Press, 2004.

Langellier, Kristin M., and Eric E. Peterson. "Shifting Contexts in Personal Narrative Performance." *The Sage Handbook of Performance Studies*, edited by D. Soyini Madison and Judith Hamera, Thousand Oaks, 2006, pp. 151–168.

Littlewood, Jane, and Michael Pickering. "Heard the One about the White Middle-Class Heterosexual Father-in-Law?" *Because I Tell a Joke or Two: Comedy, Politics, and Social Difference*, edited by Stephen Wagg, Routledge, 1998, pp. 291–312.

Lockyer, Sharon, and Lynn Myers. "'It's About Expecting the Unexpected': Live Stand-Up Comedy from the Audiences' Perspective." *Journal of Audience and Reception Studies*, vol. 8 no. 2, 2011, pp. 165–188.

Loffreda, Beth, and Claudia Rankine. "Introduction." *The Racial Imaginary: Writers on Race in the Life of the Mind*, edited Beth Loffreda, Claudia Rankine, and Max King Cap, Fence Books, 2015, pp. 13–22.

Lowder, J. Bryan. "Ricky Gervais Made Trans Jokes at the Golden Globes but Good News They Failed Miserably." *Slate Magazine.* The Slate Group, January 10, 2016, www.slate.com/blogs/outward/2016/01/10/ricky_gervais_made_trans_jokes_in_his_golden_globes_monologue_and_they_failed.html/.

Lowrey, Lacy, Valerie R. Renegar, and Charles E. Goehring. "When God Gives You AIDS … Make Lemon-AIDS: Ironic Persona and Perspective by Incongruity in Sarah Silverman's Jesus Is Magic." *Western Journal of Communication*, vol. 78 no. 1, 2014, pp. 58–77, doi:10.1080/10570314.2013.792387.

Luciani, Curtis. "The Best Response We've Heard to Daniel Tosh's 'Misquoted' Rape Jokes." CultureMap. Austin, March 25, 2013, http://austin.culturemap.com/news detail/07-12-12-14-37-the-best-response-weve-heard-to-daniel-toshs-misquoted-rape-jokes/.

Lukainoff, Greg, and Jonathan Haidt. "The Coddling of the American Mind." *The Atlantic.* Atlantic Media Company, September 2015, www.theatlantic.com/magazine/archive/2015/09/the-coddling-of-the-american-mind/399356/.

Lyons, Margaret. "Why Seth MacFarlane's Misogyny Matters." Vulture. New York Media, February 25, 2013, www.vulture.com/2013/02/why-seth-macfarlanes-misogyny-matters.html#/.

Ma, Kai. "Margaret Cho's Golden Globes Skit was Minstrelsy, Not Comedy." *Time.* January 13, 2015, http://time.com/3665825/margaret-cho-golden-globes-minstrelsy-comedy/.

McDonald, Soraya Nadia. "Amy Schumer Responds to Criticism by Insisting She's Not Racist, Just Funny." *The Washington Post Arts and Entertainment.* The Washington Post, June 29, 2015, www.washingtonpost.com/news/arts-and-entertainment/wp/2015/06/29/amy-schumer-responds-to-criticism-by-insisting-shes-not-racist-just-funny/.

Madison, D. Soyini. "Lost in Translation: The Mirror or the Hammer." *Text & Performance Quarterly.* vol. 34 no. 1, 2014, pp. 111–112, doi:10.1080/10462937.2013.853826 .

MAANA. "Guy Aoki vs. Sarah Silverman on Politically Incorrect." YouTube. February 26, 2015, https://www.youtube.com/watch?v=VsNoO8xMs04/.

Maglio, Tony. "Sarah Silverman Regrets Wearing 'Most Racist Blackface' in Comedy Central Sketch." The Wrap. October 30, 2015, http://www.thewrap.com/sarah-silverman-black-face-watch-what-happens-live-andy-cohen-racist-comedy-central/.

Maloy, Simon. "The 20 Worst Racial Attacks Limbaugh's Advertisers Have Sponsored." Media Matters for America. March 7, 2012, www.mediamatters.org/blog/2012/03/07/the-20-worst-racial-attacks-limbaughs-advertise/184776/.

Martin, Judith N., Robert L. Krizek, Thomas K. Nakayama, and Lisa Bradford. "Exploring Whiteness: A Study of Self Labels for White Americans." *Communication Quarterly*, vol. 44 no.2, 1996, pp. 125–144.

Marwick, Alice E., and Danah Boyd. "I Tweet Honestly, I Tweet Passionately: Twitter Users, Context Collapse, and the Imagined Audience." *New Media & Society*, vol. 13 no. 1, 2011, pp. 114–133, doi:10.1177/1461444810365313.

Meyer, Moe, editor. *The Politics and Poetics of Camp*. Routledge, 1994.

Meyer, Moe. "Introduction: Reclaiming the Discourse of Camp." *The Politics and Poetics of Camp*. Routledge, 1994, pp. 1–19.

Miller, Margo. "Masculinity and Male Intimacy in Nineties Sitcoms: Seinfeld and the Ironic Dismissal." *The New Queer Aesthetic on Television: Essays on Recent Programming*, edited by James R. Keller and Leslie Stratyner, McFarland, 2006, pp. 147–159.

Muñoz, Jose. *Disidentifications: Queers of Color and the Performance of Politics*. University of Minnesota Press, 1999.

Muñoz, Jose. "Feeling Brown: Ethnicity and Affect in Ricardo Bracho's The Sweetest Hangover and Other STDs." *Theatre Journal*, vol. 52 no. 1, 2000, pp. 67–79, doi:10.1353/tj.2000.0020.

Nachman, Gerald. "Curing the Body Politics: Dick Gregory." *Seriously Funny: Rebel Comedians of the 1950s and 1960s*, Pantheon, 2004, pp. 480–508.

Nakayama, Thomas K., and Robert L. Krizek. "Whiteness: A Strategic Rhetoric." *Quarterly Journal of Speech*, vol. 81 no. 3, 1995, pp. 291–309.

Nelson, T.G.A."Chapter 1: Laughter." *Comedy: The Theory of Comedy in Literature, Drama, and Cinema*, Oxford University Press, 1990, pp. 1–18.

"Not a Very P.C. Thing to Say." *NY Magazine News & Politics*. New York Media, January 27, 2015, www.nymag.com/daily/intelligencer/2015/01/not-a-very-pc-thing-to-say.html/.

Odell, Amy. "Comedy Club Owner Says Daniel Tosh Incident Has Been Misunderstood." *BuzzFeed*. BuzzFeed Inc., July 10, 2012, www.buzzfeed.com/amyodell/comedy-club-owner-says-daniel-tosh-incident-has-be?utm_term=.fbyeAoGpK#.jvE9zO7xG/.

Oldenburg, Ann. "Golden Globes Bit with Margaret Cho Racist?" *USA Today*. January 12, 2015, http://www.usatoday.com/story/life/people/2015/01/12/margaret-cho-north-korean-golden-globes-racist-racism/21623491/.

Owen, Susan A., and Peter Ehrenhaus. "Communities of Memory, Entanglements, and the Claims of the Past on the Present: Trauma through The Green Mile." *Critical Studies in Media Communication*, vol. 27, no. 2, 2010, pp. 131–154.

"Oscars 2016: Host Chris Rock Rapped over Asian-American Joke." *BBC News*. March 1, 2016, http://www.bbc.com/news/entertainment-arts-35693784/.

Page, Clarence. "College Kids Can't Take a Joke. " *Chicago Tribune Nation & World*. Chicago Tribune, February 4, 2015, www.chicagotribune.com/news/nationworld/ct-college-students-prudes-comics-perspec-0204-20150203-column.html/.

Papacharissi, Zizi. "A Networked Self: Identity Performance and Sociability on Social Network Sites." *Frontiers in New Media Research*, edited by Francis L. F. Lee, Louis Leung, Jack L. Qiu, and Donna S.C. Chu, Routledge, 2013, pp. 207–221.

Park-Fuller, Linda M."Audiencing the Audience: Playback Theatre, Performative Writing, and Social Activism." *Text and Performance Quarterly*, vol. 23 no. 3, 2003, pp. 288–310.

Paskin, Willa. "Seth MacFarlane, Misogynistic Oscar Host." *Salon*. Salon Media Group Inc., February 25, 2013, www.salon.com/2013/02/25/seth_MacFarlane_misogynistic_oscar_host/.

Patrick Henry College. "Patrick Henry College Newsmakers Interview: Dr. Ben Carson." YouTube. March 20, 2012, www.youtube.com/watch?feature=player_embedded&v=orY6M0Ex0BM#!/.

Pearl, Monica B. "AIDS and New Queer Cinema." *New Queer Cinema: A Critical Reader*, edited by Michele Aaron, Rutgers University Press, 2004, pp. 23–35.

Pelias, Ronald J, and James VanOosting. "A Paradigm for Performance Studies." *Quarterly Journal of Speech*, vol. 73 no. 2, May 1987, pp. 219–231.

Pelle, Susan. "The 'Grotesque' Pussy: Transformational Shame in Margaret Cho's Standup Performances." *Text & Performance Quarterly*, vol. 30 no. 1, January 2010, pp. 21–37, doi:10.1080/10462930903366977.

Peterson, Michael. *Straight White Male: Performance Art Monologues*. University of Mississippi Press, 1997.

Pierce, Jennifer L. *Racing for Innocence: Whiteness, Gender, and the Backlash against Affirmative Action*. Stanford University Press, 2012.

Poniewozik, James. "American Dud: Seth MacFarlane's Awkward Oscars." Time Television. Time Inc., February 25, 2013, www.entertainment.time.com/2013/02/25/american-dud-seth-MacFarlanes-awkward-oscars/.

Pozner, Jennifer L."Louis C.K. on Daniel Tosh's Rape Joke: Are Comedy and Feminism Enemies?" *The Daily Beast*. Daily Beast Co., July 18, 2012, www.thedailybeast.com/articles/2012/07/18/daniel-tosh-rape-joke-are-comedy-and-feminism-enemies.html/.

"President Barack Obama." WTF Podcast. Interview by Marc Maron, episode 63, Square Space, June 22, 2015, www.wtfpod.com/podcast/episodes/episode_613_-_president_barack_obama/.

Puckrik, Katie. "The Queen of Mean." *Guardian News*. The Guardian Media, October 6, 2007, www.theguardian.com/media/2007/oct/06/comedy.arts/.

Quirk, Sophie. "Containing the Audience: The 'Room' in Stand-Up Comedy." *Journal of Audience and Reception Studies*, vol. 8 no. 2, November 2011, pp. 219–238.

Radloff, Jessica. "Seth MacFarlane Wants to Talk: The Family Guy Creator on His Holiday Album and His Softer Side." *Glamour*. Conde Nast, November 12, 2014, www.glamour.com/story/seth-MacFarlane-wants-to-talk/.

Rappoport, Leon. "In Defense of Ethnic Humor and Its Role in Our Multicultural Society." *Punchlines: The Case for Racial, Ethnic, and Gender Humor*, Praeger Publishers, 2005, pp. 149–161.

Rayner, Alice. "Creating the Audience: It's All in the Timing." *The Laughing Stalk: Live Comedy and Its Audiences*, edited by Judith Batalion, Parlor Press, 2012, pp. 28–39.

"Rebel Wilson Makes Fun of Oscars Diversity Row in Show-Stealing Baftas Speech: Video." *Guardian Baftas 2016*. Guardian News and Media Limited, February14, 2016, www.theguardian.com/film/video/2016/feb/15/rebel-wilsons-makes-fun-of-oscars-diversity-row-in-show-stealing-baftas-speech-video?CMP=twt_a-film_b-gdnfilm/.

Reyes, R. Salvador. "Story Theory: Confessions of a Literary Darwinist." *Tottenville Review*. Blog, July 14, 2011, www.tottenville.wordpress.com/2011/07/14/story-theory-confessions-of-a-literary-darwinist/.

Rich, Katey, and Kristy Puchko. “Yes, Seth MacFarlane’s Oscar Jokes Were Sexist, and Yes It Matters.” *CinemaBlend*. Gateway Media, February 25, 2013, www.cinemablend.com/new/Yes-Seth-MacFarlane-Oscar-Jokes-Were-Sexist-Yes-It-Matters-35994.html/.

“Ricky Gervais on Controversial Jokes, Celebrities and Special Correspondents.” *NPR Weekend Edition Movie Interviews*. NPR, May 1, 2016, www.npr.org/2016/05/01/476078487/ricky-gervais-on-controversial-jokes-celebrities-and-special-correspondents/.

“Roast of Charlie Sheen.” Comedy Central Roast, directed by Joel Gallen. Performances by Amy Schumer, Mike Tyson, William Shatner, and Charlie Sheen. Comedy Partners. 2011.

Ronson, Jon. *So You’ve Been Publically Shamed*. Riverhead Books, 2015.

Rosen, Christopher. “Oscar Producers: Seth MacFarlane Boob Song Was Satire.” *Huffington Post Entertainment*. TheHuffingtonPost.com Inc., March 17, 2013, www.huffingtonpost.com/2013/03/17/oscar-producers-seth-macfarlane_n_2895591.html/.

Ross, Andrew. “Uses of Camp.” *Camp Grounds: Style and Homosexuality*, edited by David Bergman, University of Massachusetts Press, 1993, pp. 54–77.

Rush, George, *et al.*“Halle Berry Earns Top Dollar in Swordfish.” *NY Daily News*. May 15, 2001, www.nydailynews.com/archives/gossip/halle-berry-earns-top-dollar-swordfish-article-1.915299/.

Rushfield, Richard. “Last Night, Patton Oswalt Went on an Epic Twitter Rampage and Here It Is.” *HitFlix The Dartboard*. HitFlix Inc., April 1, 2015, www.hitfix.com/the-dartboard/last-night-patton-oswalt-went-on-the-most-epic-twitter-ramage-and-here-it-is/.

Scarpetta, Fabriola, and Anna Spagnolli. “The Interactional Context of Humor in Stand-up Comedy.” *Research on Language and Social Interaction*, vol. 42 no. 3, August 2009, pp. 210–230, doi:10.1080/08351810903089159.

Scaunich, Sandi. “Stand-up Comedian Jim Jefferies’ Misogynist Jokes Fall Flat.” *The Age*. Fairfax Media, April 2, 2015, www.theage.com.au/comment/standup-comedian-jim-jefferies-misogynist-jokes-fall-flat-20150401-1mciqq.html/.

Schneider, Rebecca. *The Explicit Body in Performance*. Routledge, 1997.

Scott, Karla D.“Broadening the View of Black Language Use: Toward a Better Understanding of Words and Worlds.” *Our Voices: Essays in Culture, Ethnicity, and Communication*, edited by Alberto González, Marsha Houston, and Victoria Chen, Oxford University Press, 2007, pp. 183–189.

Sedgwick, Eve Kosofsky. “Paranoid Reading and Reparative Reading: Or, You’re So Paranoid, You Probably Think This Introduction Is about You.” *Novel Gazing: Queer Readings in Fiction*, Duke University Press, 1997, pp. 1–37.

Selfa, Lance. “The Crusade against Political Correctness.” *Socialist Worker Comment*. International Socialist Organization, December 8, 2015, www.socialistworker.org/2015/12/08/the-crusade-against-political-correctness/.

@SethMacFarlane. “I demand an immediate apology. – everyone about everything.” Twitter, April 28, 2015, 3:57 p.m., twitter.com/sethmacfarlane/status/593187429810470912.

Shugart, Helene A.“Postmodern Irony as Subversive Strategy.” *Western Journal of Communication*, vol. 63 no. 4, 1999, pp. 433–455.

Shugart, Helene A.“Parody and Subversive Performance: Denaturalizing Gender and Reconstituting Desire in Ellen.” *Text & Performance Quarterly*, vol. 21 no. 2, April 2001, pp. 95–113.

Shugart, Helene A. and Catherine E. Waggoner. *Making Camp: Rhetorics of Transgression in U.S. Popular Culture*. University of Alabama Press, 2008.

Sieczkowski, Cavan. "Jerry Seinfeld Explains His Issue with Political Correctness with Gay French King Joke." *Huffington Post Entertainment*. TheHuffingtonPost.com Inc., June 10, 2015, www.huffingtonpost.com/2015/06/10/jerry-seinfeld-political-/correctness_n_7552132.html/.

Silman, Anna. "Sarah Silverman Pushes Back against Creepy P.C. Culture Backlash: You Have to Listen to the College-aged, because They Lead the Revolution." *Salon*. Salon Media Group Inc., September 15, 2015, www.salon.com/2015/09/15/sarah_silverman_pushes_back_against_creepy_p_c_culture_backlash_you_have_to_listen_to_the_college_aged_because_they_lead_the_revolution/.

Silverman, Sarah. *The Bedwetter: Stories of Courage, Redemption, and Pee*. Harper-Collins, 2010.

Sims, David. "Amy Schumer and the Growing Pains of Comedy." *The Atlantic*. June 30, 2015, http://www.theatlantic.com/entertainment/archive/2015/06/amy-schumer-race/397226/.

Snetiker, Marc. "Darren Criss Apologizes for Caitlyn Jenner Joke During Hedwig and the Angry Inch." *News: LGBT Entertainment*. Entertainment Weekly Inc., June 26, 2015, www.ew.com/article/2015/06/26/darren-criss-caitlyn-jenner-joke/.

Soloman, Akiba. "8 Reasons Why I Hated Chris Rock's Oscar Monologue." *Color Lines*. Race Forward, February 29, 2016, https://www.colorlines.com/articles/8-reasons-why-i-hated-chris-rocks-oscars-monologue/.

Sontag, Susan. "Notes on Camp." *A Susan Sontag Reader*, Vintage Books, 1983, pp. 105–119.

Stone, Laurie. *Laughing in the Dark: A Decade of Subversive Comedy*. Ecco Press, 1997.

Taylor, Diana. "Performance and/as History." *The Drama Review*, vol. 50 no. 1, 2006, pp. 67–86.

"The Puppy Episode."*Ellen*, created by Neal Marlens. Performed by Ellen DeGeneres. Season 4, episode 22 and 23. The Black Marlens Company, 1997.

"Top 10 Most Controversial Comedians." *Entertainment.ie*. Entertainment Media Network, www.entertainment.ie/comedy/feature/Top-10-most-controversial-comedians/209/4239.htm/.

Toure. "Tina Fey and 30 Rock Persistently Touch the Third Rail that is Blackface." Mediaite. December 11, 2010, www.mediaite.com/online/tina-fey-and-30-rock-persistently-touch-the-third-rail-that-is-blackface/.

Trujillo, Nick. "Hegemonic Masculinity on the Mound: Media Representations of Nolan Ryan and American Sports Culture." *Critical Studies in Mass Communication*, vol. 8 no. 3, 1991, pp. 290–308.

Warren, John T., and Amy K. Kilgard. "Staging Stain upon the Snow: Performance as a Critical Enfleshment of Whiteness." *Text and Performance Quarterly*, vol. 21 no. 4, 2001, pp. 261–276.

Weaver, Simon. "Definitions of the Humorous in Chris Rock and Russell Peters Fan Blogs: A Discussion of the Problem of Incongruity." *Journal of Audience and Reception Studies*, vol. 8 no. 2, 2011, pp. 257–275.

West, Lindy. "An Open Letter to White Male Comedians." *Jezebel*. Gawker Media, May 10, 2013, www.jezebel.com/an-open-letter-to-white-male-comedians-497503334/.

Wheeler, Brad. "Gilbert Gottfried on the Age of Internet: 'Every Joke Now Has to Come with an Apology' ." *The Globe and Mail Theater & Performance*. The Globe and Mail Inc., November 3, 2013, www.theglobeandmail.com/arts/theatre-and-performance/gottfried-on-the-age-of-internet-every-joke-now-has-to-come-with-an-apology-at-the-end/article15214481/.

Wheeler, Brad. "Jane Fonda is not Pumped about the Boob Song." *Jezebel*. Gawker Media, February 28, 2013, www.jezebel.com/5987736/jane-fonda-is-not-pumped-about-the-boob-song.

Williams, Ray. "Anti-Intellectualism and the Dumbing Down of America." *Psychology Today*. Sussex Publishers, July 7, 2014, www.psychologytoday.com/blog/wired-success/201407/anti-intellectualism-and-the-dumbing-down-america/.

Wilson, Adam. "Play It Cool, Bro." *New Republic*. February 28, 2013, www.newrepublic.com/article/112550/seth-macfarlane-oscars-review-we-saw-your-boobs-ruins-it-us-men/.

Wilson, Nathan A. "Divisive Comedy: A Critical Examination of Audience Power." *Journal of Audience and Reception Studies*, vol. 8 no. 2, 2011, pp. 276–291.

Wilson, Olivia. "10 Male Comedians Who Think Sexist Jokes Are Funny." *Crushable Entertainment*. Defy Media, March 12, 2014, http://www.crushable.com/2014/03/12/entertainment/sexism-in-comedy-misogyny/.

Wood, Julia T. *Gendered Lives: Communication, Gender, and Culture*. 7th ed., Wadsworth Publisher, 2007.

Worthen, William B. "Drama, Performativity, and Performance." *PMLA*, vol. 113 no. 5, 1998, pp. 1093–1107, doi:10.2307/463244.

Zakarin, Jordan. "Gilbert Gottfried Fired as Aflac Duck after Japanese Tsunami Tweets." *The Huffington Post Entertainment*. TheHuffingtonPost.com Inc., March 14, 2011, www.huffingtonpost.com/2011/03/14/gilbert-gottfried-fired-aflac_n_835692.html?/.

Zakarin, Jordan. "Michael Fassbender's Penis Is Hollywood's New Obsession." *The Huffington Post Entertainment*. TheHuffingtonPost.com Inc., January 23, 2012, www.huffingtonpost.com/2012/01/23/michael-fassbenders-penis-hollywoods-new-obsession_n_1224116.html/.

Zingsheim, Jason and Dustin B. Goltz. "The Intersectional Workings of Whiteness: A Representative Anecdote." *Review of Education, Pedagogy, and Cultural Studies*, vol. 33 no. 3, 2011, pp. 215–241.

Zoglin, Richard. *Comedy at the Edge: How Stand-Up in the 1970s Changed America*. Bloomsbury USA, 2008.

Index

www.ingramcontent.com/pod-product-compliance
Ingram Content Group UK Ltd.
Pitfield, Milton Keynes, MK11 3LW, UK
UKHW011011180926
475701UK00004B/679
9780367202132